ENDLESSE WORKE

Jonathan Goldberg is an associate professor
in the Department of English
at Temple University.

JONATHAN GOLDBERG

ENDLESSE WORKE

SPENSER AND THE STRUCTURES OF DISCOURSE

THE JOHNS HOPKINS UNIVERSITY PRESS
Baltimore and London

This book has been brought to publication with the generous
assistance of the Andrew W. Mellon Foundation.

The Johns Hopkins University Press, Baltimore, Maryland 21218
The Johns Hopkins Press Ltd., London

Library of Congress Cataloging in Publication Data

Goldberg, Jonathan.
  Endlesse worke.

Includes bibliographical references and index.
1. Spenser, Edmund, 1552?-1599. Faerie queene.
2. Spenser, Edmund, 1552?-1599—Technique.
3. Narration (Rhetoric)
4. Structuralism (Literary analysis)
I. Title.
PR2358.G6   821'.3   81-4906
ISBN 0-8018-2608-X   AACR2

for Julia and Abigail
and in memory of my mother

Farther on, further in, the prospect develops—
is that a town? At least the road starts there, curving
up from the lake where it leaves the ghost of itself
curving down, and life—what passes for life—passes:
another drover, someone with a donkey going
home, and a meeting between two human beings;
they are too far, or we are, to see more from here
than their meeting. They embrace: not as lovers do,
or enemies—just two human souls in a frank
community of pain. Then the road moves up, past
the sixteen buildings to the wilds.

—Richard Howard, *"Purgatory*, formerly *Paradise"*

CONTENTS

FIGURES

FOREWORDS

The aim of this study is to present, as briefly and as cogently as I can, a way of reading Spenser. My primary concern is to elucidate some features of Spenserian narration; for reasons that will become clear from my argument, I have found book IV an appropriate site for these observations—about influence, about narrative self-reflexiveness, about the location of the text in the world of discourse—and have drawn upon insights nurtured by structuralism, and especially on *S/Z* by Roland Barthes, in formulating my remarks. However, because in this book I am mainly interested not in critical theory but in *The Faerie Queene*, I have not attempted a metacritical chapter on my relationship to structuralist criticism or its relationship to previous criticism of Spenser. I have relegated such questions to notes supporting the text. A few of these are rather extensive and present the briefest of essays into critical and theoretical matters.

The relationship of *Endlesse Worke* to previous criticism of *The Faerie Queene* could be summarized in this way: I believe it could be argued that precisely because much that is valuable in Spenser criticism is conservative in nature, certain features of the text that I am interested in discussing—features that have always disturbed and provoked its readers—have been confronted only in part. Spenser's text offers continuous disequilibrium, frequent disruptions in narration, and characters who exist to disappear. Most often, when criticism takes stock of such traits of the narrative, it considers them as problems that could only be elucidated by pointing to some principle other than narration. Thematic unity, rhetorical addresses, allegorical meanings, are called forward in the service of explanation—often with the intention of explaining away—these disturbing features of the text. The frustrations of reading are thereby neglected, and so is something vital to the nature of Spenserian narration.

The reasons for this are not hard to understand. "We are all fulfill-ment men, *pleromatists*," Frank Kermode writes in his study of the in-terpretation of narration, *The Genesis of Secrecy*.[1] For him, the aim of reading, the point of interpreting, is to produce closure. If we can have satisfying readings, satisfying readings are what we want. Yet, this is a desire often frustrated, not only by difficult modern texts but also, as Kermode demonstrates, in the oldest gospel. In Mark, the reader tra-verses a path filled with pitfalls, strange lacunae, peculiar interruptions, and seemingly pointless reiterations. At the end a key to the mystery is not offered; instead there is, Kermode argues, the irreducible discovery of Secrecy. Interpretation, for Kermode, may be the need to complete, but narratives seem to be generated through the frustration of that need. That, at least as I understand it, is where Kermode's final eloquent sen-tence leaves us:

> World and book, it may be, are hopelessly plural, endlessly disap-pointing; we stand alone before them, aware of their arbitrariness and impenetrability, knowing that they may be narratives only be-cause of our impudent intervention, and susceptible of interpreta-tion only by our hermetic tricks. Hot for secrets, our only conversa-tion may be with guardians who know less and see less than we can; and our sole hope and pleasure is in the perception of a momentary radiance, before the door of disappointment is finally shut on us.
> (p. 145)

Of few texts is that experience more true than *The Faerie Queene*. In the pages that follow, I do not aim at interpretation or fulfillment, but, rather, at describing the narrative principles that induce frustration, that deny closure, but that also produce the disturbed and disturbing narrative procedures of Spenser's text. The generation of the text and its production is my subject.

Contributing to an issue of *Critical Inquiry* devoted to narration,

---

1. (Cambridge, Mass.: Harvard University Press, 1979), p. 72. Kermode opens his study by noting that modernism did not invent the fractured text (p. 15), and he closes by proclaiming Mark as an ultimately mysterious and frustrat-ing text (see pp. 143–45). At the center of Kermode's inquiry into narration is a set of oppositions: how narration drives us deeper and deeper into its secret struc-tures and how interpretation is forever filling in the gaps to produce meaning and closure. For Kermode, this is what narration does and what interpretation aims at; yet—and here is the opposition—Mark is ultimately elusive, and the reader is finally frustrated. Kermode solves this problem hermeneutically by say-ing that Mark itself is generated from its contradictions (see, e.g., pp. 140–41). This is to land on the side of resolution. In my understanding of the fractured text, it seems more faithful to it not to produce a closure that it fails to offer, and so, it is with endless work that I end. Kermode ends his book there too, but seems not to want his final words to sum up his endeavor. His oppositions mean to master an ambivalence.

Hayden White reminds us that satisfying narratives, those that answer to our "desire to have real events display . . . coherence, integrity, fullness, and closure," have already subjected "real events" to a narrative model; not only that, they offer "an image of life that is and can only be imaginary."[2] Spenser's text does not correspond to this imaginary version of the real; nor does it answer the hermeneutic desire for fulfillment. Its narrative nonetheless answers needs and desires even if it fails to offer the satisfactions of imagined fullness. In following Spenser's narration, I have not pursued the closures of formalist criticism, have failed to invoke theme or allegory as explanatory principles, and have not aimed at the production of meaning as something separable from the text. These are not, I would argue, the critical activities that Spenserian narrative seems to call for. Rather, it is in the narration itself that the poem defines its own procedures and its readers' relation to the text.

These narrative features lead me to describe the poem in terms that have not been applied seriously to *The Faerie Queene* before; but my procedures are not divorced from the work of previous critics of the poem.[3] I admire many of my predecessors. Among them, Paul Alpers, Harry Berger, Jr., Angus Fletcher, William Nelson, and Rosemond Tuve have been especially important to me. Although notes in the pages that follow record specific debts—and differences—I would not want to begin this book without acknowledging more generally the affinities I feel to those who have made my work possible. To describe their contributions in a phrase or two belies the richness and complexity of their writing. It is, nonetheless, Tuve's fundamental insistence on narrative as the medium of meaning in allegory that I draw upon ("an author must

2. "The Value of Narrativity," *Critical Inquiry* 7 (1980): 27. White's essay is important for its suggestion that the three modes of narration that he considers—annal, chronicle, and history—cannot be distinguished on the basis of truthfulness. Each subscribes to a view of narration and of life, none of which is inherently closer to reality than any other. This is a valuable insight to bring to *The Faerie Queene*, since it may keep us from "rescuing" it by describing it as if it were a novel, or a spiritual handbook. In "Freud and Dora: Story, History, Case History," *Partisan Review* 41 (1974): 12–23, 89–108, Steven Marcus points to an assumption of Freud's that is probably shared by many readers, "that a coherent story is in some manner connected with mental health. . . . Human life is, ideally, a connected and coherent story . . ." (p. 92). The consequence of this is that " 'reality' turns out to be something that for all practical purposes is indistinguishable from a systematic fictional creation" (p. 100). Again, Marcus's point is a useful reminder that what we expect from narration should be put in question.

3. Maureen Quilligan's study, *The Language of Allegory* (Ithaca: Cornell University Press, 1979), bears some superficial resemblances to the terms I use. Quilligan argues that allegory is generated from wordplay (see pp. 15, 22, 53, 68, and 156 for characteristic restatements of the thesis that allegories are "about language"). This leads Quilligan at one moment (p. 239) to associate allegorical texts with what Roland Barthes calls the writerly, a point I develop below. However, Quilligan does not take this connection seriously, because her

be permitted to tell stories, and not draw up schemes''); Nelson's demonstration of the insistent refiguration that allows theme to be embodied in
multiple forms; Berger's pointing to the "conspicuously irrelevant" episode and the disposable character as regular narrative features; Alpers's
denial that Spenser aims at constructing a world and his more recent
emphasis on the provisional nature of Spenserian narration;[4] Fletcher's
willingness to read book V in terms of multiple matrices that cut across
and against each other and that extend its thematic concerns beyond a
narrowly conceived Renaissance mind—it is upon such insights that I
feel I have depended in writing this book. These critical positions, along
with the panglossic urges of what will surely remain the largest book
ever written on *The Faerie Queene*, testify in their various ways to the
impossibility of reducing Spenser's text to one-to-one allegorical meanings, or to new-critical coherent patterns of image, or to a thematics that
makes the poem a set of commonplaces of Renaissance or Christian
thought. This is a text that, as I argue in the pages that follow, generates
itself precisely out of its own instability, self-consuming, if I may borrow
Stanley Fish's term (it is not my largest debt to him); written under erasure, if that is the Derridean equivalent.

Crudely speaking, every reader of *The Faerie Queene* knows how
difficult the poem is; criticism has, in trying to make the task of reading
easier, often forgotten to account for what made it difficult in the first
place. What it is like to read the poem has often been ignored. This book
does not aim at making the reader's work more difficult, but simply at
describing the features of Spenserian narration that make this, to use
Kermode's language, a fractured—and fracturing—text.

---

model for language is not structuralist. She believes that allegory reflects "the
culture's assumptions about the ability of language to state or reveal values" (p.
221). Hence, despite her assertions that allegories generate themselves out of
their own words, Quilligan's real argument is that allegories point at ultimate
truths and demand that their readers come to ultimate understandings. Allegories may be "about language," but, for Quilligan, language refers to the real and
the true; ultimately, then, Quilligan's allegories become homiletics, always referring outside of themselves, since language does and since allegories are all
grounded in the Word. In the pages that follow, Spenser's text is not viewed in so
limiting a pretext, nor are his words either so narrowly self-generating (Quilligan's allegories are extended systems of puns, new-critical playgrounds), nor so
comfortably referential. In short, although Quilligan and I occasionally share
a term—even, at times, write sentences that sound remarkably similar—we are
making fundamentally opposing arguments. I should add that I read *The
Language of Allegory* after writing *Endlesse Worke*.
    4. In "Narration in *The Faerie Queene*," *ELH* 44 (1977): 19–39, esp. pp.
27 and 35. "The hallmark of Spenserian narration is confidence in locutions
which are at the same time understood to be provisional" and "The definitive
reality is human discourse." Alpers is more sanguine than I am about Spenserian confidence; he is also committed to seeing the second half of *The Faerie
Queene* as a turning away in large measure from its earlier narrative principles.
Still, although our terms are quite different, I believe that he and I are frequently

Temple University provided me with support for the writing of this book, which I am grateful for, but I am most thankful for the opportunity I have had over the years to teach Spenser, and for the many students who have sharpened my perceptions and understanding. Much in the pages that follow is deeply indebted to Doris Braendel, Debra Scott Panichelli, and Mary Schmelzer; to Joseph Woolf Lewis, Rhona Moser Silver, Jeanne Silverthorne, Cynthia Simon; and, more anciently, to James Voss, Louise Wright, and even to Howard Zenker, who probably will not remember his contribution. They all have my thanks.

This book found its definitive form in the summer of 1979, which I spent in Peter Saccio's house in Etna, New Hampshire, and it was no doubt the combination of the beauty and serenity of the Connecticut River valley and the warmth of many friends there which made this possible. Among them, Donald Pease, Richard and Sarah Corum, Nancy Vickers, Brenda Silver, Paul Tobias, Elizabeth Ermarth, Thomas Vargish, and Robert and Mary Kelley must be mentioned. Under the ghostly presence of Maude Adams, and thanks to the genial hospitality of Howard Tharsing and Thomas Stehling, these introductory words were drafted. For their help in securing the illustrations for this book, in addition to Nancy Vickers and Stephen Orgel, I would like to thank Roy Strong, Jane Tompkins, Leo Braudy, and Eugene Chiaverelli. Other dear friends have, over the years, been firm supporters. They will know who they are, and how much they have meant, without being named.

One friend, one reader, however, must be set apart. Stephen Orgel has lived with this book as it was being produced, and there is no page in it that has not profited from his wisdom. Without him, this—and so much else—would not be possible. If this book is not dedicated to him, it is only because he knows that beyond friendship there are other claims and because he can be sure that the next book will be.

---

seeing the same phenomena. I would characterize the turn of narration as a turning back that highlights the provisional nature of human discourse as the only reality in *The Faerie Queene*.

ENDLESSE WORKE

PRETEXTS

In 1596, the second half of *The Faerie Queene*, books IV to VI, appeared for the first time, preceded by a new edition of books I to III. Some minor textual changes had been made in the first half of the poem, and one major one: the final stanzas of book III had been canceled and, in their place, three new stanzas were provided. Displaced were the five stanzas leading to the union of Scudamour and Amoret; replacing them were stanzas in which Amoret discovered no lover awaiting her, in which Scudamour, "misdeeming" (III.xii.45.5) her situation and his own, had abandoned her, and in which Britomart, instead of witnessing their union, discovered their loss and failed meeting; "thereat her noble hart was stonisht sore" (44.5).[1] This major revision, this moment of sore astonishment, although it is unique in the textual history of the poem, highlights central tendencies of narration in *The Faerie Queene*. The deliberate cancelation of an ending carries with it an implicit assumption: that narration cannot progress beyond an ending—any ending. What this means, in a broad sense, is easily recognized by any reader of *The Faerie Queene*, for the poem is not merely finally unfinished, but frustratingly incomplete and inconclusive throughout, even when it encourages its readers to expect conclusions. This is characteristic of Spenserian narration, and it is characteristically problematic. How, then, does narration progress in *The Faerie Queene*, and what are the virtues of, the pleasures offered by, a broken text? Raising these questions, the revisionary juncture between books III and IV seems to call into question the very nature of Spenser's narrative.

    The new ending—in which Scudamour, Amoret, and Britomart

---

1. All citations from Spenser are drawn from *The Poetical Works of Edmund Spenser*, ed. J. C. Smith and E. de Selincourt (London: Oxford University Press, 1912).

are each at a loss—evidently links narrative progress, or the possibility of going forward, to frustration. It thereby exaggerates one aspect of the original ending. For in the first edition, although Amoret and Scuda-mour shared a "long embracement" in which they virtually had "growne together quite," Britomart, standing aside, "halfe envying their blesse," remained as far from her own love, Arthegall, as she had ever been. Book III appears to be organized around Britomart's quest (it opens and closes the book), and many readers share her feelings when it arrives at its only partly satisfactory conclusion. They, too, want more satisfaction, with a firmer and fuller ending. The reader has been led to believe that Britomart will reach her goal (books I and II offer strong precedents for that expectation), and the minor felicities of the original conclusion do not really compensate for the anticipated meeting of Bri-tomart and Arthegall. The 1596 ending, however, refuses us even the partial and displaced satisfaction of the first ending and draws all the characters, and the reader too, into a situation of general frustration that appears to be necessary to generate further narration. It seems arguable, and I will want to maintain the point, that this revision clarifies the nature of narrative progress throughout the poem and suggests the pe-culiar pleasures this text offers.

For one thing, the new ending makes demands upon the reader to revaluate notions of narrative satisfaction, to defer or even to deny the pleasures of conclusions for those of expectations, and to recognize as well that failed endings are part of the design of the poem.[2] Even in the first version, Britomart's position, solitary and half envious, had been a disturbing element, perhaps a blot on an otherwise happy ending. Yet,

---

2. The ending of book I is the first strong instance of narrative distur-bance, both in the deferral of the marriage of Una and the Red Crosse knight (perfectly plausible thematically, but not fully satisfactory in terms of the ro-mance conventions of the narration) and, more strongly, in the way in which the knight's departure returns Una to the state of mourning in which she was first found (cf. I.xii.41.9 and I.i.4.6). Book II ends with Guyon at his goal; but some readers have been disturbed by his ruthless destructivity: does it exemplify tem-perance? In *Renaissance Self-Fashioning* (Chicago: University of Chicago Press, 1980), pp. 157–92, Stephen Greenblatt reviews the discussion of this issue and offers answers in terms of the cultural matrices towards which I move in the concluding chapters of this study. The questioning of what Greenblatt calls "virtuous violence" and the ways in which "each self-constituting act is haunted by inadequacy and loss" (p. 179), occurs throughout *The Faerie Queene*. When book III opens, Britomart's defeat of Guyon may, retrospectively, be putting Guyon in his place, undoing that overreaction to the pleasures of the flesh. Fi-nally, the new ending to book III may serve to highlight the defects even in the happy ending originally provided. Harry Berger, Jr., has argued this point, not-ing that there is something cloyingly unnatural in an embrace that renders Scu-damour and Amoret "like two senceles stocks" (see "Busirane and the War Be-tween the Sexes: An Interpretation of *The Faerie Queene* III.xi–xii," *English Literary Renaissance* 1 [1971]:99–121).

in fact, Britomart's plight fulfills a pattern in the text: Britomart begins and ends book III in the same situation, and a pair of parallel wounds in her first and last adventures might be said to symbolize her career of frustrated love. Britomart's first adventure concludes with a wound received from Gardante (III.i.65), and her final victory, the rescue of Amoret, culminates with the same wound again, this time inflicted by Busyrane (III.xii.33). Repetition makes it clear that it is the same wound a second time. The first wound is "not deepe" (65.6), the latter equally superficial; "nothing deepe imprest" (33.7). In the first instance, the arrow is "seene/To gore her side" (65.5–6), the second wound "empurpled her faire brest" (33.5). Drops of blood at the beginning vermeil "her lilly smocke" (65.9) and "silken skin" (65.7), and at the end "her snowie chest" (33.4) is "empurpled" (33.5). If Britomart's final situation, however much it may disappoint a reader's expectations, nonetheless represents, in these repetitions, a kind of closure, Amoret's revised position—alone, and abandoned—echoes Britomart's. The principle of repetition thus offers a different kind of completion from the original hermaphroditic embrace, but one that also clearly satisfies a demand of the text. Furthermore, Amoret is now not merely doubling Britomart but also exemplifying another of the poem's structural precepts. At the moment of Britomart's victory over Busyrane, Amoret's riven heart had been restored to her, and she was once again, Spenser's text says, "perfect hole" (xii.38.9). In the new ending, the ambivalence of "hole" is more fully taken into account. Instead of the complicated mixture of resolution and frustration that had once ended book III, the reader is being asked to take as the pleasure of the text this moment of doubled loss, fulfillment through want, "perfect hole"—a paradox that nonetheless satisfies continuing structural demands in the text's language, imagery, and theme.

The new ending, I would argue, gives a taste of the kind of narrative that lies ahead, and most readers, I suspect, would ҅ǥ҅ҽҽ that the final installment of *The Faerie Queene* does not include the pleasures of resolution that characterize the opening books. I will want to suggest that those failed pleasures *are* the pleasures of this text. Furthermore, I would venture to say that the revised ending of book III does not merely fulfill the patterns of repeated wounds and "perfect hole" that have been pointed out. It also draws attention to all the erosions of the quest structure in book III that keep Britomart from seeming to be the kind of hero that the Red Crosse knight and Guyon appear to be. No matter how compellingly human Britomart appears (and most readers find her more dramatic than the heroes of the first two books), hers is in fact a less completely sustained presence in the text than either the Red Crosse knight's or Guyon's. True, these two heroes are both occasionally—at times, quite perplexingly—absent from their books, but never for long; Britomart, on the other hand, disappears for four consecutive cantos at

the center of book III, and she disappears, moreover, just after a moment
of triumph, her defeat of Marinell, when, we are told, "all was in her
powre" (iv.18.9).

Here is the passage describing her departure; Cymoent is lamenting her wounded son:

> But none of all those curses overtooke
> The warlike Maid, th'ensample of that might,
> But fairely well she thriv'd, and well did brooke
> Her noble deeds, ne her right course for ought forsooke.
>
> Yet did false *Archimage* her still pursew,
> To bring to passe his mischievous intent,
> Now that he had her singled from the crew
> Of courteous knights, the Prince, and Faery gent,
> Whom late in chace of beautie excellent
> She left, pursewing that same foster strong;
> Of whose foule outrage they impatient,
> And full of fiery zeale, him followed long,
> To reskew her from shame, and to revenge her wrong.
>
> (III.iv.44.6–9; 45)

The syntax and shifting pronoun references confuse Britomart here,
"her" in 44.9, with a "her" in the next line, which does not refer to
Britomart but to an as yet unnamed maiden, Florimell; to add to the
reader's confusion the name of Archimago is suddenly, but only momentarily and virtually inexplicably, present: he is mentioned nowhere
else in book III. Britomart disappears here, merging into a surrogate; she
reappears four cantos later, after book III has passed through its symbolic center, the Garden of Adonis, and after Britomart has been repeatedly
replaced by surrogates—Florimell, Belphoebe, Amoret, and Hellenore.
When she once again becomes the protagonist, she journeys on but fails
to reach her goal. Finally, the new ending doubles her frustration with
Amoret's and thereby robs Britomart's rescue of Amoret of its conclusive
force; nonetheless, this episode represents a fitting end to a career that
has been consistently eroded by the very structures of narration in book
III. Although we may finish the book in expectation of a happy ending,
the new conclusion must focus our attention on all the signs that the
narrative has been offering that urge readers to give up these expectations: the disappearance of the heroine, her failure to be present at the
center of the book, her insubstantial victory, her repeated wounds. This
undermining of the hero, and with it, the weakening of the quest as a
principle of narrative structure, are, however, minimal when compared
with what happens in the next book of *The Faerie Queene*. We scarcely

need to get past the opening to see that the erosions of narration high-lighted by the new ending of book III have become the central features of narration in book IV.

In its title, "The Legend of Cambel and Telamond, Or of Friend-ship," book IV promises familiar narrative strategies: the book is about a virtue and its hero (the pair of heroes is unique, but appropriate enough for exemplifying the virtue of friendship). But in the name of one of these heroes, Telamond, the title presents a puzzle that is a complement to the new ending of book III, for Telamond appears nowhere in the poem, and his name is merely a word on the title page. The implications for narration seem even more radical than the disappearance of the hero or the frustrated resolution in book III. In *The Kindly Flame*, Thomas Roche addresses this problem when he deciphers Telamond to mean "perfect world," and, without much difficulty, attaches the name to the cosmic implications of the three brothers, Priamond, Diamond, and Triamond, and their curious battle with Cambel for the hand of his sister, Canacee.[3] Telamond, in that case, is nothing more than a slip of the pen, a mere substitute name for Triamond, the hero who does appear in the poem. But what might such a slip or substitution actually mean?

If we go back once again to the previous book, we can perhaps see, by means of a small example, where narration seems to be heading in this slip, for there is a similar one early in book III. As Britomart travels with the Red Crosse knight after their departure from Malecasta's castle, she converses with him; as the versicle to canto ii puts it: *"The Redcrosse knight to Britomart / describeth Artegall."* Four stanzas later, however, the text reports her not with the Red Crosse knight but "travelling with *Guyon* by the way" (ii.4.1), and it is not until the end of a long flashback that the name of her original companion reappears: "through speaches with the *Redcrosse* knight, / She learned had th'estate of *Arthegall*" (iv.4.1–2). Whatever readers make of this shuffling of names—the re-placement of Guyon for the Red Crosse knight—it seems at the time a very minor disturbance, although retrospectively it may undermine the stability of the identities of the heroes in the first two books of the poem. The implication seems to be that any hero is all heroes, that all heroes are the same hero. When this event is followed, as it is almost immediately, by Britomart's disappearance, we may well be led to consider the possi-bility that the true structure of narration in *The Faerie Queene*, even in its opening books, is not described by the quest centered on the career of a single figure. Hence, when book IV opens with its error, the naming of a

---

3. Thomas P. Roche, Jr., *The Kindly Flame* (Princeton: Princeton Uni-versity Press, 1964), pp. 16–31. "The legend of Cambell and Telamond is in one allegorical sense a metaphysics of friendship and in another the symbolic state-ment of the metaphysics of *discordia concors*" (p. 17).

hero who fails to appear at all—at least under that name—it may be making, however obliquely, a statement about the overall nature of narration in *The Faerie Queene.*

What would the implications of this statement be? Telamond, the "perfect world," is announced but fails to appear. On one side of this name (a signifier without a signified) we have Britomart joined to Amoret in loss, "perfect hole"; on the other side, at the very close of book IV, we face an ultimate act of deferred narration in the story of Florimell and Marinell, "which," Spenser's narrator says, "to another place I leave to be perfected" (IV.xii.35.9). That final line, like the new ending of book III, indicates that narrative structure in *The Faerie Queene* is not closed and complete, but instead describes a kind of loop, moving here from "perfect" to "to be perfected," from closure ("tela" derives from *telos,* end) to openness, from the world ("-mond") to "another place." This is a structure of undoing or destructuring, a loop threading the void, moving from Telamond, the "perfect world" that is not present in the text, to the admission that perfection lies elsewhere, in "another place" that is also not in this text. The text moves from absence to absence, doubling back upon itself and yet never ending at all. Book IV thus concludes with an explicit statement about deferred closure that sums up what narrative structure, with its erosion of the stability of character and its undermining of the conclusive quest, seemed to be preparing. The shape of book IV, to put it briefly, would seem to be this: Telamond is the name of an absence; Triamond, the name given in place of and as a substitute for this one, is itself not a narrative entity—first, because his is a substitute name, but also because he is one of a triad with his brothers, Priamond and Diamond, and because he is paired with his alter ego, Cambel. Triamond and Cambel, the joint heroes of book IV, appear, moreover, in only four cantos of the book, mainly in a long flashback. And by the fifth canto, Triamond and Cambel, the presumed heroes of the book, have disappeared from the poem—forever. With their absence, book IV would seem to have abandoned entirely the assumption that plot moves character towards a goal, or that the protagonists embody theme. These radical disturbances of narration, I would argue, lay bare the nature of narration throughout *The Faerie Queene.*

Book IV calls into question definitions of Spenserian narration that are centered on the questing hero. Even in its most idiosyncratic feature, the pair of disappearing heroes, it bears implications for the entire poem, undermining the notion of the single and singular protagonist. True, in every other book there is nominally only one hero. Yet the pairing in book IV draws attention to how these single heroes are regularly presented—paired, like Guyon and the Palmer, or Arthegall and Talus; or replaced, like Calidore by Calepine, or Britomart by half a dozen maidens. Look, for instance, at how the Red Crosse knight enters the poem:

> A Gentle Knight was pricking on the plaine,
>   Y cladd in mightie armes and silver shielde,
>   Wherein old dints of deepe wounds did remaine,
>   The cruell markes of many' a bloudy fielde;
>   Yet armes till that time did he never wield:
>   His angry steede did chide his foming bitt,
>   As much disdayning to the curbe to yield:
>   Full iolly knight he seemd, and faire did sitt,
> As one for knightly giusts and fierce encounters fitt.
>
> (I.i.1)

Even in this opening stanza, in which he is a knight riding alone, the Red Crosse knight comes clad in arms that bear the "cruell markes" of many battles, though we are told that he has never fought before. In other words, the Red Crosse knight enters the poem clothed as another; the "bloudie Crosse he bore" (2.1) names him only through a sign—as the Red Crosse knight—and it is a sign of someone else. Furthermore, the quest he is on provides him with a companion, Una, who, despite her name, is hardly single in appearance. She is a veiled lady, and the veil serves as an indication that there is more to her than meets the eye, offering an invitation to think of her in terms of surface and depth. Moreover, she does not travel alone; as first presented, she is accompanied by a dwarf and, briefly, by a symbolic lamb. In other words, from the start, the single knight has a double identity, or no identity of his own, while his companion, who is both his truth, the object of his troth, and Truth itself, seems endlessly decipherable. Una's "oneness" serves as a reflection of and an index to the unity of the Red Crosse knight; it is manifested multiply and represented as external to himself. The end of the quest, endlessly deferred, promises the marriage of the knight to Una. Only in a conclusion to *The Faerie Queene* that the poem never provides will the Red Crosse knight, marrying his unity, truly be one. Until then, the knight's identity—his singleness—is only the product of his relationship with, and differentiation from, others. Hence, throughout book I, the Red Crosse knight is set against the images of himself that populate the poem; images that he is at times mistaken for, just as he himself, from the start of his adventure, mistakes images, or just as Una comes clear only against the various forms of Duessa. Narration in book I is negotiated within these margins of difference, between deferred unity and seeming to be one: "Full iolly knight he seemd, and faire did sitt, / As one for knightly giusts and fierce encounters fitt": how he seems, what he is like, not who or what he is, are, from the first, how the Red Crosse knight is identified. When *The Faerie Queene* begins again in book IV, the meaning of this differential characterization and this condition for knightly action is at last defined openly in the twinned heroes of the book.

If even the condition of being single and having an identity involves a relationship with another, then we can see that the central concerns of book IV reveal crucial facts about the structures of discourse in *The Faerie Queene*. For book IV is explicitly about groups and regroupings, and the meanings it considers are those that involve relationships. Here, for instance, is how Cambel and Triamond are described when they undergo the wondrous transformation that makes them friends instead of professed enemies: "Wonder it is that sudden change to see: / Instead of strokes, each other kissed glad, / And lovely haulst from feare of treason free, / And plighted hands for ever friends to be" (IV.iii.49.2–5). Their change is measured physically as a movement in place and of replacement, "instead" being the crucial word to mark their differentiation. Instead of blows, kisses are exchanged, instead of raising hands against "each other," hands are joined; fear of each other turns into friendship with another, and the new binding is one that takes place in an embrace free "from feare of treason." Their sudden and momentary reconciliation in these lines is determined by psychological forces and social demands. Cultural values *situate* and *move* them to replace their antagonism with friendship. They are re-placed. Indeed, throughout book IV, the figures move in groups in ways that resemble the trajectory of some unknown, mapped by an algebraic formula onto a functional grid. In these equations X is the individual, placed and replaced in relational matrices. In its groups and in its motion, book IV reveals that narration in *The Faerie Queene* functions as a grid on which different positions and relationships define an actor from moment to moment.

To summarize. The fundamental quality of narration in book IV, that book whose place in the poem is made by the displacement of an ending, is, then, not a progression toward a conclusion, but a deferral, leaving an ending "to be perfected" in "another place"; the fundamental quality, as the narrator calls it, is "endlesse worke" (xii.1.9).[4] Such work involves seemingly endless acts of undoing, denial, and frustration. Because of it, narration is best measured in losses, the loss of a

---

4. This quality of narrative is related to what Harry Berger, Jr., terms "The Spenserian Dynamics," *Studies in English Literature* 8 (1968):1–18, and I am indebted to his emphasis on the need to go beyond resolution, to maintain differences. We part company on the notion of an "evolutionary model" (p. 10) as the motor in this dynamism and in viewing the process almost entirely in psychological terms, although his idea of a horizontal vector, problematizing the boundary between in and out, is one that informs my reading of Spenser throughout.

definitive ending or the loss of an individual hero. "Instead" of the pleasures of the text that come from completion and stability, this is a text
populated with faceless knights (as C. S. Lewis called them) and their
ladies moving in flux, constantly resituated, momentarily lodged in relationships from which they are as quickly dislodged, inevitably undone. Here, for instance, is what happens to that perfect pair of friends,
the heroes of book IV, Triamond and Cambel cemented "for ever"
(iii.49.5) in the lines we just looked at. Hardly a canto later, they have
become simply two names in a list: "first *Cambello* brought . . . / His
faire *Cambina*. . . . / Next did Sir *Triamond* . . . / The face of his
deare *Canacee* unheale. . . . / And after her did *Paridell* produce / His
false *Duessa*" (v.10–11). They are now merely elements in a formulaic
situation in which distinctions and differences have disappeared, the
presentation of a series of ladies in the beauty contest given by Satyrane.
Heroism and distinct individuality are eroded by these matrices, for they
allow endless shifting and substitution. Hence, at the beauty contest, the
names of the heroes are in no way different from the names of Paridell or
Sir Ferramont—the latter, a knight whose name appears only twice in
the whole of *The Faerie Queene*, once in this set of stanzas. And the
ladies, listed as beloved objects, possessions, *productions*, soon converge
as well: "And after these an hundred Ladies moe / Appear'd in place,
the which each other did outgoe" (v.11.8–9). A hundred ladies pass
through a place, a site on a map, a location on a functional grid; when
they pass through this place they "appear'd in place" of "each other,"
different only by replacing one another in a virtually endless sequence of
substitutions.

The features of narration in *The Faerie Queene* that are so crucial
to book IV are strikingly elucidated by the critical terminology provided
by Roland Barthes in *S/Z*.[5] Barthes opposes what he calls the readerly

5. All citations from Roland Barthes, *S/Z*, trans. Richard Miller (New
York: Hill & Wang, 1974 [1970]). *S/Z* presents a reading of Balzac's *Sarrasine* to
demonstrate the readerly/writerly opposition. Like most structuralist literary
criticism, Barthes's *S/Z* is concerned with deconstructing the illusion that the
so-called Classical text simply reproduces reality. A writerly reading aims both
at revealing that the text is one that the reader produces, and at restoring to a text
its primacy as language. The definition of language that Barthes employs is
structuralist and is indebted to Ferdinand de Saussure's *Course in General Lin-
guistics*, trans. Wade Baskin (New York: McGraw Hill, 1966 [1915]), especially
to two key notions: (1) that the relationship between signifier and signified,
which taken together constitute the sign, is arbitrary, not referential; and (2) that
what separates one signifier from another is a difference (see, e.g., p. 118, "a
segment of language can never in the final analysis be based on anything except
its noncoincidence with the rest. *Arbitrary* and *differential* are two correlative
qualities," and p. 120, with its crucial statement, "in language there are only
differences . . . differences *without positive terms*.") These ideas have been the
founding principles in structuralism, influencing Claude Lévi-Strauss, Jacques
Derrida, and Jacques Lacan. In *S/Z*, Barthes depends on Derrida's ideas about

and the writerly text; in his terms, *The Faerie Queene* would fall within the latter category. The writerly text, as Barthes describes it, demands and produces readings that go counter to the conventions of narration found in what he calls Classical texts, those texts that are based on the mimesis of such supposedly ordinary and natural processes as sequentiality (opening followed by closure, beginning by ending) or that depend upon empirical commonplaces about a fixed locus of activity and a stable actor therein.

The writerly text, on the other hand, calls these assumptions into question. Unlike the readerly text, which is enslaved to sequence, the writerly text, which is also the text produced by writerly reading, is open, endless, and reversible, a "galaxy of signifiers, not a structure of signifieds" (p. 5). In other words, whereas the readerly text aims at representation (signifieds), the writerly text is committed to what Derrida describes as play in a centerless void, or, in his word, *freeplay*. The readerly text drives toward signification, and its words mean to name things. The writerly text plays with signifiers, and its names are the names of names

---

what he calls *différance*, a term that contains at once identity and difference.

   In seeing Spenser as the poet of deferred endings and the creator of characters who are paired differentials, I use this crucial Derridean concept (it is elucidated in *Of Grammatology*, trans. Gayatri Spivak [Baltimore: Johns Hopkins University Press, 1974], pp. 44 ff., in the course of a discussion of Saussure, and at greater length in the essay entitled "Differance" in *Speech and Phenomena and Other Essays on Husserl's Theory of Signs*, trans. David B. Allison [Evanston, Ill.: Northwestern University Press, 1973]: pp. 129–60). Another crucial term that Barthes and I use is the *supplement*. Again, *Of Grammatology*, esp. pp. 269 ff. offers the fullest discussion. It is also briefly, but cogently, explained in Derrida's essay, "Structure, Sign, and Play in the Discourse of the Human Sciences," in *The Structuralist Controversy*, ed. Richard Macksey and Eugenio Donato (Baltimore: Johns Hopkins Press, 1970, p. 260), as an excess that covers a lack. The chain of signifiers endlessly generates itself; in doing so it both replaces a lost center and adds to it. That lost center can be called *presence, fullness*—any term that conveys the notion of a closed and centered structure. Derridean deconstruction takes place when there is no center, or by decentering structures that claim to have centers. (Barthes, it should be added, also uses the Lacanian notion that the central lack is castration; and Barthes's economic analyses make use of Lévi-Straussian notions about exchange; these also have a place in my analysis of Spenser).

   Although structuralist criticism has aimed at deconstructing certain privileged notions about representation in classical and postclassical texts, its suitability to preclassical texts is intimated by Barthes in the opening pages of his essay "To Write: An Intransitive Verb?" (in *The Structuralist Controversy*, pp. 134–45). Before the eighteenth century, literature is frankly rhetorical, and interpretation arrives at describing the moral effect of a text by beginning with its verbal techniques. Think, for instance, of one reader of Spenser that we know about, E.K., the editor/commentator supplied for *The Shepheardes Calender*. E.K. is concerned mainly with the linguistic value of the text; he notes with pleasure rhetorical niceties; he elucidates the text by citing other texts, classical antecedents, contemporary handbooks and dictionaries. Moral meanings follow rhetorical ones. These features of Renaissance culture have been described brief-

linked in the endless chain of words (in Spenser: Telamond is replaced by Triamond; Priamond and Diamond are regenerated in Triamond; Triamond is joined to Cambel—he can wear his arms, take his name, stand in his place). The readerly text offers its reader the word as a product, an object; the name as a thing, an object of communication. The writerly text defers, demands the "endlesse worke" of play, the discovery of and the dissolving of differences into deferred identity and unity. The readerly text is single, solid, the author's work; the writerly text is infinite, replete, broken, empty, arbitrary, structured and deconstructed in its reading, which is its rewriting, produced by reader and author at once. The writerly text is an "endlesse worke" of substitution, sequences of names in place of other names, structures of difference, deferred identities. It plays upon a void; it occupies the place of loss—where Britomart's wound is extended to Amoret, where Amoret is "perfect hole." This is the space of the text.

The new ending to book III carries these meanings for narration in *The Faerie Queene*, and book IV is the place in the text where its narra-

---

ly but acutely in Michel Foucault's *The Order of Things* (New York: Random House, Vintage Books, 1970 [1966]), pp. 17–44. Foucault describes the ways in which the entire world was seen as a text (*liber creaturae*), which could only be elucidated by reference to other texts. Knowledge was endless and endlessly verbal, and some categories that we would erect—boundaries, for instance, between fact and fiction—do not hold in the Renaissance. The features that I consider in Spenser's text, what I refer to as his undoings and deferrals, might be called deconstructions, too; indeed, as Foucault shows, the very shape of knowledge in the Renaissance is deconstructive, an endless work of supplementarity, the provision of lists that fail to exhaust the prose of the world. If words can be endlessly replaced, then none is adequate, and none is final. Ends can never be reached in the universe that Foucault describes; no category is ever filled or is entirely discrete.

In order to deconstruct the classical text, Barthes stars (cuts and splices) *Sarrasine*, breaking up the text into units that are arbitrary in length and in content; the "naturalness" of the text, its mimetic quality, is thereby disturbed. *The Faerie Queene* breaks itself; written in predetermined stanzaic units that shape each piece of narration to fit this arbitrary unit, the text cannot use its textual space to provide emphases; indeed, as Paul Alpers shows in *The Poetry of "The Faerie Queene"* (Princeton: Princeton University Press, 1967), the text subordinates mimesis to rhetoric: "The lines are organized not by the narrative events that give rise to them (and that, in another poem, they would be imitating), but by the groupings imposed by various verbal means" (p. 37).

Although Alpers correctly emphasizes the dynamics of Spenserian narration, he also points to ways in which the stanza form functions almost as a static object. In book I, for instance, the stanzas are so homologous that the fifth line of many stanzas provides a pivotal paradox. No matter how variously stanzas are constructed, narration cannot be felt to progress "naturally" when every ninth line is a cumulative alexandrine or when a (literal) margin must be traversed by the reader in order to read the following stanza. Hence, Alpers argues, *The Faerie Queene* is not a world or a set of moral judgments, but an ongoing engagement with the reader's responsiveness to the rhetorical organization and verbal structures of the poem.

tive principles are most fully revealed. From its vantage point the nature
of *The Faerie Queene* as a writerly text comes clear. From the critical site
of book IV, the entire text can be reviewed. If we were to begin reading
the poem from this perspective, what would be revealed? Let us look at
the proem to *The Faerie Queene*.

1

Lo I the man, whose Muse whilome did maske,
    As time her taught, in lowly Shepheards weeds,
    Am now enforst a far unfitter taske,
    For trumpets sterne to chaunge mine Oaten reeds,
    And sing of Knights and Ladies gentle deeds;
    Whose prayses having slept in silence long,
    Me, all too meane, the sacred Muse areeds
    To blazon broad emongst her learned throng:
Fierce warres and faithfull loves shall moralize my song.

2

Helpe then, O holy Virgin chiefe of nine,
    Thy weaker Novice to performe thy will,
    Lay forth out of thine everlasting scryne
    The antique rolles, which there lye hidden still,
    Of Faerie knights and fairest *Tanaquill*,
    Whom that most noble Briton Prince so long
    Sought through the world, and suffered so much ill,
    That I must rue his undeserved wrong:
O helpe thou my weake wit, and sharpen my dull tong.

3

And thou most dreaded impe of highest *Iove*,
    Faire *Venus* sonne, that with thy cruell dart
    At that good knight so cunningly didst rove,
    That glorious fire it kindled in his hart,
    Lay now thy deadly Heben bow apart,
    And with thy mother milde come to mine ayde:
    Come both, and with you bring triumphant *Mart*,
    In loves and gentle iollities arrayd,
After his murdrous spoiles and bloudy rage allayd.

4

And with them eke, O Goddesse heavenly bright,
    Mirrour of grace and Maiestie divine,
    Great Lady of the greatest Isle, whose light
    Like *Phoebus* lampe throughout the world doth shine,
    Shed thy faire beames into my feeble eyne,

And raise my thoughts too humble and too vile,
To thinke of that true glorious type of thine,
The argument of mine afflicted stile:
The which to heare, vouchsafe, O dearest dred a-while.

The function of the proem to *The Faerie Queene* is to begin self-reflexively by offering an account of its origin. Its opening is a story that aims at telling where the text comes from, what it speaks about, and to whom it speaks. Yet, as the proem proceeds, these three distinct thematic areas are intermingled and confused, and with them such classical narrative categories as "before" and "after" coalesce. Boundaries, like the one between "inside" and "outside," collapse, and so, too, do distinctions between persons. These four stanzas offer a series of names which are perhaps the names of as many different persons, perhaps only a set of synonyms. The text begins with a man and his Muse; by the second stanza they have either become, or have been replaced by, a Novice and a Virgin. Is the Virgin the same as the Muse? Can a poet who begins by declaring that his Muse has been with him throughout his career now be a Novice? Is the situation in stanza two a continuation of the one in the initial stanza, or a new and antecedent beginning? Or is it a reversal perhaps? All three? A reader might well assume that answers to these dilemmas lie ahead. But such questions are not resolved by reading further; rather, the third stanza adds its own confusion, multiplying the names and stories being told. Two figures adduced in stanza two, "*Tanaquill*" and the "Briton Prince," are now the poem's subject, and the poet and his Muse, Novice and Virgin, have disappeared, perhaps having been absorbed into this other story. But the names of the central figures in this story have also disappeared: in the third stanza Eros, periphrastically named, and Mars and Venus form a new cast of characters around "that good knight," who, although twice named, has yet to be given a proper name. By the last stanza, when the poet / Muse relationship reappears, the "I" is invoking a "dearest dred" under a variety of ambiguous epithets: who is the "Goddesse heavenly bright" (4.1), the Muse? the Virgin? Venus? Diana? Why "Mirrour of grace and Maiestie"? We would expect not a reflection, but the source. Who is the "Great Lady of the greatest Isle" (4.3)? Venus on Cytherea? Queen Elizabeth at home?[6]

6. For a reading of the proem to *The Faerie Queene* couched entirely in terms of its function as an address to Queen Elizabeth, see Thomas H. Cain, *Praise in "The Faerie Queene"* (Lincoln: University of Nebraska Press, 1978), pp. 37–57. Cain notices, as I do, the echoes of epic; what I refer to as the ritual of the temple, he calls a hymn, and for him, the poet's praise of the queen links him to Orpheus. Although Cain's reading adds some interesting support to mine—for instance, by noting the mingling of the erotic and epic strains (pp. 42–43), the confusion of the identity of the muse (pp. 44 ff.), and, especially, the derivation of "scryne" from the imperial formula *in scrinio pectoris omnia* (p. 49)—his emphasis on Spenser fulfilling the conventions of praise keeps him from engaging the problematization of writing which seems central to the proem.

The crucial point raised by these questions is that, even in an opening invocation, the story's characters are constantly getting lost in each other. "Character," in fact, is hardly the right word for figures so easily exchanged; figures are what they should be called: names, words written on a page, signifiers without signifieds. In the first stanza, the "I" can best be described in such a fashion and is so designated, for the text begins with a voice whose assertion of presence ("Lo I the man") echoes against, and ultimately replaces, the other, antecedent voices to which the opening phrase alludes. A Barthesian maxim, that the writerly must "de-originate the utterance" (p. 21), banishing the magisterial divine Author for the sake of the text produced by the writerly reading of it, is adhered to in the translation of the Virgilian *"Ille ego"* that opens *The Faerie Queene*. This text begins as the echo of another text. And at once "I the man" is not alone, neither as text nor in situation, for he is presented linked to a Muse, immediately doubled with a surrogate who is palpably other and yet an intimate part of the career that is being reviewed. So the double irony of this heroic assertion of self, "Lo I the man," is that it finds a voice only in another's words and in being coupled with another in order to tell its history. In these substitutive relationships, the "I" is in danger of disappearing, even syntactically, virtually from the moment he appears, behind his Muse's skirt: "I the man, whose Muse . . . did maske / . . . in lowly Shepheards weeds."

Yet, ironically, the assertions of "I the man" are meant to be conventionally heroical; indeed, this is an epic gesture. Virgil's epic presence in the opening lines is reinforced when it is followed immediately by the promise of Ariosto's romantic epic, of "Fierce warres and faithfull loves" (1.9). Moreover, these "shall moralize my song," thereby invoking other texts, biblical exegesis, and, more subversively, the *Ovide moralisé*, which *The Faerie Queene* imitates in its combination of interwoven stories and moral meanings, the "Accidents" and "intendments" of narration as Spenser calls them in the Letter to Ralegh (p. 408). "Moralize" bears yet another meaning, one that oversteps one more boundary, at once overdetermining and undermining the stability of the text. Not only does this voice echo within the epic tradition—classical, Christian, and contemporary—it also speaks within the *reading* of these texts. Not only does "moralize" refer to an element in a narrative—the moral that is part of the tale—it also names a Renaissance habit of reading in which the understanding of a text is to "moralize" it correctly. The production of the text thus includes a reading as well as a writing: that is what "moralize" intimates. *"In the text, only the reader speaks"* (S/Z, p. 151). Whose voice, we may ask, is asserted as this text opens? Is it, indeed, a *voice* at all?

The "I" lays claims to be a voice by asking to be heard as it produces its song; but it is, by its own admission, a voice produced by habits of

reading, not hearing, and what it sings is a text provided by the Muse
"Out of thine everlasting scryne / The antique rolles."[7] "Me, all too
meane, the sacred Muse areeds": the voice decribes itself as summoned by
the Muse to tell the story in the "scryne," but "areeds" conceals a pun
that may suggest that the poet's voice is itself a text that the Muse has
read. The story he has to tell is his own story, for it is the story of how the
voice is produced: "Me, all too meane." "Meane" designates a stylistic
level (*sermo humile*), and the career encompassed—I am the man who
writes epic, but once I wrote pastoral—is the history of genres. The voice
is inscribed in genre, "enforst": and the pressure of time (this Muse, after
all, has been taught by time) is the exigency of literary history. The career in the first stanza subscribes to Aristotle's hierarchy of genres in the
Poetics, from pastoral to epic, the structure which Virgilian biography
apes. The poet's life can only be a text. In this light the "I" is not an
independent character and is certainly not the divine Author producing
the readerly text; rather, the "I" is the product of the requirements of the
text, the voice that the Muse demands when it "areeds."

But even here we have neither reached a beginning, nor an end.
Questions still remain. Does the Muse have this priority, does it produce
the text and create the "I"? Is it not the voice that demands a Muse? The
first line does seem to assert an "I" who has a Muse, and immediately,
that Muse is herself hardly independent, but is instead burdened with a
disguise and subjected to time (taught: does this mean forced, or given a
proper, moral, education?). Her situation is echoed in the poet's, for he is
forced to shift his clothing to weeds "far unfitter," to substitute epic
trumpets for his pastoral pipes. The Muse's mask in time is a dependent
clause in the poet's story. We cannot finally make the distinctions that
would answer our questions. What we can know is that, either way, the
story being told involves surrogacy and shifting places: in other words,
the occupation of the poet. Hence, the first stanza closes with a further
entrance into the mutual and shared textual situation of Muse and poet.
When the singer will blazon forth the sleeping praises that have "slept in
silence long," he will write—a blazon is a literary form, a catalog of parts

7. The reversal here is extremely significant since a normative boundary
is crossed. The opposition of speaking and writing is analogous to the opposition of nature and culture, of interiority and exteriority. As Derrida argues in *Of
Grammatology* (pp. 6 ff.), this opposition is weighted in terms of value and
sequence, so that the terms nature-inside-speech are granted priority and value,
spirituality. However, they can be reversed, and *Of Grammatology* is intent upon the reversal that allows writing-culture-exteriority to precede or replace the
opposing terms. When we approach Spenser's writerly text, one thing we
mean—and one thing that Spenser's text clearly conveys—is that writing comes
before representation. Voice in the proem is an artifact, a cultural construct, an
echo of other texts; nature is made by art.

that never covers the whole.[8] He will write, but he will also be written in
the text that the Muse "areeds"; he will write an endless catalog as inadequate in its prolixity as the story is now in its undivulged and silent
form. And whose story appears in this blazon, the Muse's or the poet's?
To answer this question, the boundary it implies must be crossed. And it
is, for behind both the instructed, masked Muse and the "enforst" (1.3)
voice of the poet, there is a power producing the text, one that dissolves
the terms of this question. The enforcement of the poet and Muse is, after
all, the echo of the condition of the hero within the undivulged epic text,
fato profugus; both Muse and poet are inside the text and nowhere else.
That epic condition still obtains when poet and Muse have been replaced, in the second stanza, by their subject matter, the Prince and Tanaquill. That boundary has now been explicitly violated, and the supposition that "I" and the Muse are somehow the "outside" (the
producers) of a text in which the Prince and Tanaquill are "inside" (the
story) is no longer tenable. By the end of the first stanza of the proem, we
may already suspect that to enter the space of the Spenserian text is to
cross these boundaries to the loss of our security. The questions, and the
reversals, drive us deeper into this textual sphere in which the inside is
the outside.

   As I have suggested, the second stanza clarifies nothing. First the
"I" and the Muse are refigured in the Novice and the Virgin; then this
severely chaste couple is replaced by Tanaquill and the Briton Prince
with his difficult quest. By the third stanza the quest will be explicitly
sexual—the blazon fulfilled—and possibly tainted in the figures of Venus and Mars and the questioning of the parentage of Cupid, who replaces Tanaquill as the Prince's driving force. This adds to the reader's
difficulties, since Tanaquill is a famous Roman matron, as legitimate in
her relationship with her husband Tarquin as Mars and Venus are illicit
in theirs. The text began with a moralized song; but can love and war,
the realms of Venus and Mars, be moralized? And then—in fulfillment?

---

   8. "The blazon consists of predicating a single subject, beauty, upon a
certain number of anatomical attributes: *she was beautiful for her arms, neck,
eyebrows, eyelashes, etc.*: the adjective becomes subject and the substantive becomes predicate. Similarly with the striptease. . . . Striptease and blazon refer
to the very destiny of the sentence . . . : the sentence can never constitute a *total*;
meanings can be listed, not admixed: the total, the sum are for language the
promised lands, glimpsed *at the end* of enumeration. . . . As a genre, the blazon expresses the belief that a *complete* inventory can reproduce a *total* body, as
if the extremity of enumeration could devise a new category, that of totality"
(*S/Z*, pp. 113–14). The form derives from medieval techniques of description,
amplificatio, and becomes a recognizable genre in the sixteenth century with
such poets as Clémont Marot and Maurice Scève. On this, see the forthcoming
study by Nancy J. Vickers, "The Anatomy of Beauty: Woman's Body and Renaissance Blazon."

in contradiction?—the second stanza enters the precincts of a Roman temple. And after? Cytherea?

Each crossing of the blank space on the page into another stanza seems to traverse a boundary between different stories. The text opens with a story about a literary career, inside the voice of genre and the history of texts. But by the second stanza, we are located in a temple, and, as the invocation suggests, a ritual is begun. The voice of that ritual never ceases, as we can tell by the litany of names produced to the end of the proem. Then, by the middle of the second stanza, we cross yet another boundary when we enter a text inside the text, and the hidden story written in "antique rolles" (2.4) is transcribed. When that text itself has been entered, another reversal has occurred. Whereas in the first stanza, the Muse seems to have chosen this poet because he had the story to tell, now it is the other way around. He implores the "holy Virgin chiefe of nine" (Clio? Calliope?) to tell him the story stored up in her "everlasting scryne" (2.3). The possibility that it might be his story no longer seems operable; but perhaps the distinction is now a matter of indifference—if he and the Muse are one, it would all be the same. If this is true, however, then storytelling must be an arbitrary act, and authorial priority undiscoverable, if not irrelevant.

The second stanza extends the principles of the reversibility of the text and opens up the possibility of endless substitution. We observe here a shift in locale: the Roman temple with its rituals of power replaces the world of shepherds and knights. The link between them, as one might expect, is textual. The "scryne" that holds the text is both a shrine (the temple reduplicated) and a chest for documents, the storehouse of the word. This double meaning permits yet another shift, one in which a reversal of priority occurs. Whereas the "I" in the first stanza asserted himself vocally as a singer, a voice with a song, and yet was "read" as the bearer of a text, in the second stanza, "scryne" affirms that the text— writing—comes before the voice. The prior text, already written and stored in the "scryne," is the story of Tanaquill and the Briton Prince, as yet unwritten to our eyes because not yet read, still silent before us. To make theirs the original story constitutes a reversal, for it is as if the story told (or to be told) produced the storyteller, as if reading were the (re)-writing of the text, and as if epic came before pastoral. Yet these reversals come closer to a beginning principle: Tanaquill and the Prince at first repeat the relationship between poet and Muse, Novice and Virgin. In his abasement, in which the Novice bows to the "will" (2.2) of the Virgin, lies the connection; the Prince, too, is in a position of submission, suffering for Tanaquill. The pattern of repetition and substitution has priority and undermines all beginning stories, all stable selves: *Fato profugus.*

What is this beginning story? Who, for instance, is Tanaquill?

Spenser fails to provide her with an identity until her one other appearance in *The Faerie Queene*, in the Elfin history that Guyon reads (II.x.76.4). There, Tanaquill almost immediately becomes another name for Gloriana, a connection that the reader might well expect to be made in the proem. But the name Gloriana does not appear in the proem to *The Faerie Queene* (it is, we could say, a significant absence), perhaps because Tanaquill, as the powerful wife behind Tarquin's throne, is not a comfortable identification for Elizabeth. If the name is to be explained at all, its source must lie "inside" the text as the latest substitute in a series that had begun in the proem with the romance designations "Knights and Ladies" (1.5), and that is furthered and only minimally differentiated in the repetition, "Faerie knights and fairest *Tanaquill*" (2.5), an arbitrary articulation that produces her name as readily as the false declension of "fairest" from "Faerie" ("Faire *Venus*" [3.2] will soon appear). Hence, although the name *Tanaquill* at first invites the reader to think of an "outside" of the text (i.e., Elizabeth), when this fails to elucidate the name, the reader realizes that the text is not simply referential and that it offers no easy access to what lies "outside" it; similarly, and coincidentally, the poet seizes the same possibility, the same delusion, of an "outside" when he views the Briton Prince, as he says, with rue (2.8). To do this, he acts as if he himself were "outside" the text. Is this move the narrator's attempt to avoid Tanaquill's power as she harasses the Prince and causes his "undeserved wrong" (2.8)? Is Tanaquill Juno to the Prince's Aeneas? What is his wrong, the quest or the failure? And is the narrator outside the text? No more so than Tanaquill; she is produced by the text. He rues his own surrogate, for the Prince's quest is an analogue for the production of the poem, as we can see when the request to relieve the Prince turns into a plea on the narrator's part, "come to mine ayde" (3.6). Both act under equally stern commands. Even the compassionate response that appeared to locate the narrator outside the story is dictated: "I must rue," the narrator reports. *Must.*

We are not finished with Tanaquill when we arrive at this overlapping, for yet another prior text is reversed at this point. The Roman seriousness of the second stanza not only problematizes the poem's beginning; it stumbles across a most unlikely and yet undeniable source for *The Faerie Queene*, although, like so many other important antecedent texts, this one is not explicitly named. The text is Chaucer's *Sir Thopas*. When the proem produces Tanaquill, it is not only Rome that the name invokes; Tanaquill, as her second appearance in the text shows, is also an Elfin name drawn from the book of Faery history. In that second reading, her name spells romance. And certainly romance as much as—if not more than—epic stands behind *The Faerie Queene*; its central plot, Arthur's quest for a queen seen in a dream, is familiar to romance, so much so that Chaucer chooses it first for himself to retell in

The Canterbury Tales. Such a literary story can only be treated to the play of texts.

No doubt it is one of the wonders of *The Faerie Queene* that it can relocate—and dislocate—itself in this way. To go from the precincts of the temple to the tale of *Sir Thopas* is to traverse literary history at a gallop. However, a metamorphic principle exists in English history, from Troy to Troynovant, and in literary history too, from epic to romance and, finally, to parody of romance. The latter is the particular province of Chaucer and is perhaps one reason for Spenser's attraction to this English forebear. *The Faerie Queene* is so fully the rewriting of epic and romance (which is, as Barthes says, the condition of the writerly text) that it establishes a literary space that is located, in its play of text against text, on the deadpan side of parody. The text is inevitably in this mode when it tells of the quest of the Briton Prince, a supplementary story of the repairing of a loss. Against that windy fragment, *Sir Thopas*, this text offers its own story, which, as we keep seeing, is no single story at all, but the possibility of beginning anew, refiguring, re-entering, crossing normative limits in ways that keep narration going, but going where?

This is precisely Harry Bailly's complaint about Geoffrey's story:[9]

> 'By God,' quod he, 'for pleynly, at a word,
> Thy drasty rymyng is nat worth a toord!
> Thou doost noght elles but despendest tyme.'
>
> (11. 929–31)

It is irresponsible, Harry Bailly says, simply to spin a tale out of itself. *Sir Thopas* barely gets started because of its digressiveness, because the word *bird*, for example, demands a list of birds before the next narrative incident can be told. By so doing, the story not only parodies romance but also plays with the supplementary quality of language. Nonetheless, it does present the basic elements of the framing story for *The Faerie Queene*, the quest of Arthur hidden in the "scryne." Sir Thopas has his dream and makes his way to Fairyland to seek its fulfillment, and it is

---

9. All citations from *The Works of Geoffrey Chaucer*, ed. F. N. Robinson (Boston: Houghton Mifflin, 1957). *Sir Thopas* is suggested as a parallel for Arthur's dream in editor Hugh Maclean's note to I.ix.13 in *Edmund Spenser's Poetry* (New York: W. W. Norton, 1968). Robinson notes the transformation of Pleyndamour into Spenser's Blandamour (p. 740, n. 897), which I allude to below. The relation of Chaucer and Spenser can perhaps be elucidated by Barthes's discussion of irony and parody in *S/Z*, pp. 44–45, and its provocative question, "What could a parody be that did not advertise itself as such?," a question implicitly answered by the writerly text. A. Bartlett Giamatti addresses the relationship between Chaucer and Spenser, and particularly between *Sir Thopas* and the story of Arthur, in *Play of Double Senses: Spenser's "Faerie Queene"* (Englewood Cliffs, N.J.: Prentice-Hall, 1975), pp. 47–52; he sees Sir Thopas and Arthur as "closely related . . . opposite views" (p. 51), burlesque and serious. Barthes's terms, it seems to me, allow us to go beyond this opposition.

there that Spenser locates his text. Harry Bailly allows Chaucer to go no
further; he insists that a text that claims to be nothing more than a text
cannot be tolerated. Yet before he is silenced, Chaucer makes his point
about narration and provides a model that can be rewritten endlessly; the
model list of substitutions, formulas, and repetitions reveals an essential
feature of narration:

> Now holde youre mouth, *par charitee*,
> Both knyght and lady free,
>   And herkneth to my spelle;
> Of bataille and of chivalry,
> And of ladyes love-drury
>   Anon I wol yow telle.
>
> Men speken of romances of prys,
> Of Horn child and of Ypotys,
>   Of Beves and sir Gy,
> Of sir Lybeux and Pleyndamour,—
> But sir Thopas, he bereth the flour
>   Of roial chivalry!

(ll. 891–902)

Chaucer's reverberating names—Pleyndamour will become Blandamour in book IV—and the assertions of epic and romance intentions,
"bataille and . . . chivalry," echo as *The Faerie Queene* opens with its
assertions and substitutions.

The second stanza of the proem confirms the echo of texts: even
"Briton Prince" is no proper name, designating as easily Arthur as Sir
Thopas—or even the Red Crosse knight, whose career from rustic clown
to knight is certainly written into the initial movement from pastoral to
epic/romance. So Tanaquill is, finally, a name produced by a pen and
drawn from a Roman/romance archive. The text circulates its elements.
The structure of the second stanza, moving from "Helpe" to "O helpe"
is meaningful in this respect, for the stanza, doubling back upon itself,
beginning again, makes no progress; it simply repeats and recombines.
In this circle, the stability of the speaker is lost in his text, much as the
teller of *Sir Thopas* who, banished as a lewd rhymster, a moment later
turns to offer the moral tedium of *Melibee*; that name is deferred in *The
Faerie Queene* until book VI, but the move has already occurred.

After all these attempted beginnings, the proem seems, in the third
stanza, finally ready to stay with a story. "And" at its opening appears to
offer the innocent sign of continuity and sequentiality. Yet, "and" begins the final stanza as well, and rather than continuity, it signals further
dizzying recombinations, accumulations, and accretions, excesses. Narration, having moved from epic to romance, now tries out myth, then

leaves it in the final stanza for what appears to be the social world of writing. The last version of the relationships of power that have been refigured in each stanza—between poet and Muse, knight and lady—is that between the poet and his patron, a social story that we might assume to be an "outside," an external limit to this text; yet, the litany of names at the opening of the last stanza suggests just the opposite, that this relationship is central to the production of the text and is as far "inside" it as we can penetrate. "And," then, leads us on a route that, however contradictory to the norms of readerly narration, with its forward motion and continuity, is the path of the writerly text.

These "ands" carry us toward the depths of a lack. They, along with more new names, are all somehow beside the point, signs of irresolution, failures at providing references and signifieds. The names are periphrases hiding names, never the last word. The "ands," formally ligatures, mask discontinuity. These lacks and refusals present what Barthes would call lures for the reader, for they intimate that there is an "inside" to the text, a last resting place, some center where the real truths and genuine names that the surface barely shows would finally emerge. Barthes's terms suit no text so well as *The Faerie Queene*: "Writing extenuates . . . the hallucination of the *inside*, for it has no other substance than the interstice" (p. 208). The text undergoes continuous reconstitution in the empty spaces between stanzas. Denying that where it has been has any conclusive force, the last word always produces a new one; one name readily becomes another. These productive denials undo the stability of narration even as they account for the generation of the text. So, after the moralization of the first stanza and the circularity of the second stanza, the last stanzas begin with "and." "And" gives the show away, laying bare the procedures of narration. These ligatures defeat both grammatical order and categorical distinctions, and when "and" becomes "and with," as it does almost immediately, combinative supplementarity and freeplay follow, making havoc of the solid pretenses of nouns and the endstops of predication. A string of *ands* (at 3.1, 3.6, 3.7, 3.8, 3.9, 4.1, 4.2, 4.6 [twice]) keeps reminding the reader that words in the text are in place of other words, that the text generates itself through substitutions. Finally, as the last word of the proem, "a-while" leaves the text pausing in an interim time that results from the two infinitives at which it has arrived, "to thinke," "to heare." "A-while" describes the time of narration in *The Faerie Queene*; it is unlocated and deferred, an interim in which seemingly endless replacements occur.

As I have been suggesting, these opening lines of *The Faerie Queene*, themselves an account of the nature of narration, now move toward their goal, toward a hearer, the "dearest dred" who has been generated in the text from the Muse of the opening lines and the Muse's subject matter, the central figure in her text, Tanaquill, a surrogate for both the Muse and this final figure. We cannot know where to locate this hearer, nor, in that reversible time that the infinitive signifies, can we distinguish the figure being produced from the figure producing; this hearer is at once inside and outside the text. What about the narration does she reveal? First, that this narrator has been undone in "his" doing, the production of the poem; he began unfit as shepherd, was "far unfit- ter" as epic poet, and finally, is "too humble and too vile" (4.6) to con- ceive the poem that he is somehow producing. The narrator is located on the boundaries of absorption by the text; this is one fact about narration being told here. A second is that the power of the text resides in its nu- merous metamorphoses; the dreaded hearer is the last in a chain of pow- ers. Finally, to situate ourselves, reading this text means seeing this final discursive space as ours as well.

Reading this text is also our undoing. Categorical distinctions dis- appear. After the third stanza, for instance, we can no longer separate producing from being produced, the activity of reading from the actual- ity of the text; nor can the negations of the text (its manifest undoings negotiated in absences, lacks, denials, breaks) be divorced from its ability to continue. Thus, in the third stanza, when another version of the quest of the Briton Prince is offered, this time motivated by the cruelty of the "impe of highest *Iove*, / Faire *Venus* sonne" (3.1–2) rather than by Ta- naquill, the narrative—and narration in general—enacts its own prin- ciple of perpetuation through undoing, both by recasting the story into a new version and by substituting the causative principle. Cupid, the substitute cause, goes without a proper name and is instead twice named periphrastically, as "dreaded impe of *Iove*" and "faire *Venus* sonne." Direct naming is avoided, and the double avoidance conveys ambiva- lence in the attributes—dread and beauty—and, more significantly, in the manner of production, imp and son. Eros is both a child and an offshoot, a graft produced naturally and also artificially in the text and as the text's figure for production. His disturbing function is to be an image of the generation of the text. The ambivalence in such production is further clarified when the narrator asks for the Prince's relief—"Lay now thy deadly Heben bow apart"—a request that translates into his desire to be free of the burden of narration. Were he so joined, he would cut off both the story and storytelling; asking for the Prince's relief merges the "inside" and "outside" of the text in equal and reciprocal acts of undoing. Paradoxically, the effect of the request in the very next line is not dissolution, but instead, generative and productive: Cupid, Venus, and Mars appear in the text as new names, new stories. Moreover, unlike Venus and Jove, these are the mythologically correct (if undeni- ably immoral) family of Cupid.

A beginning, however tainted, is arrived at, and the pains of questing and authoring are rewarded in this return of the text to its problematic instigator, Eros, refigured in this fashion. But once again, this beginning is not an end, and so although the antithetical "glorious fire" (3.4) may have been extinguished, and the terms of the request overcome, in the arrival of the new set of figures it is, inevitably, rekindled at once. Eros's flame may be calmed and his bow may be put aside, but the arrival of Mars dressed up "in loves and gentle iollities" (3.8) simply inverts Eros. The story is, once again, refigured, and at the end, the stanza names the abyss over which it has passed in these transformations, in this process of production, denial, substitution, and reproduction when it says it puts behind it "murdrous spoiles and bloudy rage."

Whose spoils and rage are these: Cupid's or Mars's? We cannot know when Cupid and Mars have merged. Is this meeting how love and war are moralized? And can these be said to be behind or to be "allayd" in the final line, or when the text proceeds? Doesn't the text in this very line arrive at its legitimate beginning, at the words that come before it? *"At nunc horrentia Martis / Arma virumque cano. . . ."*

Metamorphosed into the "dearest dred" (4.9) of the concluding stanza, the "dreaded impe" does not disappear at all; he puts in a final appearance. Who is this last figure, this final word, this dread? Again, although common sense might make a reader wish to substitute the name of Elizabeth, the text avoids her name and problematizes that response. A series of appositions, in which syntactic distinctions are defeated, ends in the "dearest dred": that periphrastic, metonymic designation is a final piece of surrogacy. Even her numinosity is the product of her arrival with a light like Phoebus's, doubly surrounded, echoing another's attribute and name. Nor is she independent of the speaker, for she can be read as his light, within him, and is produced as the object of his act, "to thinke"; but it is equally true that he is cast down ("afflicted") by this argument, that what he produces undermines him and produces him as well. That is, she is also the text, "the argument of mine afflicted stile" (4.8), its subject and object at once, its source and its reader. Power in the text is, in these transformations, no longer the erotic motive behind the Prince but what produces the poem in its reading. Familiar relations, nagging questions about the borderline between inside and outside, producers and produced, earlier figured in various couples—narrator/Muse, Novice/Virgin, Prince/Tanaquill—are once more refigured. The narrator ambivalently asks to be heard, subjecting himself to the hearer and at the same time asserts that he produces her. His desire to be heard becomes the desire of the "dearest dred" to hear. Like the questing hero, he relieves his desire by giving it up and investing another with the power to remove it. Hence, his power becomes hers, his relief no different from his frustration. Not to be frustrated in desire, he desires not to desire. This is itself so small a satisfaction, and so palpably self-destructive, that it is not merely an extension of frustration but its intensification. It is this paradoxical desire, in which the voice of narration is situated, that the reader shares as well.

The opening stanzas of *The Faerie Queene* offer a paradigm for the reader's situation in relation to the text and for the desire it generates. On the one hand, the text offers its lures in endless substitution and deferral; but the lures remain teasing, and the whetted desires lead to frustration. The text plays with the reader in the circulation of words liberated from the need to name objects, relationships, or sequences. Reading, the plea-sure of the text in this freeplay is also what leads to frustration. What makes the text and the reader go on when production defeats itself? An answer to this question is given in the text through a series of names for the power of the text. First it is called the Muse, a power before the text, in other texts; finally it is named as the "dearest dred," a power "outside" the text which amalgamates a Roman wife, a Roman virgin, and the Roman goddess of love. "Dearest dred" concisely names the greatest power in the text, the form ("argument") and substance ("stile"), the content of the text, the producer of the text, its "true glorious type" (4.7). This is the power that defeats the narrator, humbling him and casting him down; this is the power that generates his desire, the desire to write, to be written, and to be destroyed in the process. Is this a consummation devoutly to be wished? The space of narration is, in a word, where loss and excess meet, where orgasm would be no different from castration, where the triple goddess (Venus, virgin, and wife) is satisfied. This is the desire the reader participates in, generated in this undoing, violating norms, boundaries, limits. As Barthes says: "In narrative (and this is perhaps its "definition"), the symbolic and the operative are non-decidable, subject to the rule of an *and/or*" (*S/Z*, p. 77). Such is the nature of the text and its fatally ambivalent pleasures.

Ben Jonson was right more fully than he realized when he declared in *Timber* that Spenser "in affecting the Ancients, writ no Language";[10] it is not merely because Spenser's vocabulary is so often archaic that his is "no Language." True, this quality alone means that words in *The Faerie Queene* do not have the immediacy of reference that current words appear to have, that rather than seeming to point transparently to things, they send us to our dictionaries (E.K. gives us some clues as to what Spenser's readers did). When such searches prove fruitless, we are reminded that the meanings of words are determined inside a text as a matter of differences. In *The Faerie Queene*, how difficult it is to fix

10. *Ben Jonson*, ed. C. H. Herford, Percy Simpson, and Evelyn Simpson, 11 vols. (Oxford: Clarendon Press, 1925–52), 8:618.

meanings in the endless flood of signifiers, always, it seems, equally far from arriving at a signified. This reveals something about the nature of language even as it defeats the communicative function of language. And it is, as the proem to *The Faerie Queene* demonstrates, crucial to Spenserian narrative with its suppression of even such privileged signifieds as the names of the hero and heroine. The text thrives on periphrases produced by such evasions. As Spenser avowed in the Letter to Ralegh, the queen "beareth two persons" (p. 407) and so is sometimes called Gloriana, sometimes Belphoebe; two names instead of one, this is crucial to Spenserian narration. Further, Spenser adds, the queen's name as "beautifull Lady" has been arrived at by "fashioning her name according to [Ralegh's] . . . excellent conceipt of Cynthia, (Phoebe and Cynthia being both names of Diana.)" Names are explained through other names, and the doubling of names is an intertextual phenomenon that spills over the boundaries between texts; within such an understanding of narration, Spenser locates *The Faerie Queene*: "I have followed all the antique Poets" (p. 407), he tells Ralegh. All.

Narration does not merely generate itself from the virtually endless chain of signifiers, the legions of endless words. Syntactical structures are also produced in this fecund and frustrating manner. Every reader of the text knows about those startling elisions when the syntax of a stanza suddenly veers in midpoint never to return to its original point of departure. The last stanza of the initial proem provides a fine example of this. Its relation to stanza 3 is syntactically unclear; moreover, somewhere in the center of stanza 4 the goddess initially invoked becomes the "dearest dred." In the governing sentence, "And with them . . . / Shed . . . O dearest dred," the "you" implicitly invoked at the beginning of the sentence is not the same as the "dearest dred" set in grammatical apposition to it. She should be one of those that "come with" the power invoked, not the power itself; one cannot tell where the metamorphosis occurs. The reader is simply carried from one figure to another, and although logic demands attention to differences, the syntax of the stanza proclaims a profound indifference, leveling items in apposition into identifications. What comes with is the same as what comes. Nothing comes alone. Even when the syntax is clear, vague pronoun references can accomplish similar effects, as we saw earlier when Britomart disappeared into Florimell. In short, the sliding syntax and vocabulary of the poem dissolve all the normative boundaries that a readerly text would preserve. We can no longer be sure of the distinctions between inside and outside, first and last, self and other. As book IV makes explicit in that gratuitous narrative gesture in its title, *The Faerie Queene* has no place for Telamond, the closed and perfected world of the readerly. The text is not a product or an object; it is a demanding production, demanding both on the reader, and on the writer.

From book IV on, the problematic of production is an explicit and central concern of the text, and the questions raised in the initial proem to *The Faerie Queene* about the place of the narrator and narration dominate the text. Is the narrator the producer of the text? Does he contain it? Does it come from him? Or, is he produced by the text, a voice made first by the words on the page? Is the poem's source a Muse or a "dred," desire or its frustration? If we look ahead to the last book of *The Faerie Queene*, we might find in the figure of Matilde one paradoxical answer to these questions about source. Bereft, bewailing her lack of issue, Matilde is given as her own a child rescued from the mouth of a bear (VI.iv). Since Matilde's estranged husband is named Sir Bruin, the child is, through a pun, his fitting heir. Matilde demonstrates that a child—one's own child—can be gotten even if it is not begotten. The babe is generated doubly, like Cupid in the proem to *The Faerie Queene*, imp and child. And the Matilde episode seems to illuminate in this strange birth the erotics of the production of the text, the birth of a word. The vexed question of the production of the text is conveyed in the narrator's relationship to it, especially, after book IV, in his weariness, a sign that at once signifies his depletion in writing and his experience of being in the text and under its power. From book IV on, *The Faerie Queene* examines what it means if the text, like Matilde's child, can *"be gotten, not begotten"* (VI.iv.32.7). Thus, Spenser's poem is not a world, complete, closed, and referential, but a process demanding endless doing and "endlesse worke," because it relentlessly undoes itself, denying closure. The text establishes its space between *"be gotten"* and *"begotten."*

No better vantage point for viewing Spenser and the structures of discourse exists than book IV of the poem because it is there that these structures are both enacted and thematized. Its central theme, friendship, has a broad semiological scope in the sixteenth century, and the word and idea embraces the cosmos as well as human relationships. As Michel Foucault points out, *friendship* is one term in the extremely rich "semantic web of resemblance in the sixteenth century"; and, crucially, *friendship* is a word embedded in and descriptive of the endless chain that structures discourse.[11] The role of the brothers Priamond, Dia-

---

11. Foucault's list of words for resemblance in the sixteenth century includes: *"Amicitia, Aequalitas (contractus, consensus, matrimonium, societas, pax, et similia), Consonantia, Concertus, Continuum, Paritas, Proportio, Similitudo, Conjunctio, Copula"* (*The Order of Things*, p. 17).
Friendship is but one term in an extensive sequence of words that describes the relationships between all things in the cosmos, in society, and in the psyche. Both the standard treatment of friendship in Renaissance literature—Laurens J. Mills, *One Soul in Bodies Twain: Friendship in Tudor Literature and Stuart Drama* (Bloomington: Indiana University Press, 1937)—and in Spenser—Charles G. Smith, *Spenser's Theory of Friendship* (Baltimore: Johns Hopkins Press, 1935)—begin by noting that friendship is understood as a cosmic

mond, and Triamond in book IV exhibits this. They present a picture of the three worlds of Pico's cabbalistic cosmos, but they also figure the structure of the triple soul, and in their actions they engage in the crucial personal and public relationships that book IV depicts, friendship and marriage, cognate phenomena. Friends share one soul, the commonplace goes; and the marriage service insists that man and wife are similarly joined. *Friendship* is the word that covers all these structures. How things and objects are related—in blood, in spirit, in affection, in society—this is what friendship means; how they enter into structures where one can be taken for another—this is what friends do. Friendship

---

force. The idea goes back to antiquity and is variously associated with Pythagorean harmonies, the Platonic tetrad, analogies between microcosm and macrocosm, etc. The literature on these topics is, of course, extensive. A recent application of them to Renaissance poetry is by S. K. Heninger, Jr., *Touches of Sweet Harmony: Pythagorean Cosmology and Renaissance Poetics* (San Marino, Calif.: Huntington Library, 1974), a book that continues the critical tradition of E.M.W. Tillyard, *The Elizabethan World Picture* (London: Chatto & Windus, 1943) and C. S. Lewis, *The Discarded Image* (Cambridge: At the University Press, 1964).

Roche's rather theological reading of book IV is also undertaken in these metaphysical terms, as is James Nohrnberg's *The Analogy of "The Faerie Queene"* (Princeton: Princeton University Press, 1976). Nohrnberg's critical method of endless analogization means, as he says, to locate the poem in the matrix that a universe of correspondences provides (pp. 785–86). All these approaches assume that a Renaissance text in some way gains stability and order from replicating verbally the assumed harmonic structure of the universe. However, that point of view fails to see that a structure of replications and echoes makes the whole sphere of difference problematical. Rudolf Allers addresses this question in "Microcosmus from Anaximandros to Paracelsus," *Traditio* 2 (1944):319–407, esp. pp. 390 ff. What he sees is that the "human" is a difficult category to establish if the universe is one and if all things in it are structurally the same.

Plato's *Timaeus* is the founding text for the metaphysical and cosmological principles of the harmonic universe; however, Plato also saw the human problems, and raises them in the *Lysis*, his dialogue on friendship. If friendship is a relationship between two virtuous people, what lack in a virtuous man (who should be self-sufficient) causes him to seek another? and, if friends are equals, what can the same want with or from the same? Desires, as Socrates points out, are for things unlike. What desire, then, can underly friendship? The *Lysis* contributes another Socratic irony to western thought, for while it affirms that friendship is a great value, it can find no way to describe what it is; nor does the language of the friendship of the universe, with its *concordia discors*, seem to be the answer. Friendship depends upon there being at once a lack and a perfection in two friends; it is thus a word for a problematic difference and supplementation. As Barry Weller so elegantly and persuasively argues in "The Rhetoric of Friendship in Montaigne's *Essais*," *New Literary History* 9 (1978):503–23, one way to handle these difficulties, from the *Laelius* of Cicero on, has been to place friendship in an elegiac mode; in it, the problem of loss attaches itself to the writing which replaces the dead/lost/absent friend and writing itself becomes a memorial to and substitute for the absent other self and, therefore, for the absent writer himself, who is absorbed into his alter ego and who, although in one sense providing his text, is, in another sense, memorialized in it. Weller locates friendship in its textual matrix, and it is in this area that book IV of *The Faerie Queene* is inevitably located.

is not simply a term that names an analogical universe but the very word for the structure of discourse with its possibilities of substitution, exchange, and union, one word in place of another, one story in place of another.

Deferral keeps in play the problematic relationship between identity and difference, and deferral is necessitated by these very same problems in the relationship between friends. At Satyrane's tournament, Cambel appears in Triamond's armor, Triamond in Cambel's; each wins the other's victory. But then, who has won? And, is either one? Explicitly, an answer is deferred in the text and by the text:

> Then all with one consent did yeeld the prize
> To *Triamond* and *Cambell* as the best.
> But *Triamond* to *Cambell* it relest.
> And *Cambell* it to *Triamond* transferd;
> Each labouring t'advance the others gest,
> And make his praise before his owne preferd:
> So that the doome was to another day differd.

(IV.iv.36.3–9)

Treated as an ideal and indistinguishable pair, the two as one, Cambel and Triamond can receive social approbation (society speaks here with one voice, "all with one consent"). When differentiation is attempted, however, the heroes blur in the indistinct exchanges of transference and release; striving towards identification, Cambel and Triamond produce a text, "the others gest," each advancing the other's story, each deferring to the other. Deference blots out difference; identification remains problematic and self-identification seems impossible. In such a situation, judgment must be "to another day differd," deferred. The deferral caused by the problematic nature of friendship is essential to the discursive principles of *The Faerie Queene* and to the frustrating pleasures of the text.

These principles and problems can also be seen in the Letter to Ralegh. For "knowing how doubtfully all Allegories may be construed" (p. 407), Spenser goes on to justify the "clowdily enwrapped" text as necessary to give pleasure to those who would be put off by simple and straightforward moralizing; yet this enwrapment, he admits, is also the likely source of the displeasure the text causes, giving rise to "gealous opinions and misconstructions." What gives pleasure gives displeasure. The incitement to narrative pleasure that the letter alludes to—the variety of stories, their endless interconnected play, the deferral of an explanation of a beginning—putting off the problem of connecting narrative and meaning, or of finding what is central and what peripheral, the structural design that defers the beginning until the end—offering instead of the "wel-head of the History" (p. 408) the circles and repetitions of twelve feasts on twelve feast days with their twelve quests in twelve books—these pleasures assure a principle of frustration. The book remains always in "the middest" ("a Poet thrusteth into the middest"), and the text occupies an interstice, an interim ("a-while"); like Amoret, it is "perfect hole." The reader, fashioned by reading, is educated in frustration.

The Faerie Queene is a powerful text and its fascination results from its otherness, the writerly qualities that free it from the responsibility to reproduce reality as it is ordinarily perceived. And although it may be a text open to Harry Bailly's charge of irresponsibility to a world outside itself, it is certainly aware of itself, intent, from book IV on, upon its own operations.[12] The troubled and weary narrator of book IV, watching the central figures disappear, viewing the endless reshuffling of faceless knights and ladies, operating on the edge of an abyss in which he too may be lost, is encountering as well that void where the reader plays before the vast and powerful indifference of the text, learning the pleasures of being made subject to it.

12. The self-referentiality of narration in the second half of The Faerie Queene is brilliantly explored by Harry Berger, Jr., in "The Prospect of Imagination: Spenser and the Limits of Poetry," SEL 1 (1961):93–120, and was recently examined again by Stan Hinton, "The Poet and His Narrator: Spenser's Epic Voice," ELH 41(1974):165–81. Although I do not agree with Hinton's assumptions about authoring, he correctly notes the increased sense of the problems in narration in book IV (see pp. 174 ff.) and the narrator's inadequacies in handling his storytelling function. Berger emphasizes the conflict between poetry and actuality, one that the notion of the writerly text further explicates. An exploration of narrator and narration in book IV is offered by Judith H. Anderson, "Whatever Happened to Amoret? The Poet's Role in Book IV of 'The Faerie Queene,' " Criticism 13 (1971):180–200; although I am not comfortable with the critical vocabulary of her essay, I certainly agree that the narrator's presence in the poem is crucial in book IV and that stories in book IV frequently seem meaningless, flat, and unsatisfactory. However, unlike Anderson, I do not think that the problem in book IV is caused by external pressures, but by the nature of narration itself. Isabel G. MacCaffrey, in Spenser's Allegory: The Anatomy of Imagination (Princeton: Princeton University Press, 1976), also pays attention to problems in language and narration in the second half of The Faerie Queene (see pp. 314 ff.), but her list of imaginative triumphs in book IV is simply a set of misperceptions. On p. 328 she includes the union of Amoret and Scudamour, the "epiphany" of Arthegall and Britomart, the reconciliation of Belphoebe and Timias, the betrothal of Marinell and Florimell, and the completion of The Squire's Tale among the imaginative triumphs; these are, however, imagined. Amoret and Scudamour are not united in book IV; nor are Britomart and Arthegall, who separate after their engagement; and the future of Marinell and Florimell, as we have seen, is left hanging as a deferred ending. I agree with MacCaffrey about the "enfeeblement of structural forms in Book IV," but not about the "many plot-resolutions" (p. 336), none of which is satisfactory, and most of which—alas—do not even occur. More fundamentally, the poem cannot be dedicated to replicating "uninvented reality" (p. 333) if reality (nature) itself is a textual invention.

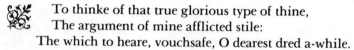

> To thinke of that true glorious type of thine,
> The argument of mine afflicted stile:
> The which to heare, vouchsafe, O dearest dred a-while.

The movement from "argument" to "afflicted stile" is a summary movement, a brief demonstration of what I have been suggesting in this chapter. The "argument," the text of the poem, refers back to the "glorious type," which is itself another name for the "dearest dred," who is the desired reader of the text. The writer's text becomes the reader's. But this transforms the text and writer, and the text so produced is also "afflicted," cast down, unworthy, subjected to precisely what makes it, and makes it glorious. In the movement from "argument" to "afflicted" the text is advanced and withdrawn; what the narrator is thinking of stands at the beginning side of this motion; at its end is the "afflicted stile" that the powerful other may deign "to heare." Between "to thinke" and "to heare," there is a gulf between two opposing powers in which an annihilative and productive transformation occurs. That abyss is the space of the text, of the production of the text. It is where the reader must be to produce it and to be produced by it. Then the reader would be the true alter ego for the narrator of a text which, as the three "ofs" of this closing statement intimate, is so deeply inside an endless series of containers that the boundary between inside and outside is hallucinatory.

OTHER VOICES, OTHER TEXTS

Absorption into other voices, subservience to other texts: this is the problem encountered in Spenserian narration. The narrator, simply in order to tell a tale, represents himself as being in the service of a text that comes before him, imposed upon by demands that are "outside" his text, usurped, so that his voice belongs to a ventriloquist, his text the text of another. The contextualization of book IV—the book is explicitly situated in relation to Chaucer's *Squire's Tale*—appears to be a way of acknowledging and confronting this problem. Book IV defines its narrative work as the provision of an ending to Chaucer's unfinished and broken tale. Narration in book IV means to supply what Chaucer's tale lacks: an ending. By making narration in book IV supplement that lack, it might well seem that writing is being allowed a free sphere of operation, that writing will occur precisely where nothing had ever been written before. Indeed, it could seem that having defined the narrative in this way, the problem of narration might be resolved. The limits upon the new writing—the supplied ending—would be in that case only the existant parts of *The Squire's Tale*, a text clearly situated before the new one, but limited nonetheless in its influence on the ending supplied. This is not, however, at all how the situation is defined. Instead, the problematization of narration is insistently affirmed; the problem of other voices remains an essential and inescapable condition of narration.

The narrator of book IV reports that there once was an ending to *The Squire's Tale*, but that had been lost, "wicked Time" having "robd the world of threasure endlesse deare" (IV.ii.33.1, 4). If that is true, then the task of narration is not to invent a suitable and new ending, but to rediscover a text that once existed and now no longer does. The "new" text must somehow coincide with that lost text. To provide that text, the narrator must abandon his voice entirely to Chaucer's, effecting a loss of voice so complete as to permit Chaucer to write through him, making his text a rewriting in another's voice. In other words, he has to occupy precisely the same relationship to Chaucer as Chaucer's squire does. This recognition will prove crucial for narration in book IV.

The tale the narrator must tell is simultaneously already written and lost, both completed and obliterated; in a word—ended.

> Then pardon, O most sacred happie spirit,
>   That I thy labours lost may thus revive,
>   And steale from thee the meede of thy due merit,
>   That none durst ever whilest thou wast alive,
>   And being dead in vaine yet many strive:
>   Ne dare I like, but through infusion sweete
>   Of thine owne spirit, which doth in me survive,
>   I follow here the footing of thy feete,
> That with thy meaning so I may the rather meete.
>
> (IV.ii.34)

To "revive" the lost story depends upon "infusion sweete," the incorporation of the spirit of the other; nothing less than complete absorption will do. In following "the footing of thy feete" the narrator is not merely assuming the language of the prior text and the rhythms that its words create; he is also pursuing that prior text as if it were a series of traces or footprints that needed to be followed, as if those ghostly demarcations could be followed.[1] The lost text is at once producing the narrator's voice and leading him on his way; to write (to produce the text anew), he needs

---

1. These terms are used earlier in the poem, when the Palmer defines Guyon's quest in relation to the Red Crosse knight's: "But wretched we, where ye have left your marke, / Must now anew begin, like race to runne; / God guide thee, *Guyon*, well to end thy warke, / And to the wished haven bring thy weary barke" (II.i.32.6–9). In book IV, the "marke" has become a Derridean "trace," the sign of an absence, a usage hinted at in the proem to book II, where the location of the text can only be arrived at by "tracing" the "fine footing" (4.5) that leads to Faery land. New beginnings are revisions, and the path of Guyon is also already written; his sea journey is the epic path of the *Aeneid*—and the poet's activity as well (cf.I.xii.42 for a typical use of the image of the sea journey for writing).

Spenser's reason for believing that *The Squire's Tale* was once completed lies in the indications in Chaucer's text that the tale was once complete; although the tale breaks off in mid-sentence, the following link treats the story as if it were complete, indeed, in the Franklin's estimation, exemplary: "In feith, Squier, thow hast thee wel yquit" (1. 673). He praises its eloquence and wishes his own son were as accomplished as the squire is. Since the tale is, in fact, rhetorically inept and always draws our attention to that, the Franklin's remarks are no doubt part of a sustained irony that surrounds the narrative, including its incomplete/complete status, the kind of allegorical irony that Alice S. Miskimin describes in *The Renaissance Chaucer* (New Haven: Yale University Press, 1975). The problems of authority and self-impersonation that Miskimin claims characterize Chaucerian narration but that are overcome by Spenser are in fact

to retrace that earlier path and to pursue his own obliteration. He needs to produce the lost text.

Defining the task of narration in this way places the narrator under an obviously impossible burden. A lost text is to be restored; yet the lost text is treated as if it still exists because it once did. That it can no longer be found does not mean that at one time there were not words, authoritative words, concluding *The Squire's Tale*. The absent text places an even greater demand upon the narrator than the presence of a completed text to be imitated would do. It exacerbates the situation of narrative absorption. If all later texts must act as if antecedent texts are lacking in some way that it can remedy; and, equally, if all later texts labor under the fear that the antecedent text is so complete as to deny any possibility that anything can be added to it, an antecedent text like *The Squire's Tale*,

---

present in both poets. As most critics of *The Squire's Tale* comment—(including Robinson in his note to 11.63 ff.)—Chaucer's tale is characterized by excessive *occupatio*. Literally, *occupatio* means that the speaker attempts to occupy the place of his audience, that is, to remove their objections by voicing them before the audience has a chance to do so. The effect of the technique is to draw attention to the narrator and the problems of narration. These have been variously interpreted. Harry Berger, Jr., for instance, argues that "the teller and his act of telling get in the way of what is told" ("The F-Fragment of *The Canterbury Tales*: Part I," *Chaucer Review* 1[1966]: 91), and Trevor Whitlock claims that "the emptiness of romance" is being revealed (*A Reading of the Canterbury Tales* [Cambridge: At the University Press, 1968], p. 166). Certainly, as even these two remarks suggest, the tale is arguably about the conditions of narration, and about literary history as well. The Franklin's familial hope reflects ironically on the squire's family (and literary) situation; his tale is a pale imitation of *his* father's romance, *The Knight's Tale*; Spenser shows his awareness of these family links when *his* Squire/narrator, the Squire of Dames, begins talking by quoting Chaucer's knight ("Whylome as antique stories tellen us" IV.ii.32.1; cf. "Whilom, as olde stories tellen us" *KT* 1.859), and when he replicates his narrator's relationship to Chaucer in the infusion of souls of the three "-mond" brothers.

An understanding of literary history as a version of family dynamics has been central to Harold Bloom's vision of literary history since *The Anxiety of Influence* (London: Oxford University Press, 1973) and is also implicit in the idea of the daemonic so forcefully presented by Angus Fletcher in *Allegory: The Theory of a Symbolic Mode* (Ithaca: Cornell University Press, 1964). The situation of the text of book IV in relationship to a disembodied but spiritually antecedent voice is daemonic. On this, see also Nohrnberg, *The Analogy of "The Faerie Queene"* (Princeton: Princeton University Press, 1976), pp. 771 ff., for an interesting discussion. Finally, on the substitution of one narrative for another as an essential hermeneutic act, literally (Hermes as robber, boundary crosser, master of languages), see Kermode, *The Genesis of Secrecy* (Cambridge, Mass.: Harvard University Press, 1979), pp. 1–2, 8, 10, and for the more general implications of this situation, see pp. 106 ff. and the discussion of intercalation in chapter vi; e.g.: "more story is needed, as a supplement, if the story is to make sense." Spenser's graveyard encounter with Chaucer issues in a hermetic ending when Cambina arrives in iii.42 brandishing the caduceus that she uses to enforce reconciliation, the union of the figures from Chaucer's text with the figures supplied in Spenser's: "and mighty spirites bound with mightier band" (iii.48.7).

which is so complete—and so void—exaggerates the situation of all writing. As Spenser locates himself, to write in order to restore a once written but now lost text is, in a sense, the condition of all writing. But, as we shall see, in the terms that Spenser establishes in book IV of *The Faerie Queene*, when writing fulfills that demand, it does so in such a way as to make the later text itself a lost text, situated in the place defined by a lost and antecedent text. Writing takes place in the space of an absence which is at the same time the space of the demand of another voice.

To enter into the lost text and to find a voice there is a most radical version of the loss of the narrator's voice to the voice of another. In book IV, that loss of voice is suffered at the very moment that the problematic situation of the text in relation to and as replacement for the lost text is announced. The confrontation with the spirit of Chaucer occurs at the point in book IV at which Cambel and Canacee, the characters from *The Squire's Tale*, have just appeared with Cambina and Triamond, the characters supplied in Spenser's poem as a way of ending Chaucer's story. Since the four characters are not recognized by others in the text, the Squire of Dames is sent out to parley. He returns and provides their names, and it is his indirect discourse and not the narrator's that seems to continue into the stanza cited above, in which the relationship of book IV to *The Squire's Tale* is described. Here are the stanzas leading up to it.

> They sent that Squire afore, to understand,
> What mote they be: who viewing them more neare
> Returned readie newes, that those same weare
> Two of the prowest Knights in Faery lond;
> And those two Ladies their two lovers deare,
> Couragious *Cambell*, and stout *Triamond*,
> With *Canacee* and *Cambine* linckt in lovely bond.
>
> Whylome as antique stories tellen us,
> Those two were foes the fellonest on ground,
> And battell made the dreddest daungerous,
> That ever shrilling trumpet did resound;
> Though now their acts be no where to be found,
> As that renowmed Poet them compyled,
> With warlike numbers and Heroicke sound,
> Dan *Chaucer*, well of English undefyled,
> On Fames eternall beadroll worthie to be fyled.

(IV.ii.31.3–9; 32)

It is not clear who is speaking here, especially when we pass from stanzas 31 to 32, whether we hear the narrator of *The Faerie Queene* or a voice inside the text, the Squire of Dames. Telling the story of the lost text, the narrator of book IV enters the voice of a Squire *in* his text who proceeds to tell a version of *The Squire's Tale* and to situate his discourse in relationship to Chaucer's story. A stanza later he will declare his problematical inhabitation through "infusion sweete" (34.6). He continues for the next canto and a half to tell "their acts . . . no where to be found" (32.5) in this voice. The fading of voice into voice that occurs in the space between stanzas 31 and 32—which delivers the narrator and squire at once—intimates the condition of narration in producing an ending for the lost and already written text.

To narrate is to enter other voices. This is a narrative fact that Spenser found by following Chaucer's lead in *The Squire's Tale*. As I suggested a moment ago, the narrator occupies the relationship of Chaucer's squire to his author. Chaucer's tale commences, after all, by placing his squire in the position of having to fulfill someone else's demands, those of his fellow pilgrims. Of course this is not unprecedented in *The Canterbury Tales*; others are expected to tell tales too. But the invitation to the squire carries a greater demand than is usual.

> "Squier, com neer, if it youre wille be,
> And sey somwhat of love; for certes ye
> Konnen theron as muche as any man."
>   "Nay, sire," quod he, "but I wol seye as I kan
> With hertly wyl; for I wol nat rebelle
> Agayn youre lust; a tale wol I telle.
> Have me excused if I speke amys;
> My wyl is good, and lo, my tale is this."
>
> (11. 1–8)

We notice at once the insistent repetition of the word *will* in various forms, as well as its synonym "lust"; the forthcoming squire's tale is placed even before it begins in a problematic space, fulfilling the commanding will of an other (is the "sire" his father, the knight?). Moreover, the demand to tell is coupled with what the squire treats as an act of misrecognition. This act is part of the demand: Come here, the "sire" says, and if you'd like, tell the story that you (among many) are qualified to tell. But the squire's "nay" denies that it is his desire to tell or that he has any particular expertise in the area designated. His agreement to narrate becomes part of a social bargain in which his own sense of himself is sacrificed to the communal demand (not to tell would be to "rebelle") that he speak and tell a tale that confirms the group's (mis)identification of him.[2] Their "lust" shapes his willingness to tell the tale, and

---

2. Since the squire is also agreeing that he has no particular expertise (implicit in "as muche as any man") his protesting "nay" is also an assent. Hence I place "mis-" in parentheses, to indicate that he has been, at the same time, correctly and incorrectly identified. Misrecognition, misidentification, and elsewhere in my text, misrepresentation, are my attempts to find English equivalents for Jacques Lacan's crucial term, *méconnaissance*. Lacan argues that in various ways at crucial stages of development the subject is subjected to

the good "wyl" he promises lies in his desire to satisfy them. "My wyl is good," he says, "and lo, my tale is this." Acceding to the will of another, his own good will is, however, something different from the tale; with all the good will in the world, the squire cannot promise that his tale will be a good one. All he can promise to do is to tell a tale since that is what has been asked of him.

No sooner has the tale begun, than it is interrupted by the squire's *occupatio*, his need to excuse his inability to tell the tale well. The story is, initially, a simple one—a strange knight appears at King Cambyus-kan's birthday feast bearing four gifts for the king and his daughter, Canacee— yet the squire has trouble with every element in this formula-ic romance. He cannot describe Canacee's beauty because [he] "dar nat undertake so heigh a thyng. / Myn Englissh eek is insufficient," he ex-plains (11. 36–37); not wishing to waste time, he nonetheless takes twelve lines to explain why he is unable to describe the king's clothing and the food served at the feast (11. 63–75). Before he presents the knight's description of the magical properties of the four gifts he bears— mirror, ring, sword, and horse—the squire interrupts himself to say that he cannot hope to reduplicate the knight's words; his excuses by now sound quite familiar: "I kan nat sowne his stile, / Ne kan nat clymben over so heigh a style" (11. 105–6)—although his pun points provocative-

others and that these acts make self-recognition something that occurs through others (this is the *stade de miroir*), make speaking an entrance into someone else's language (the Symbolic stage), and make desire the desire of an Other, for a lost, hallucinatory integrity. In Lacan's theories, the "I" is split from the start because of others, and original unity is a fantasy. Although Lacan does not pre-sent these (or other) ideas particularly systematically, they can be found in *Ecrits*, trans. Alan Sheridan (New York: W. W. Norton, 1977), esp. in the essay on the mirror stage and in the well-known essays on language, "The Function and Field of Speech" and "The Agency of the Letter." Particularly useful introduc-tions to Lacan's ideas are Anthony Wilden's "Lacan and the Discourse of the Other," in *The Language of The Self* (New York: Delta, 1968) and Richard Wollheim's "The Cabinet of Dr. Lacan," *New York Review of Books*, 25 Janu-ary 1979, 36–45, which also includes further recent bibliography.

Although I work from the introduction to *The Squire's Tale* that ap-pears in modern editions, the major editions of Chaucer in the sixteenth century did not print this link. However, this need not mean that Spenser was unaware of what we now regard as the authoritative text. There were many more Chaucer manuscripts extant in the sixteenth century than there are now, and readers then were not confined to printed books. The analysis of *The Squire's Tale* that I offer reinforces the meanings to be read in the invitation to the squire to tell his tale. Although Spenser could have known the link from manuscripts, he could also recognize what it implies about tale-telling from the tale itself. And the text of *The Squire's Tale*, in manuscripts and in sixteenth-century printings, is sub-stantially the same as in modern editions. The classic studies arguing the likeli-hood that Spenser read widely in manuscripts are collected in *Essays by Rose-mond Tuve*, ed. Thomas P. Roche, Jr. (Princeton: Princeton University Press, 1970), pp. 49–162; see esp. pp. 113–18.

ly beyond the limits it names. Once the gifts have been described, the festivities resume, again with the expected protestations, this time that the "forme of daunces" is too "unkouthe" (11. 283–90) for the deficient narrator. Hardly any story gets told because of all these interruptions and protestations of inability, and to the virtual exclusion of anything else, the first part of the tale seems to be about the difficulty the squire is having telling the story.

The theme of the first part of *The Squire's Tale* matches this narrative situation. If the tale is unsatisfactory as narration and is about the difficulty and dissatisfactions of narration, it is also a tale whose subject is desire and its satisfaction. That is what the knight's gifts correspond to: what the squire cannot describe satisfactorily are gifts of indescribable satisfaction. The mirror that enables its bearer instantly to know friend from foe, the sword that both wounds and heals, the ring that provides extraordinary knowledge—of the language of birds and the powers of simples—and the flying horse; these are explicitly designed to satisfy the desires of their intended recipients, the king and his daughter. However, those assembled at Cambyuskan's court are in much the same position as the squire's audience. They can only express bewilderment at these objects when the strange knight presents them—they keep wondering what the gifts mean and how they work. They too are not told the secrets. Whereas the king and his daughter have their wishes fulfilled, the courtiers are piqued and frustrated in their desire to understand the objects. The squire spends more than seventy lines (11. 189–262) listing their opinions about the gifts and registering their confusion only finally to label the courtiers' talk as mere "jangle" (1. 261). The judgment, however, is self-reflexive. Their inabilities match. Just as they are unable to penetrate the meaning of the gifts, so too is the squire. They ask the same questions. How does the sword work? the squire asks; his answer is that it "is unknowe, algates unto me" (1. 246). That is all he can say. But what is hidden is imparted by the knight to the king, a secret knowledge presented in the text as a promise to be fulfilled elsewhere. Here is the knight's promise to the king, and we should note again the repetitions of *will* and its synonyms, especially list, for they point to the desires that are promised satisfaction as the knight talks about the flying horse and its secrets.

> 'Sire, ther is namoore to seyne,
> But, whan yow list to ryden anywhere,
> Ye mooten trille a pyn, stant in his ere,
> Which I shall telle yow bitwix us two.
> Ye moote nempne hym to what place also,
> Or to what contree, that yow list to ryde.

And whan ye come ther as yow list abyde,
Bidde hym descende, and trille another pyn,
For therin lith th'effect of al the gyn,
And he wol doun descende and doon youre wille,
And in that place he wol abyde stille.

(ll. 314–24)

The example shows that this secret satisfaction of desire, the promise of
an offstage revelation of the workings of the pins of this pegasus, is the
only desire satisfied as the first part of *The Squire's Tale* draws to a close.
The king and his daughter receive their gifts and have their pleasures,
and no further words of explanation are offered about these matters. Nor
can they be, for the knight shares secrets that the squire—the narrator—
does not know. The reader of the tale, the teller of the tale, and the wit-
nesses to the presentation of the gifts in the tale (Cambyuskan's court) all
suffer exclusion; their pleasures are not fulfilled, their desires are not
satisfied. These frustrations seem palpably connected to the act of telling
a story.

The second part of the story addresses itself directly to these dissatisfactions. Coming to what he terms the "knotte" in his tale, the squire
admits again that the story has not been well told, acknowledging specifically that the reader is likely to be chafing at its prolixities and evasions.

The knotte why that every tale is toold,
If it be taried til that lust be coold
Of hem that han it after herkned yoore,
The savour passeth ever lenger the moore,
For fulsomnesse of his prolixitee;
And by the same resoun, thynketh me,
I sholde to the knotte condescende.

(ll. 401–7)

The desire ("lust" is the word for will here) for a good story is, as the
language indicates, as real and pressing as appetite, and needs to be satisfied; storytellers work to satisfy such desires. When they are inadequate,
as the squire is, what do they do when they arrive at such a knot, when
they must deliver or fail entirely? The squire, having managed to get
Canacee out of bed and into her garden, describes her standing before a
withered tree on which a bleeding falcon is perched. At that moment, the
squire solves the problem of narration adroitly; he steps aside and lets
the bird start talking, and the self-lacerating falcon tells Canacee her
pathetic story about abandonment and betrayal. The squire's solution is
to allow another narrator into his story; his voice disappears and a new
one picks up the thread. Canacee, having received in the first part of the
tale the gift of the ring that allows her to understand the language of

birds, now becomes the listener within a story to this new storyteller. Explicitly, at this moment, the pleasure of the gift is the satisfaction of hearing the story. The secret is no longer offstage, although the squire is. Ironic satisfactions, these; the narrator disappears into a talking falcon, and Canacee is given the pleasure of the story of the bloody bird, a story about frustrated desire.

Canacee sees the falcon lacerating herself, bleeding and swooning; understanding her plight because of the magic ring, and feeling for her, she asks, "if it be for to telle" (1. 447), that the story behind these actions be told. The falcon, descending and settling in Canacee's lap, tells her tale. She begins by commenting on Canacee's compassion for her; because Canacee has understood and felt, the falcon recognizes her as a desirable audience for her tale and as an audience that desires her tale.

> 'That pitee renneth soone in gentil herte,
> Feelynge his similitude in peynes smerte,
> Is preved alday, as men may it see,
> As wel by werk as by auctoritee;
> For gentil herte kitheth gentillesse.
> I se wel that ye han of my distresse
> Compassion, my faire Canacee.
>
> (11. 479–85)

The falcon begins her comment on Canacee's compassion with a piece of Chaucerian self-quotation. The line, "pitee renneth soone in gentil herte," appears in both *The Knight's Tale* (1. 1761) and *The Merchant's Tale* (1. 1986). So the falcon enters literally into a voice of "auctoritee" with these words, establishing herself as the narrator in precisely the same way as the squire has acquitted himself of his task, by entering into the voice of another. Either way, this seems to be an essential position for narration. Here, the falcon not only quotes words already written but also speaks in answer to Canacee's desire, compensating and rewarding her compassionate fellow feeling. Her relationship with Canacee, like her relationship with the authoritative text, is one in which she speaks for another.

Not surprisingly, the falcon's tale is about loss—her beloved tercelet betrays her; and crucially, it is about the loss of her will, even in becoming the lover of the tercelet. Desire fulfilled means losing your heart, and she insists on the word *will* as much as the squire does.

> And shortly, so ferforth this thyng is went,
> That my wyl was his willes instrument;
> This is to seyn, my wyl obeyed his wyl
> In alle thyng.
>
> (11. 567–70)

Once she has abandoned herself to him, the tercelet literally abandons
her, following the course of his restless desire. When she comes to tell
this part of her story, the falcon's explanation of the tercelet's betrayal is
couched in a striking manner. She recognizes that his behavior depends
upon his subscription to a text:

> I trowe he hadde thilke text in mynde,
> That 'alle thyng, repeirynge to his kynde,
> Gladeth hymself;' thus seyn men, as I gesse.

(ll. 607–9)

His flight does not illustrate his free will; rather, it illuminates a text: the
Boethian definition of nature, rather than nature itself, was behind the
tercelet's act. He had a "text in mynde" when he followed his desire.
"Thus seyn men, as I gesse," the falcon concludes. The play of texts here
is stunning, for it admits that the fiction is a trope and that the speaker is
a figure of speech. The tercelet fulfills his natural desire (his "kynde")
when he acts out a text, and the falcon derives her authority from a
"gesse" about what men say that reveals the text behind her voice.

The play continues when the falcon goes on to berate the perversity
of her love. What can you do with men, she says; they are just like birds
that are fed everything they could want—having their desires fulfilled—
and yet they would rather be free and eat worms:

> Men loven of propre kynde newefangelnesse,
> As briddes doon that men in cages fede.
> For though thou nyght and day take of hem hede,
> And strawe hir cage faire and softe as silk,
> And yeve hem sugre, hony, breed and milk,
> Yet right anon as that his dore is uppe,
> He with his feet wol spurne adoun his cuppe,
> And to the wode he wole, and wormes ete;
> So newefangel been they of hire mete,
> And loven novelries of propre kynde;
> No gentillesse of blood ne may hem bynde.

(ll. 610–20)

So saying, the falcon is fully revealed; the fiction that she is a talking bird
is replaced by talk about birds as (fictional) examples of human behavior. The reversal establishes narration in the play of fiction inside fiction
and in the elisions of the voice of narration from one textual situation to
another. In this explicit play on the difference between nature ("kynde")
and text ("kynde" is also genre), questioning whether or not nature is
textual and the bird's flight is natural, writing seems to have priority and
authority. Inevitably, the voice enters a text and the text maintains what
Barthes calls the "dissolve" of voices (S/Z, pp. 41 ff.), breaking down the

boundaries that would establish the differences between teller and tale, or that would maintain a single voice of narration or a single point of reference.

Narration in *The Squire's Tale* repeatedly occurs in situations of surrogacy that carry their attendant losses. The narrator (the squire) begins as the (mis)recognized communal representative; in the second part of his story, in order to satisfy his hearers, who are, he assumes, weary of the prolixity of his tale up to this point, he steps aside—explicitly withdraws—to allow another, a narrator "inside" his story, the falcon, to tell the tale. Narration now immediately locates itself in yet another act of surrogacy, for the new narrator agrees to her task only because Canacee is compassionately in her place, feeling at one with her, and requesting her to tell her story. At the climax of the story of losing her lover to another bird, another loss occurs, for her story enters antecedent texts, and their demands overwhelm hers. In both the citation from Boethius and the reversal that occurs when the falcon speaks as a person and not as a bird, text and tale seem to absorb the teller.

This absorption echoes the first half of *The Squire's Tale*. There, although neither the telling nor the hearing of a story seemed to offer any satisfaction, the story itself was about the satisfaction of desires in the gifts given to Cambyuskan and Canacee. In the second part of the story, however, it is precisely because Canacee has received one of these gifts that she can hear the falcon's troubling tale and enter into a compassionate identification with her. The satisfying gift of the first part of the tale becomes in the second part the profoundly dissatisfying capacity to be absorbed in another's grief and to hear a story.

Finally, narration in *The Squire's Tale* seems to be a process of continual absorption into the will of another; absorption is always accompanied by loss; as boundaries between tellers and tales keep dissolving, a virtually endless chain of surrogacy is generated. Not surprisingly, although the squire closes the second part of the story promising all sorts of satisfactory endings to his tale—among them that the bird will regain her mate with the aid of Canacee's brother, Cambel, and that he too will be instrumental in providing his sister with a husband, an anticipation of interlinked stories and their resolution—the third part of the tale breaks off after two lines, in the middle of an awkward sentence that has failed even to reach its predication. Ending is not what the squire can provide. Rather, as he indicated when he came to the "knotte" of his story, all he can do is defer to the voice of another.

When book IV of *The Faerie Queene* opens, we are in a similar situation, as the echoes of Chaucer's vocabulary of pity and compassion and an overt concern with narration indicate. The narrator establishes his relationship to the "piteous" stories of "lovers sad calamities" by displaying a Canacee-like compassion.

> Of lovers sad calamities of old,
>   Full many piteous stories doe remaine,
>   But none more piteous ever was ytold,
>   Then that of *Amorets* hart-binding chaine,
>   And this of *Florimels* unworthie paine:
>   The deare compassion of whose bitter fit
>   My softened heart so sorely doth constraine,
>   That I with teares full oft doe pittie it,
> And oftentimes doe wish it never had bene writ.
>
>   (i.1)

The narrator acts as if the text before him were not his own; this is at once a radical piece of misrepresentation on his own part and the crucial admission that stories are not told *in propria persona*. The "I" in this stanza is and is not designated accurately in this procedure. Since the text is treated as having already been written, and by another, the narrator positions himself not as its author but as its reader—that other—and he defines his relationship to the text in his feeling with the text. His compassion and pity provide him with the marks that the falcon had recognized in Canacee as perfect for the audience of a tale of self-laceration and loss. The narrator in book IV has collapsed author and reader self-reflexively; moreover, he performs the bird's self-laceration on himself in his act of reading, for his compassionate sympathy with the text leads him to desire its obliteration—to "wish it never had bene writ." This desire only furthers his denial of his role as author of the text; and it indicates as well that, if the text is to proceed, it will do so by undoing the "I" here, whether he is viewed as the producer of the text or as its absorbed reader. The text here, its "piteous stories," is described as something anterior to either a reader or a writer, both of whom are consumed by performing their designated roles in relation to the text, reading it, writing it—piteously absorbed.

This opening of book IV in the problematic denial of the narrator and reader predicts the shape of the entire book as it moves finally to the ultimate deferral of an ending when the story is left "to be perfected" (xii.35.9) elsewhere. The narrative of book IV takes shape between this complementary opening and close. The poem begins with a desire not to write and not to read, a desire for there to be no text that the text has already created in the reader/writer. The poem ends with the antithetical and yet parallel admission that the text that would satisfy the reader's desire and fulfill the writer's goal has not yet been written; it would exist only in some undefined "other place" that is not the place of the text. The poem ends with the infinite postponement of an ending, a denial of the text as firm and as absolute as the undoing of reader and writer with which it began. Already written and yet to be written, the space of the text—or its absence—puts the reader/writer in a position of lack: he does not gain his desire from the text. He wishes it annihilated, yet it annihilates him and finally undoes itself, gesturing toward that "other place" of satisfaction.

These difficult recognitions about the consuming text echo the basic conditions for storytelling in *The Squire's Tale*. They are the first indication of the way in which the provision of an ending for the Chaucerian fragment in *The Faerie Queene* will remain faithful to the principles Chaucer's text establishes, of what following in its steps will entail. Spenser's ending will also be an abandonment of Chaucer's text. The pretext will appear to have been annihilated. In fact, ending *The Squire's Tale* occupies little narrative space in book IV; by the conclusion of canto iii, Canacee has been married, and an ending promised by Chaucer's squire has thereby been reached. Soon after this point, the titular heroes and their brides become, as we have already seen, two among many couples at Satyrane's tournament and beauty contest, where they put in their final appearances in the text. The ending of Chaucer's story is literally their end, and whatever force the marriage of Canacee might have had as a satisfying conclusion to Chaucer's tale, it lacks any finality in book IV. The text continues beyond it, treating that ending as no ending at all, merely dismissing it and the heroes of the poem in a single gesture. The structure of *The Faerie Queene* demands twelve cantos to a book, and the actual conclusion to *The Squire's Tale* fills but a canto and a half of book IV.

It is, moreover, all flashback and narration inside narration located, as we have seen, in that undefinable voice of narrator/Squire. As a flashback alone we might view it as regression, not progress, and in voice it issues into that dizzying annihilative space that *The Squire's Tale* defines in its narrative exchanges. Ending Chaucer's story, then, at first means putting it behind, treating it as already written and yet somehow beside the point, undoing that story to allow this story its space. The old tale is dismissed—done with, abandoned—in ironic fulfillment of the gesture that opened book IV, the desire that the tale had never been written.

How then is *The Squire's Tale* ended in book IV, and what form does the narration take when that ending is supplied? If we can see these as related questions, we can begin to see answers. The ending supplied is not conclusive, but an ending that can be gone beyond. Book IV continues to find its way by further acts of annihilation and repudiation; one set of characters, for instance, is simply jettisoned, and a new one supplied in its place; one voice narrates, then another. The continuation of narration is made possible by such acts of undoing, totally undermining the stability of narration in order to narrate at all; what the text does to its master text it does to itself. This means finally that book IV so fully absorbs the voice of its source that it cannot end itself except by undoing itself. This, as *The Squire's Tale* implies, is the nature of narrative. Narrative works by entering more and more deeply into loss. Rather than supplying the loss in *The Squire's Tale*, finishing it and making it whole, book IV imitates the lacuna that the Chaucerian tale defines as the space of narration. This is where the narrator is, from the moment of his first utterance in book IV, the "wish it never had bene writ." The writing that follows confirms the wish.

When the narrator's voice dissolves into that of the Squire of Dames (ii.32), an ending for *The Squire's Tale* follows. This flashback story imitates its model in the most forthright manner. Chaucer's Canacee and Cambel remain and are simply doubled with two echoing characters. Canacee, "the learnedst Ladie in her dayes" (ii.35.2), is matched in her knowledge of nature's secret language by Cambina, "learned . . . in Magicke leare" (iii.40.1), just as the warlike and invincible Cambel, protected by Canacee's magic ring, is paralleled by the "-mond" brothers, remarkable for their love of arms, and saved from total annihilation by their mother's visit to the Fates. At first, narration finds a close in the simplest of entrances into the pregiven text: mere duplication. Chaucer's and Spenser's characters are linked in bands of friendship and marriage, and their unions provide an image of the relationship between the two texts. It would seem as if the narration has fully absorbed the preceding text, as if the ending were definitive. And it is: "So all alike did love, and loved were, / That since their days such lovers were not found elswhere" (iii.52.8–9); like echoes like, a chain of duplication tantamount to indistinctions, and the admission that they are "not found elswhere" is the precondition for dismissal. Soon after this they are not found at all. Obliteration is the ending provided.

Narration proceeds after this conclusion by returning to the story that was interrupted by completing *The Squire's Tale*. In going back—treating the flashback as a break in the story, not as part of the progress of the narrative—the narrator does not simply resume his own voice. The interruption of the narration has perhaps undermined that. Instead the narrator, even as he continues, reminds the reader of the entrance of his voice into the Squire of Dames:

> . . . now a new debate
> Stird up twixt *Scudamour* and *Paridell*,
> The which by course befals me here to tell:
> Who having those two other Knights espide
> Marching afore, as ye remember well,

> Sent forth their Squire to have them both descride,
> And eke those masked Ladies riding them beside.

> (iv.2.3–9)

He begins with a "now" and a "new" action, and takes control by referring to his "course" in telling and by his assumed superiority to a reader
who needs reminders after a break of a canto and a half. Yet the "course
befals" him—narration may, in fact, be directing the narrator, and his
statement that he is simply picking up where he left off glosses over the
implication in his words, that he may not be controlling the tale. Moreover, and this is crucial, the reminders to the reader of where we are
constitute a tissue of small, but numerous, misremembrances which,
taken together, suggest the limits of the narrator's authorial function.
The "new debate" between Scudamour and Paridell implies that there
had been an old one in progress earlier, when the narrative had broken
off; but in fact then it had been Blandamour and Paridell, not Scudamour and Paridell, who were engaged in a fight, and it was *they* who had
sent the Squire out to parley. Scudamour's name has no place in these
events. In "reminding" the reader, the narrator has replaced one name
with another, Blandamour with Scudamour. He makes other "mistakes" as well, for instance, treating the Squire as the knights' servant
("their Squire") instead of as an unattached and newly arrived member
of the group (this conflates the Squire of Dames with Scudamour's
word-brandishing squire [ii.1–2], Glauce, who is really Britomart's
squire/nurse); and, in another "error," the narrator locates the ladies
riding beside their mates when they had earlier been depicted as riding
behind. Now, moreover, they are masked; in canto ii they were not.

The "errors" have their point; they suggest how readily characters
displace each other, how fully they are enmeshed with each other, how
much what anyone is depends on the relationship between them all.
These principles apply equally well to the narrator. What "befals me
here to tell" is, as these mistakes tell us, as little under his control as were
events earlier in the poem. It is not only the break in narration that has
dissolved the narrator's voice into a surrogate narrator, the Squire of
Dames. Even before the break, in the main story, when Paridell and
Blandamour had begun the fight that the narrator now mistakenly recalls, he could see no way to end it until the Squire of Dames appeared
and stopped them.

> There they I weene would fight untill this day,
>   Had not a Squire, even he the Squire of Dames,
>   By great adventure travelled that way;
>   Who seeing both bent to so bloudy games,
>   And both of old well knowing by their names
>   Drew nigh . . .

> And then those Knights he humbly did beseech,
>   To stay their hands. . . .

(ii.20.1–6; 21.1–2)

"Inside" the narration the Squire is as much the narrator's surrogate, fulfilling his desire and his function, as he is when he joins the narrator's voice to commend the exemplary Chaucerian tale that intersects with his own. The Squire's success with Paridell and Blandamour leads him to suggest that they join together to go to Satyrane's tournament to defend their joint right to Florimell's girdle. When the narrative continues in canto iv, it is still recognizable as the Squire's and still headed in the direction he has appointed. That is, before book IV entered *The Squire's Tale* and completed it—before that completion punctuated and interrupted book IV—the narration was in the Squire's control. The narrator's reminder at the opening of canto iv, rather than establishing his authority, reminds the reader of the Squire's powers. *The Squire's Tale* is done; the Squire's tale continues.

It is *The Squire's Tale*, albeit transformed, that in fact keeps the text moving as it continues beyond its first ending of Chaucer's tale. Done, it is still not done. Satyrane's tournament, with its three-day fight to establish the proper mate for Florimell and the recipient of her magical girdle, is certainly recognizable as a retelling, or a replay, of the tournament that the three brothers waged against Cambel to win Canacee and her magic ring. And whereas the first tournament issues in marriage and a dismissal into somewhere "not found elswhere" (iii.52.9), the second tournament removes the heroes entirely from the poem. Replacement accompanies doubling, and in place of the perfect coupling of canto iii we are offered the union of Braggadocchio and (False) Florimell, latterday incarnations of Triamond and Canacee. This new couple has its double at the tournament, for the two are surrogates for the genuine winners of the tournament and beauty contest, Britomart and Amoret, an ideal—and impossible—couple. Britomart's victory upsets the chivalric ideal that had motivated the prowess of Cambel and Triamond; Amoret's, the ideal beauty of their ladies. Amoret may be the only lady who can wear the belt, but she is not the lady that the knights want or the one to whom they give the prize. The Squire of Dames, who was last mentioned at the opening of the episode, returns near its end to point its moral: "*Ungirt unblest*" he says (v.18.7). The statement applies to the episode and to its place in the narration. The narrative threads that seemed at first to have been tied up are being unwoven. This repetition is not simply duplication; it is at the same time an undoing of that earlier ending.

So the episode concludes with general dispersal. The narrator promises to follow his disappearing characters—"In which poursuit how each one did succeede, / Shall else be told in order, as it fell" (v.28.5–6)—a promise that he fails to keep. Sequence, order, and succession do not govern the narrative. Rather, the remainder of the canto is passed with Scudamour inside the Cave of Care, a location of great significance for narration. The narrator closes the canto by declaring his weariness, and that comes to be a primary characteristic of the narrator's voice in the second half of *The Faerie Queene*. Weariness is a fundamental result of being in the place of care—in the locus of compassion—for another; and all the narrator can do is once again defer an ending:

> The end whereof and daungerous event
> Shall for another canticle be spared.
> But here my wearie teeme nigh over spent
> Shall breath it selfe awhile, after so long a went.
>
> (v.46.6–9)

After this episode, the basic narrative material of *The Squire's Tale* is used again, with an even less satisfactory and more inconclusive ending. In the next canto, Arthegall and Scudamour commune (vi.9.1), joining together to form a little society bent on wreaking revenge and hostility on Britomart for her supposed wrongs, among them the victory at Satyrane's. The union of Scudamour and Arthegall, an amalgam of enmity and friendship, places them in a position others, notably Blandamour and Paridell, have been in earlier in book IV, and they replay a familiar scenario; each takes the other's part, each falls in the other's place. And the end of fighting here—as earlier—is falling in love. We have been watching the progress of "warlike wooers" (ii.38.1) throughout. So, at the end of the canto, Britomart and Arthegall are engaged. If we review the endings supplied, we can see the direction of narration: from the double marriage of canto iii, with its emphatic ceremonial and social support, we have passed through the parodic union of Braggadocchio and (False) Florimell to this engagement, at once a union and a separation. The marriage of Britomart and Arthegall is deferred. And, although their battle was modelled on the tournament for Canacee, it neither reaches its happy ending nor is its social vision broad and encompassing; community is reduced. A consummation is postponed because so much has been lost, because solutions seem so much weaker. Each repetition furthers narration, yet each reduces, denies, defers; loss is the principle of narration. One sign of this—it is a cause in the plot for the postponement of the union of Britomart and Arthegall—is the loss of Amoret. Britomart promises Scudamour that she will travel "backe to that desert forrest" (vi.47.1) where Amoret was lost, to recover "her second care" (vi.46.7). The direction of narration now, pursuing Amoret, is explicitly the motion that we have been following, a movement of return and retrogression rather than progress, a seeking out of the place where loss occurred.

> Backe to that desert forrest they retyred,
>   Where sorie *Britomart* had lost her late;
>   There they her sought, and every where inquired,
>   Where they might tydings get of her estate;
>   Yet found they none. But by what haplesse fate,
>   Or hard misfortune she was thence convayd,
>   And stolne away from her beloved mate,
>   Were long to tell; therefore I here will stay
> Untill another tyde, that I it finish may.
>
> (vi.47)

This stanza defers, putting ahead a story of what has already occurred, a story of what is lost. Here, the poem's forward motion is explicitly announced as retrogression, retirement, withdrawal; and the earlier flashback "interruption" in which *The Squire's Tale* was first ended now has become a basic structure of narration. In other words, the very form of that first ending becomes the form of the sequent narrative; deferral of narrative progress makes the next location of the text a place of loss that precedes what has occurred in the text thus far. Moving back, the text moves into itself, or refers to its own movement, for this return reveals explicitly that the text has been finding its voice only in reworking and unworking that ending with which it began. Undoing those ends, it returns to the condition of narration, which is to enter the place of loss, "Where sorie *Britomart* had lost her late" (47.2), the place of the lost text endlessly replaced without ever being restored.

Into whose voice does the narrator enter going "backe to that desert forrest"? The question has an answer we might by now expect. Again, it is the voice of surrogacy, the Squire's voice, that we hear. In this return, this backward glance, a gesture of the Squire of Dames at the moment he rescued the narrator from an early impasse and set the characters on the road to Satyrane's is repeated. When the Squire came upon Blandamour and Paridell fighting, and asked why they fought, they told him that it was because of Florimell:

> Ah gentle knights (quoth he) how may that bee,
> And she so farre astray, as none can tell.
> Fond Squire, full angry then sayd *Paridell*,
> Seest not the Ladie there before thy face?
> He looked backe.
>
> (ii.22.3–7)

The Squire's gesture, to look before by looking back and to find what is lost before his eyes, is the perfect emblem for narrative movement. For the narrative to go ahead it looks back. Going forward, the narrative confronts the loss behind the text that generates it. The story, rather than

making genuine progress, returns to what has been lost, and loses what
has been gained; going ever deeper into loss, the text enters itself and its
generating principle, born as it is from other voices, from other texts,
from those lost words spoken in another's voice.[3]

No part of book IV exemplifies the nature and direction of Spenserian narration better than the story of Timias in cantos vii and viii. Attempting to rescue Amoret from her abductor, "greedie lust," Timias
wounds her. Belphoebe catches him bending over the wounded maiden,
kissing her eyelids; assuming that she is witnessing seduction or love-
making, she storms off: "Is this the faith, she said, and said no more"
(vii.36.8). She wordlessly refuses all his attempts at explanation, and
brandishes her bow and arrows, not allowing him to say a word, forcing
him "backe . . . to retreat" (37.9). Finally, "unto those woods he
turned backe againe" (38.3) to live in solitude and grieve for his loss.

What has happened here? A Chaucerian sequence is initiated, beginning with Belphoebe's act of (mis)recognition, reading betrayal in
her lover's behavior. She sees desire in an act of compassion and reads
one for the other. In her eyes, Timias's behavior instances lust, and what
she sees produces what occurs; Timias becomes the image of Lust, retrospectively a justification of her perception but also a result of it. Timias
continues to maintain the silence imposed upon him; he shows the power of Belphoebe's abandonment by abandoning himself: he breaks his
arms, rips his clothing, lets his hair grow. "Uncomb'd, uncurl'd, and
carelesly unshed" (vii.40.6), Timias no longer resembles his former self

---

3. Book IV begins by demanding a backward look. In the third stanza of
the proem, the importance of love is argued in this way, that "who so list looke
backe to former ages, / . . . / Shall find" that all acts of wisdom and heroism
"in love were either ended or begunne: / Witnesse the father of Philosophie, / Which to his *Critias*, shaded oft from sunne, / Of love full manie lessons did apply" (Proem 3.1, 3, 5–8). Beginning and ending are indifferent matters in this backward glance, and the shape of narration as an undoing is
intimated. Moreover, to what text do these lines refer? The one described sounds
most like the *Phaedrus*, although the description is loose enough to cover any of
the dialogues in which Socrates talks with young men about love. On the one
hand, the description disperses its referent to a number of possible texts; the one
text it does specifically allude to, however, does not seem to fit; Socrates (presumably "the father of Philosophie") is not in the *Critias*, nor is its subject love.
It is, however, an unfinished dialogue, its subject is human society, and it breaks
off at the description of a meeting in the Temple of Neptune where the Atlantean
decline into covetousness is to be considered. Is book IV also supplying an end to
that Platonic fragment when it concludes in Neptune's realm and demands that
Proteus give up Florimell? By the end of the proem, book IV is, like this antecedent text, described as a lesson (5.9), so the words of the lost text alluded to (lost
both in the plenitude of dispersion and in absence) are the words in this text in
which motion is forward/backward, ending and beginning in the lessons of
love, the act of reading (lesson derives from *lectio*) a text.

but has, instead, assumed the form that Belphoebe saw, the savage that had attempted Amoret's rape. In this shape, he assumes his place within the text as a duplicate. "Who he whilome was, uneath was to be red" (vii.40.9), inscrutable as "himself" but not in his textual generation. He has been undone—alone, lost, abandoned—and slips into a form already written in the text, an identity seen before. The transformation of Timias which is so visibly his undoing also makes the narrative go backward; the text enters itself in this retrogressive movement "backe" (37.9) and "backe againe" (38.3).

Timias, then, is transformed into an antecedent figure in the text. Although the reader can readily recognize this transformation, those in the text cannot. Arthur soon appears, for instance, and does not know his own squire; he ventures a number of interpretations of this curiously mute and provocatively moving figure, recognizing at least that Timias is other than what he appears to be, that a "gentle swaine" (vii.45.6) lurks behind the savage guise. "Secret signes" (45.4) take him that far. Even this reading, however, has been prepared for in the text. In a moment that is even antecedent to the appearance of "greedie lust," Arthegall had arrived at Satyrane's tournament disguised as a savage man. For him, the form was a costume and the motto on his shield, "*Salvagesse sans finesse*, shewing secret wit" (iv.39.9), carries an invitation to decipherment. Arthur reads the transformed Timias as if he were the kind of emblematic figure with explanatory text that Arthegall's device proclaims itself to be, in which the natural man is a piece of literary play. But when Timias is in this form, the question is whether this emblematic figure of savage lust is a natural state or an artificial construct, whether Timias has become what he was or whether, devastated by the withering word of the most important other person in his life, he has accommodated himself to her sense of him by becoming what she saw. As in *The Squire's Tale*, the boundary between nature and text is called into question through this transformation, this squire's tale, and the question seems especially problematic because so many possible others condition the form and appearance of the self. As in Chaucer, the problematic nature of Timias's form coincides with the complex nature of desire.

In his transformed state, however, Timias has one certain identity. As Arthur readily sees, he is a writer.[4]

> And eke by that he saw on every tree,
> How he the name of one engraven had,
> Which likly was his liefest love to be,

---

4. "Outside" the text he is Ralegh. It is Ralegh's "owne excellent conceipt of Cynthia" (p. 407) that lies behind Belphoebe, Spenser avers in the Letter to Ralegh, as mentioned earlier. As Stephen Greenblatt argues in *Sir Walter*

For whom he now so sorely was bestad;
Which was by him *Belphebe* rightly rad.

(vii.46.1–5)

Arthur has no trouble deciphering Timias's text or reading "rightly" that name, the single word written "on every tree," and Timias's joy at hearing Arthur pronounce the name makes it clear to Arthur that the squire is the writer of the name. So Timias, who has denied himself speech because Belphoebe would not allow him to speak to her, whose every spoken response is "mum" (vii.44.5), writes one word again and again. He is silent; yet he is in his form a speaking picture, an emblem of lust, an embodied trope. The lack of speech, which makes him uncivilized, is also what makes him a cipher. As he is produced, so he produces—he writes. Writing comes before and in place of speech in this paradigmatic story, and the writing he does is itself a literary sign; it is, of course, because of other texts that Spenser's reader knows that the poet's signature is the inscription of the name of his beloved on the bark of a tree. Such writing reverses the familiar trope that makes nature into a book (*liber creaturae*); the poet makes nature his writing tablet and inscribes his text on it. The reversal is a figure for the genuineness of the

---

Ralegh: The Renaissance Man and His Roles (New Haven: Yale University Press, 1973), Ralegh's life transforms his poetic tropes into lived reality; in *The Faerie Queene*, the translation back into text occurs. In *The Queen and the Poet* (New York: Barnes & Noble, 1961), Walter Oakeshott draws comparisons between "Like to a Hermite poore" (xi in *The Poems*, ed. Agnes M. C. Latham [Cambridge, Mass.: Harvard University Press, 1962]), and the situation in IV.vii–viii (see pp. 97 ff.). There are many specific echoes of Ralegh in Spenser's text, such as the derivation of Corflambo from "the flames . . . which from my hart arise" (xi, 1.8) or Amoret's unfeeling treatment by Lust from 1.2 of "My boddy in the walls captived" (xxiii); Timias's aphasia is the silent suit of 1.30 of "Sir Walter Ralegh to the Queen" (xviii); perhaps the cryptic xxii alludes to Sclaunder (cf. "Meanings accordinge to their minds" and viii.26), and perhaps the syntax of 1.5 is remembered in AEmylia's account (cf. "art . . . weare" and vii.14.6, 15.1). In *The Oceans love*, Cynthia is named Belphoebe and identified with a dove (11. 327–8), and the metaphor of the chains of love follows: "Shee did untye the gentell chaynes of love" (1. 330). When the etymology of "world" is offered (viii.31.6) it is, possibly, Ralegh's disyllabic pronunciation that is remembered and imitated; see Latham's comments (p. 31) in a note on 1. 174. In short, in the Timias episodes, Spenser's text enters Ralegh's, being those texts into which Ralegh's life entered as well. Some of these matters are treated in Michael O'Connell's *Mirror and Veil: The Historical Dimension of Spenser's "Faerie Queene"* (Chapel Hill: University of North Carolina Press, 1977), pp. 114–24. His reading of the episode as the representation of the challenge of actuality to the poet's moral function seems to separate poetry and actuality too easily, and fails to see their continuing relationship throughout *The Faerie Queene*. The "historical dimension" of the poem is not simply its allusions to events "outside" the text, but the relationship of the text to these events and their situation in the text. I return to these questions in my consideration of "The Authority of the Other" below.

poet's love, a return to nature that is not artifice. Again, the boundary between text and nature succumbs to the shape of desire.[5]

Thus far, Timias's story seems indebted to *The Squire's Tale* thematically, and its regressive return appears to be both a rearrangement and transformation of some of the narrative elements of the antecedent text and a revelation of the basic conditions for the production of the text in place of loss. But, in the very next episode, the relationship of the story of Timias to the meanings connected with the art of storytelling in that precedent text becomes fully apparent. For yet another ending to Chaucer's story is offered, this time, however, not in terms of the marriage of Canacee, which had generated the earlier sequence of failed endings, but through her interlocutor, the talking falcon. Their fates, we recall, were interwoven in the promised conclusion of Chaucer's squire. In book IV, the falcon becomes a dove, and Timias replaces Canacee. But the situation remains the same in structure: a human being and a bird enter into a compassionate relationship in which fellow feeling and the production of a text are interwoven. As we shall see, in this version of an ending, as in those given to the Canacee story, ending overlaps with undoing: the bird and the bard are destined to disappear from the text.

The dove first appears when Timias is engaged in poeticizing,

---

5. That texts replace nature with other texts, and call those texts nature, is the playful intimation in volumes of poetry that bear names like *Silva* (Statius) or, in English, *The Forrest* or *Under-woods* (Jonson). The reversal of this trope is, as Rensselaer Lee suggests, exemplified in *As You Like It*, where Orlando not only writes the name of his beloved on the trees, but also fulfills the destiny marked out for him in his pre-text, Ariosto; on this see Lee, *Names on Trees: Ariosto into Art* (Princeton: Princeton University Press, 1977). At the point when book IV moves into its own explicit textuality in canto vii, we enter an area of "nature," rather than the castles and tournaments of the first part of book IV, a savage landscape where caves provide a basic habitat. Here, the emblematic Lust and his double Corflambo live; we find ourselves entirely in a realm of literary representation, moving among tropes for natural desire. The wild men here are like those savages from Elizabethan entertainments; for instance, the one at Kenilworth, where "one clad like a Savage man, all in ivie" greeted the queen (see John Nichols, *The Progresses and Public Processions of Queen Elizabeth*, 3 vols. [London, 1823], 1:494): here Gascoigne, disguised this time as Sylvanus to agree to her departure (pp. 515 ff.), presented her with the figure of Deepedesire—Leicester's persona—pleading, as Bruce R. Smith summarizes, "that Elizabeth would metamorphose him from a languishing plant back into a dutiful courtier. Tongues in trees indeed" ("Landscape with Figures: The Three Realms of Queen Elizabeth's Country-house Revels," *Renaissance Drama*, n.s. 8 [1977]: 58). These figures are like knights disguised for a tilt, for instance the wild man in the joust at Queen Helen's court in Sidney's *Arcadia*, II.xxi. A charming illustration of such a figure can be found in Robert Withington, *English Pageantry*, 2 vols. (Cambridge, Mass.: Harvard University Press, 1918), 1: facing p. 74; his history is told by Richard Bernheimer in *Wild Men in the Middle Ages* (Cambridge, Mass.: Harvard University Press, 1952), which includes a description of a contemporary and Lustlike savage from *The Rare and Most Wonderful Things Which Edward Webbe an Englishman Borne Hath Seene* (London, 1590). Descriptions of the inhabitants of the New World frequently transform these literary tropes, cannibalism being the attribute most often ascribed, a displacement of imperialistic desire on to the savage opponent. On this transforma-

pouring out his laments for the lost Belphoebe into the void; for although he is aphasic in human company, in solitude he can speak. The dove too has "likewise late . . . lost her dearest love" (viii.3.4), and her parallel loss provokes similar activity; in "deare compassion" (3.7) of "his undeserved smart" (3.8) she joins voices with Timias to "beare with him a part" (3.9; compare the lines with the opening stanza of book IV). In the song she sings, Timias believes he hears "his owne right name" (4.5), an act of identification which only increases his flood of tears. Yet, "her mournefull muse" (5.3) also comforts him, and in recompense he feeds her:

> And every day for guerdon of her song,
> He part of his small feast to her would share;
> That at the last of all his woe and wrong
> Companion she became, and so continued long.
>
> (viii.5.6–9)

---

tion, see Stephen Greenblatt's "Learning to Curse: Aspects of Linguistic Colonialism in the Sixteenth Century," in *First Images of America*, ed. Fredi Chiappelli (Berkeley and Los Angeles: University of California Press, 1976), pp. 566 ff. Commenting on one such description, Greenblatt notes that it is "an almost embarrasingly clinical delineation of the Freudian id" (p. 567).

This same description is as true of Spenser's Lust, Mandevillian with his ears reaching to the ground, savage trope and a phallus at once (although his huge mouth may invite a hermaphroditic reading), just as Corflambo is the act of perception that follows from his consuming form, "the powre of . . . infectious sight" (viii.47.8). For further discussion of Spenser's use of the wild man, see Donald Cheney, *Spenser's Image of Nature: Wild Man and Shepherd in "The Faerie Queene"* (New Haven: Yale University Press, 1966). For further discussions of European images of the New World, see Hugh Honour, *The New Golden Land* (New York: Pantheon Books, 1975), p. 56 for the wild man connection, pp. 5, 54–55, 64, 77, 87 ff. for cannibalism (including illustrations).

Several pertinent essays appear in *The Wild Man Within: An Image in Western Thought from the Renaissance to Romanticism*, ed. Edward Dudley and Maximillian Novak (Pittsburgh: University of Pittsburgh Press, 1972). Hayden White, in "The Forms of Wildness: Archaeology of an Idea," pp. 3–38, offers a breathtaking introduction to the subject, which ranges from the Judaeo-Christian wild man as radically other and the Greeks' polymorphous satyrs, to medieval ambivalances centered on desire and its punishing fulfillment, to Renaissance and modern noble—or at least, heuristic—savages, and to contemporary wild men within, ids, exploiters, the reminders of the costs of civilization. White's essay is not easily summarized because of its range, but it presents much material to support the figure of "greedie Lust." More limited, but nonetheless interesting, studies, are provided by Stanley L. Robe, who deals with ambivalent responses to the physical and spiritual nature of new world inhabitants and the transference of old world myths to new locales in "Wild Man and Spain's Brave new World," pp. 39–53, and by Gary B. Nash, who emphasizes the colonizing activities of the early seventeenth century in "The Image of the Indians in the Southern Colonial Mind," pp. 55–86. As Earl Miner remarks in passing (p. 88 of "The Wild Man through the Looking Glass," pp. 87–114), Englishmen did not have to look beyond Ireland to find wild men. Spenser's poem and his *View of the Present State of Ireland* amply show that; cf. Stephen Greenblatt, *Renaissance Self-Fashioning* (Chicago: University of Chicago Press, 1980), pp. 184–188, for an incisive discussion.

The episode obviously derives from the Chaucerian story. As in the second part of *The Squire's Tale*, central is the concern with that compassionate merging of speaker and audience in which one tells a story for another and tells another's story. Here, the exchange of food for word indicates that the life of the text derives from the loss shared by Timias and the dove, the source for their context, companionship, and communication.

The dove's role as alter ego and surrogate is not limited to playing the poet's double; she is Belphoebe's as well. The dove, after all, is female, and she has lost her lover; and in her loss, Timias imagines her saying his name. Clearly, the dove is a fantasized version of the beloved; the bird in fact further concretizes and enlivens the conceit involved in inscribing Belphoebe's name on a tree. She is a speaking piece of nature. Before, Timias's text was her name; now, the dove speaks his name as her text. It is because of this compensatory identification that Timias's next act is to take the heart-shaped ruby that Belphoebe had given to him and put it around the dove's neck. The gift serves as the emblem of the exchange of hearts that constituted his relationship with Belphoebe. Although it is a token of desire fulfilled, it is, quite explicitly, a wounded and bleeding heart (this recalls *The Squire's Tale*); there is loss whether desire is fulfilled or frustrated. Putting the jewel on the dove's neck, Timias takes bittersweet pleasure in this further identification of the dove with Belphoebe; and the bird, immediately upon receiving the token, flies away, to Belphoebe. She seems to be doubling Timias's pain, playing Belphoebe's part entirely, including abandoning him. Yet it is to Belphoebe that she flies, to her that she displays her gift; the identification is used as a lure to draw Belphoebe back to Timias. This accomplished, the dove disappears, and Belphoebe receives Timias back.

The dove's role has been to join compassionately with Timias in loss and to embody his loss doubly, by echoing his song—his lost speech—and by symbolizing Belphoebe—his lost love. To complete her role, and be what she signifies, she comes to be replaced by the other she has stood for. Once the dove has brought Belphoebe to Timias, she is seen no more. Having done what the poet's words desire—spoken of the lost beloved to the lost beloved and having brought her back—she can disappear. She has been like the words that take the place of loss; now she takes their place when Belphoebe assumes hers. In the fiction, the source, the end, and the only word for Timias to write is *Belphoebe*, and the dove, functioning as a replacement for this, is eminently replaceable. The dove is made to be sacrificed. With her, a piece of the Chaucerian text is transformed in this text so that the dove enacts the meaning of the falcon in that precursive script. Ending her story does not restore her to her mate, and the reason for this is clear. She is not a "character" but a trope; her function is to be the word in place of the lost beloved and to be replaced by her. She is restored to her meaning in the antecedent text, her meaning as a text. And if she is simply the text, she bears its most unsimple meaning, forcing us to wonder what the transformed Timias is if not a text, or what *Belphoebe*, that word in place of loss, is. After all, what is, finally, Timias's career if not his exile because of Belphoebe's words and silence—"Is this the faith, she said, and said no more" (vii.36.8); his exile from words—the only word he has is hers to write; and his recovery—acknowledging himself as and at her word. It is only when Belphoebe views him as *her* text that she compassionately receives him back.

> Yet nathemore his meaning she ared,
>> But wondred much at his so selcouth case,
>> And by his persons secret seemlyhed
>> Well weend, that he had beene some man of place,
>> Before misfortune did his hew deface:
>> That being mov'd with ruth she thus bespake.
>
> (viii.14.1–6)

She reads the text—"his meaning she ared"—that she made when she refused to say another word or hear one. Compassion causes speech; identification follows. Back in her good graces, Timias regains his tongue, forgets his lord, Prince Arthur, and neither he nor Belphoebe is seen again in book IV.

This paradigmatic story about the text as a replacement for loss and about the necessity of a lack for the production of a text is not merely another ending for and undoing of that crucial lost text that book IV keeps replacing. We have seen that Timias's story intersects with one squire's tale, Chaucer's; but that is not all. It also crosses another squire's tale, the one Spenser's narrator is telling when Timias's story interrupts. To see this, we must go back to the beginning of these stories in canto vii. When Amoret fled the embraces of "greedie lust" we are told that her flight was coincident with Belphoebe's pursuit of wild beasts in company with someone simply described as "that lovely boy" (vii.23.6)—presumably Timias. Then their paths cross.

> It so befell, as oft it fals in chace,
>> That each of them from other sundred were,
>> And that same gentle Squire arriv'd in place,
>> Where this same cursed caytive did appeare,
>> Pursuing that faire Lady full of feare,
>> And now he her quite overtaken had.
>
> (vii.24.1–6)

Who is this "same" squire, the same as "that lovely boy" in the stanza before or the same as a squire Amoret had heard about from AEmylia in Lust's cave and who had been replaced at their place of meeting by Lust himself? The answer, of course, is both. This is Timias; yet, his first mention in the story of Amoret confuses him with an antecedent figure from a story she has heard. And no wonder: in this stanza in which he is simply "that same gentle Squire," he and Lust, "this same cursed caytive," are "in place" (24.3). Before Belphoebe (mis)reads him as Lust, they have met in a pronoun: "And now he her quite overtaken had" (24.6). So even at first Timias is, again, overtaken by the antecedent form of Lust who overtook an antecedent squire. Tale inside of tale; squire inside of squire. Where do they meet? "In place," where Lust finds them both. That place of replacement is the location where they lose their loves, lose themselves, and become instead the very shape of desire.

When we retire "backe to that desert forrest" (vi.47.1), to the place where Amoret was lost in the arms of Lust, we enter a section of *The Faerie Queene* in which narration and loss continuously and variously, and quite overtly, meet the shape of desire. Repeatedly, desire takes the form of the wish to hear someone else's story, to enter into it compassionately, and to be lost in it because the other's story is one's own as well. Amoret is lost when she is carried off by "greedie lust" and when her shrieks fail to reach Britomart; sleep seals Britomart's ears. But once in the cave of Lust, Amoret is all ear. Someone else is there, AEmylia, and she has a story about lust and loss to tell. The conditions of her storytelling by now should be familiar to us: Amoret needs to recognize her own story in this one. The weeping maiden reminds her that they share the same place; in response, Amoret asks for a *reading* (that is her term) of the situation. Her use of that word embodies her situation; in the cave of Lust, in the place of desire, she is in someone else's story:

> Aye me (said she) where am I, or with whom?
>   Emong the living, or emong the dead?
>   What shall of me unhappy maid become?
>   Shall death be th'end, or ought else worse, aread.
>
>   (vii.11.1–4)

When the story of "a Squire of low degree" (vii.15.7) has been told, it ends with the teller's name, AEmylia, as its final word. That name answers Amoret's question about who shares her place and what that place is. For AEmylia is the name of the relationship between Amoret and AEmylia; it is their friendship, compassionate fellow feeling, that allows their tales to be one: "Ah sad *AEmylia* (then sayd *Amoret,*) / Thy ruefull plight I pitty as mine owne" (19.1–2). Friendship is that substitutive mode of identification that joins their lives in this forlorn situation.[6]

---

6. In the Renaissance, friendship, because it represents an ideal and almost unrealizable form of human relationship, is more often exemplified through fictions than through historical exempla. When we consider the list of friends in the Temple of Venus, for example (x.27), we note that all—with the exception of David and Jonathan—would have been considered fictional by

OTHER VOICES, OTHER TEXTS   57

AEmylia clarifies this in answer to Amoret's next request, that she "read" (19.3) how she has managed not to be devoured by Lust.

> Through helpe (quoth she) of this old woman here
> I have so done, as she to me hath showne.
> For ever when he burnt in lustfull fire,
> She in my stead supplide his bestiall desire.
>
> (19.6–9)

There is yet another person in the cave, a further alter ego, an old woman who "in . . . stead" (19.9) takes AEmylia's place with Lust. How is that supplementation related to the union that AEmylia and Amoret have made? It is a duplicative form, as appears in what follows. As Amoret and AEmylia "did discourse" (20.1), Lust appears in "the mouth" (20.5) of the cave. He means to rape them and then to eat them. The place of desire is characterized by the equation of discourse and sexuality. Lust's cannibalism and rape are an extreme version of a pattern of substitution. Not only do sex and talk in the cave of Lust occur in place of each other, but AEmylia's experience with the "Squire of low

---

Spenser's readers. In his treatment of friendship in *The Book Named the Governor* (ed. S. E. Lehmberg [New York: E. P. Dutton, 1962], 2:xi. ff.), Sir Thomas Elyot gives no historical exempla, as he usually does, but instead launches his longest fiction, the tale of Titus and Gesippus (pp. 136 ff.), a story of an ideal— its title declares that it presents *"the figure of perfect amity"*—friendship as exchange and sacrifice; like its model in Boccaccio's *Decameron* (X.viii), Elyot's fiction develops all its problems out of the central thesis that friends share everything and can substitute for each other. These ideals are humanly problematical, especially if the shared item is a spouse, or one's life. Another way of seeing the problem is to recall that Montaigne's essay "Of Friendship" (I.28), a celebration of his relationship with Etienne de la Boétie, is also meant to be an introduction to a book of la Boétie's. Montaigne is "particularly obliged to this work, since it served as the medium of our first acquaintance" (*The Complete Essays*, trans. Donald M. Frame [Stanford, Calif.: Stanford University Press, 1965], p. 136); ironically, by the end of the essay, Montaigne has substituted another book of la Boétie's poems for the one in question, since the text in which they met had been pirated and misunderstood. It seems consistent with the idealized friendship eulogized by Montaigne that it should be located in a reading of a book that is no longer possible. For further interpretation of the textuality of friendship, see Weller, *New Literary History* 9 (1978), esp. pp. 508–9, 517–20. In *The Faerie Queene* AEmylia's Squire of low degree derives from a medieval romance of the same title (see *Middle English Verse Romances*, ed. Donald B. Sands [New York: Holt, Rinehart & Winston, 1966], pp. 249 ff.), and Amyas and Placidas echo the world of friendship stories, for instance, that of *Amis and Amiloun* (ed. M. Leach [London: Oxford University Press, 1937]), in which the friends are so "lyche" that only clothing distinguishes them; hence, they can substitute for each other in bed and in battle. Some of the hagiographic background for such tales is found in A. H. Krappe, "The Legend of Amicus and Amelis," *Modern Language Review* 18 (1923): 152–61; Krappe makes the interesting claim that friendship traditions are likely to derive from 'primitive' ideas about twins. This idea receives further treatment in Robert Brain's fascinating *Friends and Lovers* (New York: Pocket Books, 1977), pp. 116–38.

degree" fully reveals the sequence of substitution. Her story is of a secret assignation with her beloved "in a privy place, betwixt us hight" (17.7) that leads instead to a meeting with Lust: "There was I found, contrary to my thought, / Of this accursed Carle" (18.3–4). The place of this union is where her desire goes unfulfilled and she becomes instead prey to the devouring desire of Lust, that savage who is first described as little more than a gaping mouth dripping blood (vii.5). Instead of meeting the object of her desire, the squire, desire meets her in its most undesirable form. The words of agreement between AEmylia and her squire lead to this devouring place—to that devouring mouth; and telling the story to Amoret, the situation recurs. They talk of Lust, of fobbing him off with a substitute, and when their discourse, the story, ends, Lust reappears. The shared story is repeated. Amoret flees, a squire comes to the rescue, and Belphoebe calls him Lust. One squire's tale is placed inside of another.

The squire's tale of AEmylia is not the last version of that story either. The very same story is told again, this time to Arthur. In this second account, the squire's fate, not AEmylia's, is revealed. It is, not surprisingly, exactly parallel. When he arrives where "twixt themselves" (viii.51.1) they had agreed to meet, "in stead of his *AEmylia* faire" (51.4) he is taken by a giant named Corflambo, his name as emblematic of desire as any could be, "*Corflambo* was he cald aright" (viii.49.1), the teller self-reflexively says. The giant's daughter, Poeana, attempts to seduce him and he is carried off to a dungeon where her dwarf keeps him under lock and key. The squire's trusty friend arrives and attempts to rescue him, as we might expect, by an exchange:

> The morrow next about the wonted howre,
>   The Dwarfe cald at the doore of *Amyas*,
>   To come forthwith unto his Ladies bowre.
>   In steed of whom forth came I *Placidas*.

(viii.59.1–4)

Since the two friends are "so like" (55.9), the substitution works—so well indeed that it is Placidas, not Amyas, who escapes.

The story is extraordinary, and not merely because its substitutions seem to double and redouble those in the tale AEmylia told. Finally all distinctions are lost, which seems to be the point in that amazing outcome whereby nothing is accomplished for Amyas. The story is especially extraordinary, however, as narration. It is, after all, Amyas's story; Amyas is the squire of low degree, although the narrator is Placidas. But the reader cannot know who is speaking, whether the teller is recounting his own story or not, until the moment in the story cited above when the names are supplied. At the very moment of substitution in the story, *we* know that Placidas has been substituting as the teller of Amyas's story.

We know this because Placidas supplies his name in order to take on that of Amyas, his friend. This is actually the first time that the squire has a name—he is always a "squire" before—so he is given his name just when another has taken it, and he is given it by another. Moreover, his story is not only parallel with AEmylia's: it is because Amyas is as a name cognate with AEmylia that we know that he is her squire, the one about whom she has told her story.

This second version of that squire's tale, then, has as its narrator one who enters into the place of Amyas doubly, both "inside" the story and in telling the story, and Placidas has arrived at the situation he hoped his substitution would achieve—he is where he meant Amyas to be. As book IV continues, these heady interchanges in this squire's tale continue; in the versicle to canto ix, the summary statement, *"The Squire of low degree releast / Poeana takes to wife,"* makes another of those substitutive "mistakes" that are keys to the meaning of narration. Arthur effects the double marriages that end these interwoven squires' stories, but only after a dizzying moment when, seeing both squires together, neither he nor Poeana can tell them apart (ix.11). After that, their names are not mentioned again, and it is simply two squires and their ladies who are disposed of. Once again a version of the double marriages that end *The Squire's Tale* has occurred; the end of all these squires' tales is to rediscover that ending anew.

These multiple squires' tales, these Chaucerian supplements, have driven story into story; more and more, substitution marks the entrance into a place of loss in which the desire for another coincides with the desire for storytelling and story hearing. Insistently, these stories stand "instead"; substitution is the rule both "inside" the stories and in their telling. The meeting place for all these tales, although renamed, is the locus of desire, a cave or dungeon correspondent to Lust's "wide mouth" (vii.5.5) and Corflambo's "infectious sight" (viii.47.8). This is where Timias stood kissing Amoret's eyelids and attempting to heal her wound; here Belphoebe appeared with her "sodaine glauncing eye" (vii.36.1) and her devouring word. This place of identification is one of (mis)recognition, where being named by another means to be a word in another's mouth—in his story, not one's own—substituted, effaced, lost. In the caves and dungeons through which these stories move, discourse meets the cannibalism of desire.

We can recognize why this occurs when we remark that these meanings join in a single word, *converse*, which in Spenser's period covers a broad area of social and physical familiarity as well as encompassing the modern meaning of talking with another. Moreover, in book IV, this word, in all its semiological richness, stands as the crux in an address to the reader that the narrator makes in the midst of all these squires' tales. This is a moment worth pausing over. The reader is told that this episode, the sojourn of Arthur, AEmylia, and Amoret in the house of Sclaunder, has been misread.

> Here well I weene, when as these rimes be red
>   With misregard, that some rash witted wight,
>   Whose looser thought will lightly be misled,
>   These gentle Ladies will misdeeme too light,
>   For thus conversing with this noble Knight.

(viii.29.1–5)

The address is virtually unprecedented in *The Faerie Queene*; true, occasionally, in an opening apostrophe to a canto, an implicit reader of the text is asked to reconsider an idea or a mode of behavior; in book III, for instance, men are asked to recall the heroism of women (iv.1), and women are implored to restrain their cruelty to men (xi.2). But never have these been addressed as *readers*, and it has been behavior or ideas, not the reading of the text, that have been called into question before. The only person ever addressed as a reader is the "dearest dred" of the first proem; for instance, in the proem to book IV, she is asked to "reade this lesson often" (5.9). However, in the address to the reader in the middle of book IV, it is not even reading, but assumed misreading that is in question. Although, like the "dearest dred," this reader is being asked to read, the request is couched negatively—the narrator assumes that the reader has read and has (therefore) misread. Ironically, the injunction not to misread translates into not reading at all. The chain of implied demands—avoid "misregard," do not be "misled," do not "misdeeme" —ends in "conversing," the very word for discourse that contains the misreading that the narrator wants the reader to avoid at all costs. To avoid it, the text must either not be read or must be misread. The narrator's stern counsel to the reader thus represents a denial of the text, demanding that either the reader share the desire of the narrator expressed in the first lines of book IV, the desire to unwrite the text, or the text be refused the range of possibilities contained however uncomfortably in the word *converse*, and thus in the episode of "conversing." Yet to deny the text, to misread in one way in order not to read in another, has its safeguards; it is meant, one presumes, to save the reader from the polysemous perils of the place that the narrative itself has just entered; for we are in the house of Sclaunder when the narrator addresses the reader.

Sclaunder is the most threatening representation of the voice of the other in the text. She is entirely venomous speech, a voice that embodies the worst version of the "misregard" of others.[7] Her words express a

---

7. Harry Berger, Jr., writes convincingly about Sclaunder in "A Secret Discipline: *The Faerie Queene*, Book VI" in *Form and Convention in the Poetry of Edmund Spenser*, ed. William Nelson (New York: Columbia University

"poysnous spirit" (viii.26.3) that enters the hearer's ears and pierces the heart, leaving a wounded soul:

> Her words were not, as common words are ment,
>   T'expresse the meaning of the inward mind,
>   But noysome breath, and poysnous spirit sent
>   From inward parts, with cancred malice lind,
>   And breathed forth with blast of bitter wind;
>   Which passing through the eares, would pierce the hart,
>   And wound the soule it selfe with griefe unkind:
>   For like the stings of Aspes, that kill with smart,
> Her spightfull words did pricke, and wound the inner part.
>
> (viii.26)

Hers are, in short, devouring and destructive words; to be in her mouth is to be engulfed in her malicious desire. When we recall that earlier moment when the narrator (inside the Squire of Dames' voice) had asked for the "infusion sweete" (ii.34.6) of the spirit of Chaucer, we can see Sclaunder's "poysnous spirit" as its demonic counterpart. It is that desire become dread. But where has the narration been proceeding if not towards that metamorphosis? Entering that lost voice, finding that lost text, it has not ended *The Squire's Tale* but imitated that loss again and again, never bringing the antecedent text any closer to closure; instead, it has so fully entered the voice of its precedent that all it can do is replay it in an increasingly fragmentary and unsatisfactory manner. So doing, the antecedent text seems only to be further dismembered, and narration occurs in the voice of undoing. The voice is now called Sclaunder. Precisely because the text is polysemous it can be undermined, read and misread at once; this is what leaves it open to Sclaunder and what enables her words to wound. The narrator responds to her menace with a wish to undo the text. His saving gesture imitates her and he slanders the

---

Press, 1961), p. 42: "words become a form of rending, a spiritual cannibalism whose perverse and irrational music is aimed at the nerves and the affections." On the significance of "conversation" in this context, see the etymology of "conversation" noted by A. Bartlett Giamatti in "Proteus Unbound: Some Versions of the Sea God in the Renaissance," in *The Disciplines of Criticism*, ed. Peter Demetz, Thomas Greene, and Lowry Nelson, Jr. (New Haven: Yale University Press, 1968), p. 456n. A brief but significant discussion of the idea is offered in D. J. Gordon's essay, "Name and Fame: Shakespeare's *Coriolanus*," in *The Renaissance Imagination*, ed. Stephen Orgel (Berkeley and Los Angeles: University of California Press, 1975), p. 218: "the earliest meaning of *conversation* is *living together*. The bond is language."

For typical uses of "conversation," see Lodowick Bryskett, *A Discourse of Civill Life*, ed. Thomas E. Wright (Northridge, Ca.: San Fernando Valley State College, 1970), e.g., p. 154: "civill societie and conversation"; pp. 166–67: "Conversation therefore and friendship are necessary for the accomplishment of civill felicitie, which without love cannot be."

text; to keep it from being (mis)read he denies the meanings it produces, for instance, the meanings that meet in "conversing" and that have been undercutting the solidity of discourse and storytelling throughout book IV. The narrator attempts to stop a seemingly autonomous destructiveness inherent in the text, something figured in the last action of Sclaunder when, alone, she spews out her words to an empty landscape. She is said to be like a dog chewing a bone when all substantial food is gone (viii.36); is she also like a poet—like Timias—making nature a text, speaking in the void?

Sclaunder, the embodiment of verbal undoing, spreads. The narrator, overtly trying to defeat her, and covertly caught in her destructiveness, assaults the text indirectly, and through a surrogate, the reader. He does not say now that *he* wishes the poem unwritten; instead, he would have it unread, since the reader, not the text, produces (mis)reading and missaying. Characterizing the reader in this way, the narrator operates within the patterns of the text. The reader is in the position of Belphoebe, (mis)judging Timias, in the position of Timias, maligned. This is a place in the text that covers multiple cases. The reader might as easily be called Lust or Corflambo or Sclaunder, versions of the (mis)reader in the text, that devouring other who in reading produces words on the page as the counterpart of a desire, the desire for the text. This is how the narrator (slandering?) characterizes the reader. Has he misread? Is it the reader who produces and reproduces the text as a series of increasingly fragmented and unsatisfactory versions of a lost text? Or does the text produce the reader as (mis)reader, as deconstructor of the text? Where is the reader situated in this address, inside the text or outside it? producing it or produced by it? Into whose desire has the reader entered? One answer to these questions is clear—the reader has become the narrator's surrogate; the narrator's desire, the wish to destroy the text, has been made the reader's. The reader as surrogate narrator produces the story.

Narrative surrogacy can go further; the narrator can be endlessly replaced, undone. We began with the narrator wishing to undo the text. Now the reader is in that role. In each case it is because the text seems to menace those who produce it. The narrator is threatened in his telling of the story by an antecedent other represented by a lost voice and the demand that that voice be entered since it already has the story that the narrator means to tell. This produces the condition of narration in book IV; voice inside of voice measures the depths of loss. In response, the narrator finds a further move in the realm of Sclaunder, by making the reader his surrogate; then (as we shall see) he allows a character in the text to take over his narrative function. The boundary between teller and tale is crossed anew. It is the most explicit revelation of narration as a matter of entering other voices, other texts.

After the cycle of interwoven squires' tales ends with Arthur marry-

OTHER VOICES, OTHER TEXTS   63

ing off Amyas, Placidas, AEmylia, and Poeana, repeating thereby a conclusion to *The Squire's Tale* that is no ending, book IV moves ahead by
once again going backward. Blandamour and Paridell, along with others last seen at Satyrane's tournament in canto v, reappear; Britomart
and Scudamour arrive. Old fights are fought anew; but it also looks as if
the goal of the journey "backe to that desert forrest" (vi.47.1) will finally
be reached. Amoret stands there, under Arthur's patronage, ripe for discovery by Britomart and Scudamour. Recognition and reunion seem
imminent. All Scudamour need do is look in front of him to reclaim his
wife. Instead, he repeats the Squire of Dames' gesture; he looks back.
Responding to Britomart and the crew, he tells the story of how he won
Amoret in the Temple of Venus. He goes back to a troubled beginning
when a happy ending seems to stand before him. The crew's request is
properly Chaucerian, that "as we ride together on our way, / Ye will
recount" (ix.40.6–7), and Britomart echoes the prologue to *The Squire's
Tale*: "But *Britomart* did him importune hard, / To take on him that
paine: whose great desire / He glad to satisfie, him selfe prepar'd / To
tell" (ix.41.2–5). "That paine" is the act of telling the story, and Scudamour agrees to it, assenting to "satisfie" the will, the "great desire"
(41.3) of others. What he himself desires—Amoret—is there before him.
But that desire will not be fulfilled. He never regains her, telling the
story; she remains lost, forever. Looking back, he tells the beginning of
his story, and it turns out to be the end as well. This is the final appearance of Scudamour and Amoret in *The Faerie Queene*, and there are
fearful ironies here; telling the story of how he satisfied his desire and
won his bride, Scudamour substitutes that story for regaining his bride.
And that story of beginning is left instead of an ending in reunion. Narration is unraveled, going back to the beginning, and the narrator is
effaced, receiving pain instead of satisfaction, settling into permanent
loss. Spenser's narrator is also effaced, for he undoes himself in this telling. During the space of Scudamour's devastating narration, the narrator in the tale and the narrator of the tale coalesce. The narrator of book
IV becomes this narrator in book IV. There are two narrators, then, who
are undone in this beginning story, the groundplot for book IV. The
narrator's effacement is a further sign that to narrate is to assume a function in the text that precedes the narrator. When the narrator's voice
enters Scudamour, we are reminded that "he" is not there at all except as
a voice that the text produces, disperses, and ultimately undermines and
undoes.

Canto ix closes after Scudamour has agreed to tell his story, but it
also ends with the narrator promising us that he will tell those events,
"which sith they cannot in this Canto well / Comprised be, I will them
in another tell" (ix.41.8–9). Canto x opens voicing truisms about love as
dolce amarum; anyone with some knowledge of cultural commonplaces

could be speaking here (anyone, like Chaucer's squire, who knows as much about love as anyone else).[8] It takes the reader some time to realize that Scudamour, not the narrator, is now speaking. Both are in the squire's place, Scudamour by fulfilling the will of another, although to his own discomfort and ultimate discomfiture, and the narrator by giving up his voice for another's, like the squire passing to the falcon. To put it another way, and to find an even closer antecedent for the narrator's effacement, the narrator's voice has disappeared into the double meaning prepared for in the final words in canto ix: "I will them in another tell." Stories are always told "in another," and to tell is to submit what "I will" to the demands of narration. The narrator disappears to satisfy the desire of the text. The story told by Scudamour—in substitution for the satisfaction of his desire—is itself about the satisfaction of texts, not about human desires.[9]

Here, then, is the beginning story.

The Temple of Venus is a literary trope hallowed by medieval

---

8. The canto opens, "True he it said, what ever man it sayd, / That love with gall and hony doth abound" (x.1–2), voicing a commonplace, immediately ascribing the sentence to another speaker. The voice here is located in an anonymous saying, a proverb. As Barthes says in *S/Z*, "the utterances of the cultural code are implicit proverbs: they are written in that obligative mode by which the discourse states a general will, the law of a society, making the proposition concerned ineluctable or indelible" (p. 100). In book IV, the cultural matrices of love and friendship are frequently rendered proverbially. Smith lists seven commonplaces about friendship in *Spenser's Theory of Friendship*, p. 27; their proverbial quality can be checked against Morris P. Tilley, *A Dictionary of the Proverbs in England in the Sixteenth and Seventeenth Centuries* (Ann Arbor: University of Michigan Press, 1950), pp. 242 ff., or typical texts like *The Mirrour of Friendship* (London, 1584) or W(alter) D(orke), *A Tipe or Figure of Friendship* (London, 1589), with its list of the twenty values ("for vertues sake onely" A4r) of friendship, sig. A4, a list of commonplaces. Many readers of book IV have noticed that its "flatness" comes from the frequency of its commonplaces; the point of these is to locate the text in the inevitability of cultural utterance, in a voice and in texts that preceded the text, not to endorse them. The voice speaking at the opening of canto x affirms the truth of an anonymous belief in a voice that itself becomes anonymous. We hear this voice often opening cantos in this most self-referential part of book IV: "Well said the wiseman, now prov'd true by this . . . " (viii.1); or cf. the commonplace that "the band of vertuous mind / Me seemes the gentle hart should most assured bind" (ix.1.8–9).
9. Harry Berger, Jr., has described this well in "Two Spenserian Retrospects; The Antique Temple of Venus and the Primitive Marriage of Rivers," *Texas Studies in Literature and Language* 10 (1968): 5–26. Although I do not find evolutionary schemata necessary, I agree that the Temple is a place of fragmentation and deformation, of genital tyranny in which love is a game, "a play which is irrelevant to Venus Genetrix except as an instrument" (p.8) of her purposes; for Berger these are cosmic purposes and love is inhumane in the Temple. This is true; and it must be added that cosmic forces are themselves cultural constructs, not natural facts. The nature (generation) into which Scudamour and Amoret are so unnaturally embedded is a text (generics).

romance. We could say that even the initial location of the voice in the commonplace of love as *dolce amarum* places the narrator in the text as a piece of text (it surely does not characterize or distinguish the voice speaking). As still another version of the squire, he appropriately voices these truths and launches a tale from the world of medieval romance. Predictably, his account conforms to the basic pattern of earlier endings to *The Squire's Tale*: first a joust, then the lady. The tale is, however, even more explicitly embedded in texts. The reward for this first adventure, which is also Scudamour's only adventure, is inscribed as a piece of writing. It says that the shield hanging on the pillar in the tiltyard and the maiden go together:

> And in the marble stone was written this,
> With golden letters goodly well enchaced,
> *Blessed the man that well can use his blis*:
> *Whose ever be the shield, faire Amoret be his.*

>   (x.8.6–9)

Scudamour reads this writing twice; first to whet his desire ("when I red, my heart did inly earne" 9.1); second, after defeating the twenty knights guarding the entrance to the Temple, as his reward: ". . . I repeated / The read thereof for guerdon of my paine" (10.7–8). He takes the shield; by the end of the canto, he has the maid. "*Cupids* man," he says, must have "*Venus* mayd" (x.54.7).

Why is the first part of the adventure framed with reading and re-reading? What beginning principle is this? The first reading defines the terms of the Temple; the second reading confirms Scudamour's place in that writing. He has his place when he has the shield, for it gives him his name. He becomes himself, Scudamour, at the moment of winning the shield; he becomes Cupid's man, a generic type. His identity is his attribute named in the text. The text was written before he was there to read it; the second reading makes it "his" text, the text that has produced him. "The read thereof," he says, is the prize, the reward for the "paine" (x.10.8) of fulfilling the text—reproducing it in the adventure and in the telling, for that too is the same "paine" (ix.41.3)—the reward is the prize of being absorbed into the text. Teller, character, reader; all meet in Scudamour, all serve the tale, for the tale is told through him. Scudamour's story tells how he came to be the embodiment of the already written text, how his union with Amoret fulfills a textual prescription. The text was written, "enchaced" in golden letters in the place where the generic types—Cupid's man and Venus's maid—belong, the Temple of Venus, the privy place of desire. In this beginning text, desire is satisfied, bliss achieved; in that place, in that text, Scudamour and Amoret express the fulfillment of the desire of the text. That beginning is their ending, understandably. For there can be, then, no second embrace, no recovery, only a return in discourse to that beginning end; in discourse, not in fact, is that bliss achieved.

Scudamour ends his tale with a literary allusion. He says that in carrying Amoret from the Temple he was like Orpheus when he "did recoure / His Leman from the Stygian Princes boure" (58.4–5). His allusion suppresses an ending: Orpheus looked back. Then, in place of his wife, he had the story of loss to tell. That is Scudamour's story. And, as the allusion to Orpheus affirms, it is a story about narration and desire. "Fond Squire, . . . / Seest not the Ladie there before thy face? / He looked backe . . ." (ii.22.5–7).

Twice over, Scudamour satisfies a desire inside the text; as a character he embodies the words written in the Temple yard, as a narrator he fulfills Britomart's request. Much to our dissatisfaction, demands inside the text are satisfied. The situation is similar to the one at the end of the first part of *The Squire's Tale*, when only Cambyuskan's desire was satisfied. We saw, though, that the second part of Chaucer's story took away even that satisfaction; receiving the gift meant, finally, receiving the pain. Here, too, Scudamour's satisfaction of these demands results in his undoing; rereading, recounting, is his only prize. We are in Scudamour's place, left with our desire for an ending. And what we desire is a lost text, the story of a second embrace that once closed book III of *The Faerie Queene* but was cancelled so that book IV could narrate—doubly, we can now see—in the space of lost texts, both Chaucer's and Spenser's.

This is the crucial meaning of the failure to reunite Scudamour and Amoret, for it makes clear that the relationship of book IV to book III duplicates its relationship to *The Squire's Tale*. In each case, a text deprived of an ending stands behind book IV: Chaucer's lost text, and book III without its original concluding cantos. The cancellation of that resolution is, as we now can see, a prophecy of narration in book IV, which moves only by denying the possibility of conclusive endings; in its slidings, substitutions, and replacements, the story progresses only by denying endings that were earlier possible. The story seems to undo itself in these denials, going backward rather than forward. Indeed, narrative motion might be described as metacritical, increasingly so as book IV views its own production, folding narration into narration. These stories in search of a lost ending arrive in Scudamour's story at a beginning principle, the principle of inevitable loss. Scudamour's tale forcefully insists that the end of narration is always lost and can never be restored. The text always stands in place of the lost text; its doing is undoing. With Scudamour's story, we have arrived at a point in time antecedent to both books III and IV, a beginning story in place of an ending.[10] How much further back could a text look? After this, where

10. We arrive at the place where the problematic of endings touches that of beginnings, for which see Edward W. Said, *Beginnings: Intention and Meth-*

can narration go but to the affirmation of its own undoing, making it explicit that the production of the lost text is the power of the text. This is precisely where book IV moves next.

The narrator begins this movement by admitting that his voice overlaps his surrogate's: "So ended he his tale, where I this Canto end" (x.58.9). This, the only canto in book IV in which one entire story corresponds to one marked unit of narration—the one canto that formally and visibly shows structural control and completion—the narrator claims as his own by claiming Scudamour's voice as his own. So doing, he affirms the nature of the voice of narration, always telling in another voice, yet, rightly, dissolving his voice in this affirmation. The narrator is as much a character in the story as the character in the story is the narrator. The text produces both, interchanging one with the other. The narrator is no privileged voice outside the text, no producer of it in any simple way. He is produced by it; he is the character in the text that figures the production of the text. The condition for his existence pre-conditions his existence, existing "before" and "after" him. The text goes on in the undoing of the voice. The narrator's affirmation insists that all voices in the text are the voice of another. His removal of the boundary between narrator and character, the dissolving of those two voices, is the firmest affirmation of the nature of the text and its production.

When the narrator proceeds, compassionate pity once again overwhelms him: "But ah for pittie that I have thus long / Left a fayre Ladie languishing in payne" (xi.1.1–2). He becomes the voice of the text promising amelioration, to undo what it has done, a "Ladie" will be

---

od (Baltimore: Johns Hopkins University Press, 1975), a circle that book IV of The Faerie Queene first traces in the proem's backward glance at love as an indifferent end or beginning (3.5). The place of desire is where the text is produced, at once an ending and a beginning. This is replicated in the action of the text, in its "character relations," and in the language in which differences become single words: "It often fals, (as here it earst befell) / That mortall foes doe turne to faithfull frends, / And friends profest are chaungd to foemen fell: / The cause of both, of both their minds depends, / And th'end of both likewise of both their ends" (iv.1.1–5). In these lines, the repeated event ("it often fals") is the singular beginning event ("as here . . . earst"; this is, in Said's terms, a beginning, not an origin); the oppositions between "faithfull frends" and "foemen fell" are obliterated by alliteration and by the syntactical constructions that lead these opposites to meet in "both." The metamorphic activity doubled in these lines (as "turne" and "chaungd") is clearly reversible, so that "cause" and "ends" meet in the single place that "both" designates. The final line here is almost meaningless except as a structure, "And th'end of both likewise of both their ends." "Likewise" is the metamorphic fulcrum and turn of the line; it functions as a kind of mirror for duplication, and the words that follow it repeat and reverse those that come before. What the line demonstrates is a pattern of repetition ("and" is the first word) in which forward and backward motion meet in "likewise." Beginnings are thereby deprived of originary force, inscribed as they are in a pattern of repetition.

released—and the reader will be satisfied. The promise is a lure to trick the reader into thinking that Amoret's story will continue, that her suffering will finally be relieved. However, the "Ladie" is Florimell; her seven-month imprisonment in Proteus's bower, rather than Amoret's loss, is remembered, an obvious analogue to Amoret's enslavement to Busyrane, rather than to Amoret's condition after her liberation. The text will proceed so, by telling one story in another, Amoret's in Florimell's; Amoret is undone in this rewriting, however; she dissolves into Florimell and thereby loses her entire history in book IV; for this final story returns to the end of book III and provides a new version of the liberation of Amoret from Busyrane. The story is once again retreating, undermining an old ending in its rewriting; the end of book IV will rewrite and replace the end of book III. The end of book IV thus coincides with another loss, one that affirms the power of narration at last. Denying itself—all of book IV is taken away in going back to the end of book III—it affirms itself. There is always a story to tell in place of another, in the loss of an antecedent text. This is the text's power. More loss, more gain.

Spenserian *entrelacement*, tale within tale, is, as this displaced ending suggests, fatal weaving. Early in book IV, Agape glimpses this in the cave of the Fates, one of the first images in book IV for the place of narration into which the poem moves when it enters Lust's cave with its three weird sisters. Agape found that in order to have one son she needed to sacrifice her other two:

> Then since (quoth she) the terme of each mans life
> For nought may lessened nor enlarged bee,
> Graunt this, that when ye shred with fatall knife
> His line, which is the eldest of the three,
> Which is of them the shortest, as I see,
> Eftsoones his life may passe into the next.

(ii.52.1–6)

Generation by undoing, eking of threads: such is the vision of life born of loss. This is not merely an intensely bleak view of life; it is also a principle of textual production.[11] The sacrifice Agape asks for as a favor is what the names of her sons already seem to reveal—that they were

---

11. In *Pagan Mysteries in the Renaissance* (New York: W. W. Norton, 1968), Edgar Wind describes the presentation of the three "-mond"s in ii.41–43 as "a schoolroom lesson in mystical 'explication' " (p. 210), and Roche has connected Pico's cabbalistic three worlds in the *Heptaplus* with the processes of allegory (*Kindly Flame* [Princeton: Princeton University Press, 1964], pp. 7–8). These cosmic schemata explain not only principles of analogy, as Roche claims, but principles of generativity as well, since *explication* is Cusa's term for the unfolding of the many from the One; it is also a means of discovering vestiges of the trinity, of making the equation reversible. Those neoplatonic habits of mind

made to replace each other, just as one number succeeds another by adding a single integer. Priamond, Diamond, Triamond: they share the same name save for the numerative repetition that is, in the narrative, the principle of doubling and substitution. The analogy is not fanciful. For what is it that the Fates weave and undo? The answer lies in a word; etymologically fate is "that which is spoken." The Fates speak the final word, about endings in which life is cut off so that life may be extended; in their language, doubling and undoing meet. To Agape, they tell the life of the world, or so the shared name of her three sons suggests. They are telling, too, the life of the word, double, repeated, substituted, and in all this activity undone, deferred. The end ("the terme of each mans life") places every beginning in a ghastly infusion—"his life may passe into the next"—precisely the "infusion sweete" that guides the life of narration in the voice of the lost text.

The Fates weave that hallucinatory Chaucerian border between text and nature. Weaving "the terme of each mans life," they weave the world, for etymologically (as the *OED* tells us) world means the life of man: *Wer + eld*. Hence they weave the word. And this etymological fantasy about the word/world is spun before the reader's eyes, not merely implicitly in the cave of the Fates but explicitly in the house of Sclaunder, as part of the narrator's address to the reader just after the crux about "conversing." It is the etymology of "world" that is adduced to explain misreading. Because the reader is in the world, he is likely to misread: "But when the world woxe old, it woxe warre old / (Whereof it hight) and having shortly tride / The traines of wit, in wickednesse woxe bold" (viii.31.6–8). Here is an etymology to strain the reader's wits. If the world was only named by its decline / declension from itself, what was it called before? The sentence begins by calling it "world," and takes that original name away, making "world" a second name, a name for a second beginning, in loss and in division and differentiation from itself. The world is generated as words are, and this sentence, like an epitome of

---

that Wind reveals, in which no god comes without two others, in which endless unfolding and "explicating" goes on in an attempt to remove a veil that is never finally removed—indeed, is constructed in this endless activity—are consistent with the "prose of the world" that Foucault describes and in which *The Faerie Queene* is written, so that what it says it presents in one place "enfold[ed] / In covert vele" (II.pro.5.1–2), it elsewhere describes as "mirrours more then one" (III.pro.5.6). The moment when the word for cosmos (world) and life is treated as a word marks the primacy of the text in this world. For a fascinating study of the etymological web spun by *telos*, see Richard Broxton Onians, *The Origins of European Thought about the Body, the Mind, the Soul, the World, Time, and Fate* (Cambridge: At the University Press, 1951). As its title suggests, all the issues in Spenser's text are treated in Onians's study; the chapter on *telos* (pp. 426–66) summarizes the connections, from the bonds of life to those of death, a root connection in the idea of obligation and payment.

Spenserian narration, produces the word/world as a piece of trompe l'oeil, a trick of wit. At its end, the sentence arrives to flourish in wickedness; the sentence ends where frustrated desire and desired frustration meet, in the place of wickedness, the locus of desire, where the text produces and reproduces stories of substitution and substitutes story within story.

At the end of book IV, the tale of Florimell and Marinell substitutes for that of Amoret and Scudamour. It has scarcely begun when the narrator interrupts it to tell yet another story, the marriage of the Thames and Medway, with a genuine happy ending: how "at last relenting, she to him was wed" (xi.8.9); this marriage is yet one more version of the ending the text has so often supplied for its Chaucerian source. And this time, the story is obviously about words. The marriage of two rivers translates the names on maps and the names in books into other words; it brings together the myths and folktales attached to these names. What the river marriage gives is produced and reproduced in etymology. As Roche has remarked, the conceit of this canto is etymological; it plays on the name of the Thames as the marriage of the names of two other rivers, Thame and Isis, and it extends that play.[12] The river marriage provides an extended play on words that also happen to be names on a map; the play on words is a play on words for the world, play on word/world. Narration here enters the space of its own freeplay, and quite explicitly, invention takes place in the space provided by a full—and lost—text that stands before it.

The narrator comments directly on this production of words. The voice he finds to produce what is essentially a list of names is overtly a version of the squire's voice with its apologetic insistence on its own inadequacy. Now the insistence becomes a genuinely rhetorical trope; rather than an apology it is a proclamation of power. To proclaim inability represents a triumph for the voice of narration, for it is an act of self-admission, an entrance into itself and into the condition for its pro-

---

12. *Kindly Flame*, p. 172. Nohrnberg in *The Analogy of "The Faerie Queene"* proposes that couples in the poem move toward this kind of verbal union—Britomartegall, Scudamoret, etc. (p. 607). Berger comments that "the effect of this verbal pageant is a panorama which is not merely spatial and temporal but also cultural and mental—a panorama which could only be rendered in the medium of language because its sole locus is the poetic imagination and its sole time of occurrence is the sophisticated, modern *now* of poetic utterance" (*TSLL* 10 [1968]: 21), and Jack B. Oruch, in "Spenser, Camden, and the Poetic Marriages of Rivers," *Studies in Philology* 64 (1967): 606–24, also emphasizes the verbal aspects of the canto, its subordination of topography to "the demands of poetry" (p. 617) and its feat of including, in Oruch's count, some 170 names in 400 lines (p. 618). A similar emphasis can be seen in the discussion of Giamatti, *Play of Double Senses: Spenser's "Faerie Queene"* (Englewood Cliffs, N.J.: Prentice-Hall, 1975), pp. 130–33, where the river marriage is read as a triumph of the imagination and the poet's ability to marry words and things.

duction. Narration, as the narrator says, requires "endlesse memorie" (xi.9.8) in order for recounting to occur.

> So both agreed, that this their bridale feast
>> Should for the Gods in *Proteus* house be made;
>> To which they all repayr'd, both most and least,
>> Aswell which in the mightie Ocean trade,
>> As that in rivers swim, or brookes doe wade.
>> All which not if an hundred tongues to tell,
>> And hundred mouthes, and voice of brasse I had,
>> And endlesse memorie, that mote excell,
> In order as they came, could I recount them well.
>
> (xi. 9)

The narrator enters—to his loss—the violation of limit and the loss of voice to summon up the "endlesse memorie" stored in other texts, and whose end he can never reach. His text, full to repletion as it may be, endlessly generating itself from itself and never arriving at a conclusive ending, will nonetheless never represent the fullness and order of the world; it will represent the fullness of the word, and being endless will recount in its repletion and loss. As recounting—rewriting—narration in loss defines the power of the text.

The narrator's excuses about his inadequacy thus proclaim his power.

> But what doe I their names seeke to reherse,
>> Which all the world have with their issue fild?
>> How can they all in this so narrow verse
>> Contayned be, and in small compasse hild?
>> Let them record them, that are better skild,
>> And know the moniments of passed times:
>> Onely what needeth, shall be here fulfild,
>> T'expresse some part of that great equipage,
> Which from great *Neptune* do derive their parentage.
>
> (xi.17)

He need not end the teeming issue of Neptune, which is itself endless. Nor are words meant to replicate the world. Less is more, a part will do for the whole. The aim is not to record, doubling Neptune's names with his own, nor to build monuments and enclosures. That is neither the aim, nor is it possible. Rather, the aim of narration is narration—to retell, to enter the loss, which is also the full flood of Neptune's generation. Not ending, the narrator produces endless words that nonetheless withhold and fail to coincide with the endless world. "O what an endlesse worke have I in hand" (xii.1.1), the narrator proclaims, joining in a single locution two endless ends: the endlessness of what has come before and the endlessness that lies ahead; all that he controls and all that controls—and disables—him:

> O what an endlesse worke have I in hand,
>   To count the seas abundant progeny,
>   Whose fruitfull seede farre passeth those in land,
>   And also those which wonne in th'azure sky?
>   For much more eath to tell the starres on hy,
>   Albe they endlesse seeme in estimation,
>   Then to recount the Seas posterity:
>   So fertile be the flouds in generation,
> So huge their numbers, and so numberlesse their nation.
>
> (xii.1)

In the sea, that ultimate place of beginning where the text finally arrives, the excess of "numbers" is the same as being "numberlesse," and likewise, narrative failure is narrative success. What cannot be counted can be recounted, and not reaching an end will be to occupy that fullness of the word/world which never ends. The power of the text lies in its endless recounting, a vast supplementation that fills the place of loss, the place of the lost text.

At the end of book IV (xii.29–31), Cymodoche tells Neptune that unknown to him he has in his power, within his floods, one whom she wants, Florimell. Cymodoche reads (30.6) him a name, and he, in recompense, gives up the girl. Cymodoche, in turn, delivers her to Marinell. Marinell, too weak to speak, is revived by her presence; Florimell, too fearful of possible misreading, says nothing, gives no sign of her feeling. That final moment, made possible by repeated acts of renunciation, of giving up powers and possessions and delivering them into the hands of another, is one of debilitation just short of annihilation, a silence on the perilous borders of language. Appearing to have achieved their desires, the characters say not a word. Their story is not told, and narration triumphs by not telling the story, by not letting words come in place of desire. The shortest canto thus far in *The Faerie Queene* ends, as forecast, with "endlesse worke . . . in hand" (xii.1.1) which, it concludes, "to another place I leave to be perfected" (xii.35.9).

   The only way to tell a story is never to have it end.

OTHERS, DESIRE, AND THE SELF
IN THE STRUCTURE OF THE TEXT

The "endlesse worke" of narration entails continuous revision; the narrator's work is never done, and neither is the reader's. Both come to occupy the same place in supplying the text and being located in the inability to fill satisfactorily that textual demand. Replacement, or
standing instead, becomes the location in the text for its own production, and that textual space is, in relation to what came before—book III,
The Squire's Tale—the occupation of the space of *occupatio*, the space
in which the narrative voice loses itself in the inability to tell on its own
and in its own voice. The consequences for narration are manifold, and
the primary effect, as we have seen, is that the work of narration is never
done and that its doing is always its undoing. Narrative progress is regressive, a series of replacements, and the narration takes itself away in
order for it to go on. In these undoings, reader and narrator are undone,
and the tale, failing to come to an end, spins itself out.

What, then, happens in the tale? what are these tales about? We
have seen that the answer to the question is self-reflexive, but we have
only seen, in part, what that means. These tales are about their own
production, about the relationship of the reader and the teller and the
tale. Those in the narrative take on the function of telling and receiving
stories, and their relationship (friendship/enmity) is a version of the act
of relating. But, as a review of *The Squire's Tale* also reminds us, to
reduce the story to mere self-reflexiveness would be to ignore the thematic center of the story. *The Squire's Tale* has as its subject the entangling
of desire and the desire for the story; it shows the entrapment of natural
desire in textual demands and demonstrates the impossibility of drawing the line between nature and text. The story the bird tells is about the

loss of her will to another, and about his loss as well. She is lost in him; he is lost in a text; and both, as talking birds, well-read creatures capable of quoting their authors—who create them and give them authority— present themselves as emblems of the dual demand of desire and the text. For both are made in the complicity of that double desire, both are caught and disabled—made to their undoing—in the double call of kind. The demand of desire is the desire of the text.

On the one hand, this desire shapes narrators and the act of narra- tion. But characters in Chaucer or in Spenser are not solely tale-tellers and their function in the text to reflect the text's acts of production is not to be viewed reductively. They are also caught up in other demands that shape them. In the pages that follow, the pressing question is simply: Who *acts* in Spenserian narration? If the tale and the teller are gripped by the demand of the text, how are the actions of characters to be viewed? How, to focus the question even more narrowly, is character to be viewed in such a narrative? Who is acting? What causes action? What really occurs to characters in a narrative that undoes itself? In relation to narra- tion, characters seem to exist to be undone, to be replaced by others. Although this can be seen to occur in the text, and is registered in the frequency with which characters ask for readings of their situations, rec- ognition of their textual embeddedness in others' stories, in the actions or other characters, is not overtly solely textual; nor in considering their concerns can we allow their textual situation to exclude an understand- ing of their actions in the text. Chaucer's bird talks about desire; that is her subject. It is also a central theme in book IV. It is ultimately true that the desire in the text is the desire of the text, one kind answering another. But how is that true, and what does it mean for those who act in Spenser- ian narration?

In order to answer such questions, it is necessary to see what the characters see. In the text, what they are aware of, what shapes their actions, is not the fact that they are expressions of the text—characters in a poem—although they come to see themselves in others' stories. Rather, they express desires and aversions. Although few readers of the poem are tempted to translate the ways in which these desires are expressed into representation of rounded, whole, or developed characters, most readers succumb to the lure of the proper names given Spenser's characters, and even as they recognize that an Amoret or a Florimell does not seem as real as a character in a nineteenth-century novel, they nonetheless allow Spenserian characters to reflect aspects of human behavior. Inevitably, I too have taken this lure insofar as talking about Spenser's characters and describing their actions—indeed, merely naming them—grants them a certain status, making it sound as if persons are being discussed. Yet, what I want to argue is precisely the opposite: that it is a fundamental act of misrepresentation to treat the figures in *The Faerie Queene* as if they were characters or had character.

There is, however, no critical vocabulary for the discussion of character that is not trapped by its own terminology. In treating the histories of characters, in locating their place in the text and their situations in relation to one another and in relation to what they see and reflect as their moving principle—namely, desire—I want to argue and demonstrate that characters are also placed in relation to another principle. Thematically, *desire* is also the word for this otherness. To place character in such a relation not only reduces and ultimately displaces the very notion of character with regard to those who act in Spenserian narration; it has another consequence as well. This Other—desire—this theme, also represents a lure. It does not finally explain characters by offering them new names in thematic terms, for the language that moves narration in its undoing is as severe on theme as it is on character. The gloss on the meaning of desire is, ultimately, the desire of the text— ultimately, that is, textual desire. Admittedly, this is to maintain that we cannot go further than the text and its self-reflections. That is not, however, a limiting statement; it really suggests how open this endless text is. Although taking away two of the tools regularly applied to the analysis of narration—character and theme—would seem to leave little, precisely the opposite is true.

The place of the theme in Spenser's text lies within discursive practice; characters, who are "placed" in the text to express aspects of its theme, are not, obviously, characters in the sense of persons; but they are not explained by referring to them as versions of ideas that somehow exist somewhere other than in the textual space they are allotted. To succumb to such interpretive moves, and Spenser criticism has often done so—when, for instance, Britomart becomes the embodiment of the concept of married love in some reader's interpretation—is reductive in the extreme because the actuality of the textual space in which characters move in *The Faerie Queene* is ignored and replaced by something supposedly outside it. The need for this external system of meaning can be understood. Spenserian narration generated it, for, as narrative, the poem undoes itself; it creates characters who are also undone. One response to this is to look elsewhere for what the text denies. But characters are not salvaged by being taken out of the text and referred to some other system of supposedly stable and finally reductive sets of meanings. Rather, we must see that what generates and undoes the characters in Spenser's poem establishes them in a world of discourse which is so fully responsive to such "external" systems of meaning that it has already taken them into the text and subjected them to the very narrative strategies that determine the action of the poem. Once again, there is no "outside" to this text. Characters independent of the text are not being created here, ideas outside the text are not being exemplified. Yet, if we attend to the names that pass before our eyes and to the stories told about them, we can see that these tales of what appear to be human interrelationships are not, by being expressions of the text, reduced in this self-reflexiveness but are actually broader and more significant. *The Faerie Queene* becomes a poor thing if we read it merely as a poem about characters who are reduced or stylized persons; or if it is taken to be, however learnedly, the reflection of commonplace ideas. The aim of this chapter is to redefine concepts of subject and theme in *The Faerie Queene* by recognizing the subjection of character to the structures generated in the text.[1] If other voices shape the voices in the text, we need now to see that situation

1. Another way to define the scope of this chapter would be to say that allegory offers the reader two lures. One is the set of characters who act in the text; since their actions often seem simply to serve the story at hand, it is possible for a reader to respond to characters as if they were people, reading them as human, even if deformed by certain obsessive or limited kinds of behavior. This is the lure of the proper name, in Barthes's terms (see n. 11 below). But the second lure is one that allegory, from its very definition, has always seemed to hold out: the possibility of substituting an abstraction for the name of a character, thereby leaving behind the narration and its actors for the sake of meaning. I suggest that this lure is no different from the first and that in both cases we are really being asked to take one figure for another. Characters in *The Faerie Queene* are, precisely, figures; the married Amoret, discussed below, defines a condition that pertains throughout: as we have seen from the proem to *The Faerie Queene*, nothing comes alone; everything comes with something else. But that joined otherness replicates, duplicates, and ultimately fails to provide in its other terms explanations, ends, final words. Thus, the names of characters in the poem are no different from any other words in the poem, and recourse to words "outside" the poem ignores the fact that it is precisely what happens to words in allegorical texts that make such movements to an "outside" a futile gesture.

As noted earlier, moreover, language as conceived in the sixteenth century, at least as described by Foucault, operates precisely the same way as language in *The Faerie Queene* does. Cf. the discussion of allegory that I offer in "Marvell's Nymph and the Echo of Voice," *Glyph 8: Johns Hopkins Textual Studies* (Baltimore: Johns Hopkins University Press, 1981), esp. pp. 27–32. My argument in this chapter may seem to be directed against the most naive reading of allegory, of the sort offered in the glosses to books I and II of *The Faerie Queene* in the edition of Robert Kellogg and Oliver Steele (New York: Odyssey Press, 1965); e.g., on II.iv: "For the next two cantos, and for part of a third, Guyon's enemies are chiefly representatives of excessive anger, vices of the irascible power. Undoubtedly Spenser throws these enemies of temperance in Guyon's way before he faces the temptations to excessive pleasure and desire because, as Aristotle writes, 'it is hard to fight against anger, but it is harder still to fight against pleasure' " (p. 61). This gloss treats Guyon as a person and as a representative of a virtue; it assumes a teleological narrative; and it assumes that another text with its philosophical structure fixes the meaning and direction of acts and actors. However, even the most sophisticated readers of allegory also succumb to its lures; in *The Poetry of "The Faerie Queene"* (Princeton: Princeton University Press, 1967), Alpers believes the reader is always making choices, and that, difficult as they are to make, nonetheless the terms for choice, however ambiguous, are before us. Fletcher, in his book on the subject, argues that allegory, for all its complexity, terrifies the reader into certain positions. Tuve believes that although allegory is not a set of one-to-one equations, it always offers Christian truths.

The argument I offer is far more radical than these because I cannot see that a principle that determines meaning is offered in Spenserian narration; its very endless quality denies hermeneutic closure. The text invites us, lures us, to these activities and then obliterates the possibility of interpretation. In the text,

in the text. The text behind the text is replicated by what occurs in the text. We can see this by discovering how characters are shaped by others and by their relations to others. Ultimately, we must see that the text intertwines its textual situation with stories told of interlinked desires. Finally it is Desire—of another, as an Other—that shapes discourse.

The opening of book IV is the most suggestive place to attempt to locate character in the text, precisely because its initial stanzas crucially revise the narrative that has come before. This revision redefines the status of Amoret and her relation to Scudamour; they are relocated. Changing her story, the narrative makes a demand upon the reader; we can no longer interpret what has come before in the same way. The change in the situation of the character forces the reader to revise what has been understood about what came before and about who came before. It is, suddenly, as if we were not dealing with the same character, as if the story we had just read were now not the same story. What happens in the text as book IV opens undermines the possibility of fixed character and fixed meaning. Here is the crucial opening—the entire history of Amoret and her "hart-binding chaine" (i.1.4) apparently is simply being retold, and yet it is, significantly, a new story:

> For from the time that *Scudamour* her bought
>   In perilous fight, she never ioyed day,
>   A perilous fight when he with force her brought
>   From twentie Knights, that did him all assay:
>   Yet fairely well he did them all dismay:
>   And with great glorie both the shield of love,
>   And eke the Ladie selfe he brought away,
>   Whom having wedded as did him behove,
> A new unknowen mischiefe did from him remove.

---

the figures of overwhelming desire represent the imposition of this demand of the text and its obliterative force. Although the terms of his analysis are not those I use in this chapter, I believe that Fredric Jameson's essay, "Magical Narratives: Romance as Genre," *New Literary History* 7 (1975): 135–63, lends support to my position. Jameson remarks upon the need to replace the notion of character in romance with what he calls "states" (see pp. 148–49), positions; he sees romances constituting a confrontation with "Otherness" (see pp. 140–41), and for him their resolving moment comes when the Other is recognized as a mirror (p. 161), a recognition of placement and relationship. For Jameson, these events serve an ideological function, the reflection and product of a "society torn between past and future in such a way that the alternatives are grasped as hostile but somehow unrelated worlds" (p. 158). I assume that Jameson sees the magical embrace of the Other as the fantasized solution to this dilemma. I see such moments, as I suggest below, as raising the question of differences, not as solutions, but as problematic, and as generative of further narration. On the subject of social placement, see the following chapter, "The Authority of the Other."

For that same vile Enchauntour *Busyran*,
The very selfe same day that she was wedded,
Amidst the bridale feast . . .
Brought in that mask of love which late was showen . . .

(i.2; 3.1–3,6)

In these two stanzas with their casual and rapid summary of
Amoret's history, there is a startling piece of information presented in a
typically understated manner: Amoret and Scudamour are married, and
Busyrane's abduction occurred during her wedding masque. The repetition of "wedded" is the only indication of a situation that no readers of
book III would have known, and few would have suspected until this
moment; before this, Amoret and Scudamour have simply appeared as
lovers separated by Busyrane's attempted seduction.[2] Indeed, book III
would seem to be structured and to structure its meanings precisely
around various quests for a lover—not for a lost husband. That is, the
thematic center of book III reflects stories detailing the pains and com-
plications attendant upon the desire for someone not yet attained—and,
in Britomart's case, never even seen. As dominant character, Britomart's
quest would seem to define the scope of book III; she begins with an
image of Arthegall seen in her father's mirror (is this also Canacee's
mirror?) and she ends, not by marrying Arthegall, not even by meeting
him, but by rescuing Amoret.

Understanding Amoret in the light of Britomart's career, her
rescue seems to mean that she has been released from fear of the object of
her desire and has been enabled to move from an imagined lover to a real
one. With Britomart's rescue of Amoret, we appear to have arrived at the
end of a path and to have overcome the final obstacle blocking the possibility of actually uniting with another person. Viewed in this way, the
book says that the wound Amoret receives from Busyrane manifests her
fear of self-impairment, and the closing of the wound means that there is
no reason to fear: integrity, chastity, can be maintained even in union
with another.[3] But what does the wound mean if Busyrane is recast, as he
is at the opening of book IV, as Amoret's abductor *after* marriage? Then
the full ambiguity of being rendered "perfect hole" (III.xii.38.9) comes

2. Amoret's captivity is first mentioned in III.vi.53; her story is told by
Scudamour in III.xi.10 ff. In both cases, Amoret is referred to as Scudamour's
love, not explicitly as his wife; nor do Busyrane's attempts at her chastity include
any mention of a violation of marriage vows. Scudamour's explanation of
Amoret's predicament need not cause a reader to assume that any formal ceremony joins the lovers; Busyrane, he says, "tormenteth her . . . / Because to
yield him love she doth deny, / Once to me yold, not to be yold againe"
(III.xi.17.1, 3–4). Her chastity and fidelity, her troth, is under pressure.
3. I present this interpretation in "The Mothers in Book III of *The Faerie
Queene*," *Texas Studies in Literature and Language* 17 (1975): 5–26. esp. pp. 23
ff., and as the notes in that essay suggest, it is a reading echoed by many other
critics. That essay fails, however, to clarify how provisional its reading is.

into play. The rewriting of book III revises its meaning; if something is lost, something is also added. The text contains whatever meaning it once had, and what it now has. Amoret still names the "same" character, even if she has a new history. Quietly, the text announces this. It is the "same" Busyrane, on the "selfe same day" that carried off "the Ladie selfe." "Selfe" and "same"; yet everything is different.

Although the wound remains as a token of integrity, of individual *castitas*, it is also revised and would seem to signify as well the inevitability of subjection and impairment. Britomart receives a wound too, we recall, an indication that, by the end of book III, she shares Amoret's condition. In the light of book IV, an equation of shared loss, rather than or in addition to shared integrity, is invited. Amoret has a husband, but has lost him; Britomart has a lover, but has not found him. Amoret is wounded by the loss of her husband; Britomart, because she lacks one and has one in her mind. Either way—having had or wanting to have— the shared wound would seem to mean that an "I," the self, exists only in relationship to another whom the "I" lacks. That relationship appears to be one of inevitable subjection to desire, impairment of the self, lack of fulfillment in the object. Even closed, this wound remains open, as the pun on "hole" tells us; this wound engulfs both rescuer and rescued. In the wound they are one. One, and yet two. Doubling each other, their mutual loss defines who they are. Book III appeared to end with the assurance that the self could be maintained as itself with another. Now, the self exists only with and for another. The concept of self—and thereby the notion of character—is undergoing an explicit revision through the presentation of Amoret married, and through the presentation of Amoret doubled with her companion, Britomart. What we glimpsed earlier, when we considered the first appearance of the Red Crosse knight, seen from the vantage point of the paired heroes of book IV, can now be extended. The revisionary gesture of book IV, the retelling of an old story, is also the remaking of character, the recasting of theme. The crucial difference is the removal of the concept of singularity which seemed central to book III, which indeed might be said to sum up the entire movement of the first half of *The Faerie Queene*, from its contemplation of wholeness to the confrontation with and overcoming of the possible loss of wholeness in the face of another. Otherness is, with book IV, before us. This, then, makes explicit, at the level of plot and character, what moved plot and character before. Identity—having a self—is a matter of identification with an other and being identified by others; in the revisionary opening of book IV, Britomart and Amoret remain themselves by doing two things at once—replaying old parts, and, despite the differentiation that would appear to entail (the difference between rescuer and rescued, knight and lady)—mirroring each other, losing themselves in that identification by which they are identified.

On the one hand, book IV opens on a familiar situation; Amoret remains in a state of fear, and Britomart, whose wound betokens a hidden identification, covers herself in knightly behavior:

> Thereto her feare was made so much the greater
>   Through fine abusion of that Briton mayd:
>   Who for to hide her fained sex the better,
>   And maske her wounded mind, both did and sayd
>   Full many things so doubtfull to be wayd,
>   That well she wist not what by them to gesse,
>   For other whiles to her she purpos made
>   Of love, and otherwhiles of lustfulnesse,
> That much she feard his mind would grow to some excesse.
>
> (i.7)

Amoret fears Britomart's mind, which is itself wounded. The wound explains both Amoret's fear and Britomart's behavior. The identity in the wound explains apparent differences in behavior. Amoret, rescued, views herself as delivered into her rescuer's hands. Although intent on preserving her honor, she believes that as "her lives Lord" (6.2), Britomart has a right to "so faire a pray" (4.9), and Amoret cannot fail to provide a few coy looks (5.7) as recompense. Britomart, as rescuer, plays her chivalric role to the hilt, behaving "as well became a knight" (8.9). Rather than reveal that she shares Amoret's condition and "fained sex," she threatens to turn ravisher; better that, presumably, than to strip off her disguise and reveal her own subjection to her lover, Arthegall. The narrator comments that it should "be a pleasant tale, to tell / The diverse usage and demeanure daint, / That each to other made" (5.1–3); but if this is pleasure it is a dark comedy indeed of mistaken identities and false behavior. The grimness hides a joke: were the masks to be taken off, identification could follow. But, knowing themselves one in the wound, they would know they were no different. What maintains character, selfhood, is this failed recognition. Upon this lack, they exist. Indeed, how they relate to each other—falsely, mistakenly—is imposed upon them in another way as well. If there is something hidden that would obliterate external differences and also swallow up the selves acting here, there is also something prescriptive in the behavior that moves Britomart and Amoret to hide and to put on masks.

They are moved in this initial situation by social prescriptions. How a knight behaves has been told in the review of Amoret's career. Scudamour "bought" her like a piece of property, carried her off "with force" (2.1,3); and "from the time that *Scudamour* her bought / In perilous fight, she never ioyed day" (2.1–2).[4] Amoret's sadness and fear are

---

4. Amoret is treated as a commodity, and in a system of exchanges in which a community is established upon the ravishing of women. The social form here is not merely a fantasy; it is, for instance, a founding myth for Rome,

the signs of her subjection to Scudamour's force and power. Britomart and Amoret are replaying that story again. What we know about them now, moreover—that they share, to their loss, an identity in the wound that makes them "perfect hole"—can be extended to include Scudamour. Amoret's wound is only half the story; Scudamour's chivalric rescue also hides something—his identification with his prey. He, as much as Amoret, is subjected. And when, late in book IV, he retells the story that book IV opens with, he echoes the description of Amoret. The same words cover what are apparently opposite cases and link these two in a common situation: "For since the day that first with deadly wound / My heart was launcht, and learned to have loved, / I never ioyed howre, but still with care was moved" (x.1.7–9), he says. They share echoing wounds, the absence of joy. This is how Scudamour is joined to Amoret, in the wound of love; his chivalric force is, as much as Britomart's, merely a show, a mask for a wounded mind. Both lover and

---

the rape of the Sabine women, and Ben Jonson thought it explained aspects of force in the wedding ceremony, as in his note to 1.258 of *Hymenaei*: "Their first nuptials with the Sabines were contracted by force and as with enemies" (*Selected Masques*, ed. Stephen Orgel [New Haven: Yale University Press, 1970], pp. 343–44). As Orgel notes, the wedding celebration of Prince Arthur and Katherine of Aragon in 1501 included an assault on the ladies by "the Knightes of the mount of love" (*The Jonsonian Masque* [Cambridge, Mass.: Harvard University Press, 1965], p. 23). Amoret's forceful abduction from the seat of Womanhood repeats the Roman ceremony of carrying the bride from her mother's lap (see *Hymenaei*, 11.418 ff., and Jonson's note for classical antecedents). The amount of force that was displayed at Elizabethan marriages is suggested in the almost public nature of the bride's defloration; the comments in IV.i.3 about the marriage masque seem to be confirmed in George Puttenham's description in *The Arte of English Poesie* (1589), intro. Baxter Hathaway, facsimile ed. (Kent, Ohio: Kent State University Press, 1970). In the chapter on *"The maner of reioysings at mariages and weddings"* (I.xxvi), union is presented in militaristic terms—Puttenham refers to "assaultes" (p. 67) and "warre" and to "amorous battaile" (p. 66). The function of the epithalamion and the guests' noise is simple: they cover up the screams of the wife as she is taken, "the skreeking and outcry of the young damosell feeling the first forces of her stiffe and rigorous young man" (p. 66; the salacious puns determine the 'mind' of Paridell and Blandamour). At once she becomes "the laughing lamenting spouse." The bridal ceremony closes, Puttenham reports, when the guests have been notified of defloration and "second assaultes" have occurred; the bride, he says, has been robbed of her maidenhead, yet survives these "terrible approches" (p. 67). Although not particularly accurate anthropologically, several accounts provide further information about these practices and the texts on which they are based, beginning with John F. McLennan, *Primitive Marriage: An Inquiry into the Origin of the Form of Capture in Marriage Ceremonies*, ed. Peter Rivière (Chicago: University of Chicago Press, 1970 [1865]) and including George E. Howard, *A History of Matrimonial Institutions* (New York: Humanities Press, 1964 [1904]), 1:161 ff.; and Edward Westermarck, *The History of Human Marriage*, 3 vols. (New York: Allerton Book Co., 1922), 2:240 ff. Westermarck reports that at the time of writing, marriage-by-capture was still being practiced in Wales (p. 261). For evidence of Elizabethan marriage revelry as customary and nonethless socially suspect for its licentiousness, see Chilton Latham Powell, *English Domestic Relations 1487–1653* (New York: Russell & Russell, 1972 [1917]), pp. 24–27.

beloved share a lack, are wounded. The configuration of the lost or not yet found husband illuminates a more fundamental and essential loss; having a husband, being married, is a figure for it. Six cantos into book IV, Britomart will finally have Arthegall, and then she will have him only to lose him, and then to know, or to demonstrate, that her existence is wrapped up in her loss. There is nothing here to make this a "pleasant tale" at all; in this comedy of errors, all labor under versions of a single misapprehension that one might have about someone else—that he has power, that he has what he desires—or that one might have about oneself. All are in the same position, united or separated, possessor or possessed, all are subjected. To what? to whom?—to overpowering desires.[5]

Awaking to this recognition would undermine all behavior, re-

---

5. To borrow a title from Jacques Lacan, book IV demonstrates "Structure as an Inmixing of an Otherness Prerequisite to Any Subject Whatsoever" (in Macksey and Donato, *The Structuralist Controversy* [Baltimore: Johns Hopkins Press, 1970], pp. 186–95). It is Lacan's essential premise in that essay and throughout his work that the subject is well-named since it is subjected; "the subject is always a fading thing that runs under the chain of signifiers" (p. 194) because its language is not its own. The entrance into language (the Symbolic stage) means entering into the language of another (see p. 188). In language, which *is* structure for Lacan, the subject is separated from signification. The sign, composed of signifier and signified, is split—divided—and the subject is barred from knowing signification because it speaks another's language. Lacan concludes that, "it is necessary to find the subject as a lost object" (p. 189). The subject searches for another with whom it would be one; it is split and seeks to be whole, but the other it seeks is its own loss, or the separation in which it is constituted. The subject is, Lacan says, using an arithmetic notion derived from Frege, not number one; it is formed in repetition (cf. the "-mond" brothers) and is barred from its source through repression, distortion, forgetting (the source is the initial trauma of separation in which the loss of the object constitutes the subject in loss). "The subject is the introduction of a loss in reality, yet nothing can introduce that, since by status reality is as full as possible" (p. 193); hence, the subject is single and split, broken and continuous, external (physical) and internal (mental). The subject is a "fundamental cut" (p. 193). Finally, "the question of desire is that the fading subject yearns to find itself again by means of some sort of encounter with this miraculous thing defined by the phantasm" (p. 194), i.e., a lost unity is sought in the lost object, and this is "forbidden *jouissance*" (p. 195).

Writing from a quite different analytic perspective, Roy Shafer makes a connection between the self and storytelling central to this chapter; in "Narration in the Psychoanalytic Dialogue," *Critical Inquiry* 7 (1980), he says, "the self is a telling" (p. 35); "the event is always an ongoing dialogue" (p. 53). Or, as Steven Marcus remarks, the successful end of treatment for Freud was the translation of symptoms into language, a patient coming "into possession of one's own story. It is a final act of self-appropriation, the appropriation of one's own history" (*Partisan Review* 41 [1974]: 92). Further, Marcus notes that, in his study of Dora, Freud habitually refers to her as a text and to the transference as a "new edition" of a previous story (see pp. 100–101). For a discussion of related matters, see *Diacritics* 9 (Spring, 1979), devoted to "The Tropology of Freud," and Geoffrey Hartman, ed., *Psychoanalysis and the Question of the Text* (Baltimore: Johns Hopkins University Press, 1978).

duce distinctions, roles, and appearances to a nullifying identification. The narrator treats this as a joke, thereby assuming that he stands outside this devastation. He invites the reader to join him in this view, but the opening episode itself undermines these possibilities. The narrator's reading of this "pleasant tale" is a misrecognition; the reader's attempt to put together this revisionary opening with what has come before deprives us of the meanings we once had and the characters we once thought we knew. As we are displaced by this opening, our relation to the text is revised. We are not in control of what has occurred when a married Amoret is put before our eyes. We are asked to look back, but do not quite know what we now see; we are invited to go ahead, armed with new knowledge which we know is likely to be provisional./The text, making us go on, is also making us, drawing us in. The position in which those in the text find themselves—subject to the wound, the "hart-binding chaine"—is a figure, too, for the relation of the text to those who come under its power. With this new piece of information, which punctures his earlier account, the narrator lures the reader with a "pleasant tale." The pleasure of the text lies in that alluring representation. What is our desire for the text is, in the text, the desire—that wound—that moves the characters to relate (falsely), to identify (secretly), with each other. To be themselves in each other they inevitably cross a boundary between self and other as palpable as the boundary between text and reader; as palpable, and as illusory. We are joined to the characters in the text in our shared desire. What moves us—and them—is itself in the text. This is why we need to look at the shapes of overpowering desire in the text; by understanding the desire that shapes the text, we can come to understand our relation to it.

We have already seen that the place in the text that corresponds to the place of narration is the place where those in the text enter into the locus of desire. This is the space of the text, a place of desire. In book IV, that place is, quite literally, one where the characters in the text find themselves by finding that they are at the service of their desires. Further, what they discover, by discovering desire, is that the very desire with which they constitute themselves is their undoing. What they desire is another, and it is precisely because they lack others that they come to experience that lack as an impairment to themselves. But, more urgently, they also discover that having others also robs the self of the illusion of sufficiency. Either way, desire disables any notion of the self as an entity. Furthermore, this discovery, which is a repeated event in the text, nonetheless remains a discovery about the text as well. For the text is about the coincidence of the moving paradoxes of desire with the principles of narration, storytelling, and reading. To follow the course of desire is then to unravel further what it means that the place of narration coincides with the place of desire.

Desire takes on many forms in this text, forms that are basically contradictory. Scudamour comments, opening his story: "True he it said, what ever man it sayd, / That love with gall and hony doth abound" (x.1.1–2). Because desire is conceived to be inevitably overwhelming, the force of its contradictions devastates the individual. Scudamour revaluates the abundant measures of gall and honey, and precisely because they cannot be taken if taken together, he revises his equation: "For every dram of hony therein found, / A pound of gall doth over it redound" (x.4–5). Desire is felt as something larger than the individual, mastering him. In his subjection, the subject loses himself in the wound. But the wound of desire is not all that Scudamour's statement reveals; the experience of desire transforms the lover in another way. What Scudamour says embodies what every man, any man, might say. A meaning in his statement, even if it is not a meaning he intends to apply to himself, is that lovers act out the tropes of desire and are undone as individuals by doing so. They become imprisoned in their passions, and this means that they are trapped in literary tropes. Now, as I have been suggesting, Spenser's characters in *The Faerie Queene* are not constructed along mimetic or dramatic lines; they are not meant to represent selves at all. But it is important to see that our critical recognition is not one that the characters share. Rather, in book IV, characters act as if they were selves, as if their desires were their own, and as if they were selves seeking or warding off others. When Scudamour's words find their way into prescriptions, he reports as well a loss of himself. Again and again, in the text, a character's supposition of having a self confronts the reality of subjection, a reality that is not meant merely textually, although that is how it is ultimately registered.

Thus Timias's transformation into the form of "greedie lust" is an emblem for what, in various ways, is true of every character and what they become in the text; it is analogous to Scudamour's identity as "*Cupids* man" (x.54.7). Saying this, I recognize that I appear to be flattening a distinction the text might seem to be inviting us to make—surely there is a difference between malign lust and benign Cupid. Yet it is just such distinctions that fade when characters themselves fade. When the self is transformed into the prescripted form of desire, the notion of character as a stable, coherent, whole is denied the reader. Equally devastating to the understanding of the text is this larger denial: when characters disappear into the form of desire, we find ourselves in an inherently contradictory realm that supports itself in oppositions the reader cannot reconcile. Scudamour revises honey and gall in favor of gall; readers, too, watching a character become enveloped in a term that has thematic weight precisely because of a system of differences (meaning is always a matter of differences), find, like Scudamour, that they lose their footing, moral as well as narrative, as the differences fade. In book IV, selves

struggle to be themselves, to have what they want; instead, they become
the expressions of the demands of the text and take on the shapes of
desire in the text.[6] Selves desire or fear others and become themselves by
becoming other than themselves. As they are undone—and made—so are
we, reading. Characters think they have become themselves when they
cease to be the very selves they were; and at that endpoint, when they
finally become themselves, and are finally withdrawn, they become who
they are in ways that defy interpretation of what they have become. The
crushing irony in all this is that at such moments thay have come to the
end of their desires.

To summarize: in numerous ways, the idea of the self, the idea of
character, and the possibility of interpretation are disabled by this way of
conceiving desire. The revisionary opening of book IV highlights the
idea of the self and character that operates in *The Faerie Queene*.
Amoret's marriage means that the self cannot exist without an other; yet
it presents that necessary other always as either lost or not yet found or,
most devastatingly, when found still lost, lost again. Desire always begins and ends in a lack. The self lacks and desires another. Desiring, it
subjects the self to desire. Yet whether it achieves its desire or not, has
another or continues to desire one, the self feels a lack. To preserve the
self, the lack can be concealed; and Britomart and Amoret epitomize two
possible ways of doing so. Either the mask of power—chivalry—or the
mask of beauty may be put on. These masks attempt to affirm a self that
has been rendered impotent by desire. These masks, which are the external marks of identity and difference, are hollow. They can, and as we
shall see in book IV, do become ends in themselves, self-assertions made
at the expense of others which ironically register the expense of the self
that makes them. For the desire to possess another is a way of affirming
the potency of the self, a way of masking the fear that possession by
another will dissolve the self. That fear, just like the desire, is based on a
fantasy, for everyone is in the same position and the powers of the self are
imagined. No one in this text is free from the prison of desire, no self

6. Nohrnberg has a brief but acute discussion of these matters in the final
pages of *The Analogy of "The Faerie Queene"* (Princeton: Princeton University
Press, 1976); see pp. 780 ff. on "other selves" in the second half of the poem, and
p. 770 on self as a generic designation. "In one sense the Genius in Spenser is
indeed the "Selfe," as the poet tells us (II.xii.47); but in its division from the self,
the Genius is also the other, the other in allegory tending to be the *genus*."
Nohrnberg's discussion also focuses on daemonic agency; in book IV, the daemon is manifested as the contradictory shapes of desire: Lust, Corflambo, Venus,
and Ate, among others. If one wanted to relate this conception to psychoanalytic
theory, R. D. Laing, as well as Lacan, would be worth considering, particularly
Laing's notions of the self as cast in pregiven yet unavailable and unrecognizable
parts, scripts written by a hidden dramatist that make all life phantasmagoric.
See, e.g., *The Politics of the Family* (New York: Vintage Books, 1972), particularly the section on family scenarios, pp. 77 ff.

eludes that subjection. As the characters act to dominate others or to free themselves from others, again and again they face the unreality of their own selves, their own failure of integrity. Hence, some of the characters in the text act as if they were their masks; others deny that they are. Yet either way the situation remains the same: complex and shifting combinations of self-alienation, self-division, false representation and mistaken identity characterize each of them and their relations to each other. The self ceases to be able to know itself or to name itself. The self disappears into the mask, into a literary form.

As readers, we can, at best, record such transformations, noting how characters, overmastered by desires, become the very forms they sought; we can see the doubleness in such transformations, see that fulfilled desires produce obliterated selves. Yet, to record and to see where in the text the characters are placed does not untangle their knotty situation. The combinations of false representations tallied above are not easily untied; nor, in fact, can they be. What we must recognize, and be snared by so doing, is that the location of the self in the text corresponds to two equally unfathomable places. One is the place of desire, which is the desire of the text; the other is the place of lack, which is the wound within. The space of the self is bounded by these two nullities. The wound within is, for the characters, a piece of knowledge which explains behavior; repeatedly, lovers find that instead of a self they have a wound, or what the text refers to as "the griefe of mind."

> What equall torment to the griefe of mind,
>   And pyning anguish hid in gentle hart,
>   That inly feeds it selfe with thoughts unkind,
>   And nourisheth her owne consuming smart?
>   What medicine can any Leaches art
>   Yeeld such a sore, that doth her grievance hide,
>   And will to none her maladie impart?
>   Such was the wound that *Scudamour* did gride;
> For which *Dan Phebus* selfe cannot a salve provide.

(vi.1)

That wound propels them to their own undoing; it represents the contradiction of desire "that inly feeds it selfe with thoughts unkind" (vi.1.3), at once devouring and sustaining the self.

The cure for this wound is a talking cure, to tell your tale, to "impart" the malady to another (Freud might call this transference). This is a situation in which only the text, and not the desire of the self, is satisfied. Telling tales to each other, lovers enter into each other's wounds and find themselves in each other. That mirroring state is friendship, a society of loss situated in a prison, the prison of the text itself. Ironically, the cure to the disease is the confirmation and revelation of the disease itself. Recounting their stories, these lovers reveal that they are all in the same position, subjected to desire, trapped in texts. Friendship simply confirms this situation and makes a virtue of necessity; it celebrates self-sacrifice, the absorption of self into mirroring self; it is grounded in loss and absence. Friendship, we could say, is the thematic version of the meeting of self, desire, and text. The turning of the theme of desire into the desire of the text is covered by the idea of friendship. The transformation of self into other, which is what friendship entails, is, as a textual phenomenon, the disappearance of character into the desire of the text. These overlapping phenomena, these meetings of self, desire, and text, are accomplished at those moments of shared stories we have seen before. Let us look at one of them again, this time to see what it reveals about the "griefe of mind," that underlying condition that is shared by the characters in book IV.

The meeting of the lover's desire, "that inly feeds it selfe with thoughts unkind" (vi.1.3), and the bond of friendship, the imparting of that malady to another, is perfectly illustrated when Amoret falls into the hands of "greedie lust." Separated from Britomart, lost, she is carried off to the cave where she meets AEmylia, whose story, as we have seen, is recognizably a version of her own. Indeed, the story told in the cave, when looked at for its content, is an essential history for those who are slaves to desire. For when AEmylia is, as she says, "found, contrary to my thought" (vii.18.3), she discovers that her pretensions to autonomous behavior are simply that. Acting "by secret meanes to worke / Time to my will" (vii.17.1–2) and agreeing on a "privy place" (17.7) of meeting with Amyas, AEmylia instead finds herself in the hands of a much stronger will, so strong that it is at once contrary to her own and yet an embodiment of the monstrosity of her privy desire. She falls into the hands of lust. This contradiction expresses the state of the lover's desire, and not merely because it undermines the self, at once fulfilling and frustrating desire, but also because, when desire seizes Amyas and AEmylia and deposits them in prison, they are lodged with others in the same state. Identifying differences becomes hard to define. AEmylia has the company of a hag and, later, Amoret; Amyas not only has Placidas but "above a score / Of Knights and Squires" (ix.8.4–5) as well. The lovers are not alone in their desires; they are merely two among many who are prey to Lust and Corflambo. They make a society of a sort, sharing in friendship the mutuality of loss. They are all one in this situation. But where are these lovers? Where have they been placed, replacing each other? The caves of Corflambo and Lust are eminently literary domains, their presiding geniuses two emblematic figures of desire.

The crucial and central point, then, is that desire is not simply a natural prison or a natural force. It is invested with power by the imagination, given potency in acts of social recognition. "Whence he was,"

the narrator says of Lust, "I have not red" (vii.7.7, 8). And the consequence for us as readers is that we are invited to read this unreadable
situation. We watch characters becoming the figures of their desires; we
watch them cease being selves and, joining in the prison of the text,
becoming figures. We witness textual transformations that disarm our
abilities to make distinctions, to preserve the identities of characters, and
to hold onto their meanings. Formalist criticism invites readers to take
any moment in a text as definitive and exemplary; in this text, all moments are equally provisional. This text cannot be held to mean if we are
to read the unreadable; what occurs textually conditions our understanding of theme. What are we to make of desire, how are we to understand the self, when those supposedly natural categories are revealed as
textual creations?

The compulsion and overmastering force of desire and its con-
structive and constrictive potency—which affects both the characters
and our understanding of their situation—is nowhere more apparent
than in the Temple of Venus (canto x), the place in the text inhabited by
lovers who are generic types. This canto merits a closer look, since it can
provide a fuller example of the intertwining of desire and the defeat of
character and, with it, the defeat of the reader's ability to perform those
acts of distinction which make meaning a matter of differentiation,
which lure us into believing that words in a text refer outside the text.
Scudamour's echo of Amoret speaks directly to this—"I never ioyed
howre" (x.1.9) he says; she had been described in almost the same words.
The point is that both those who appear to have strength and those who
are captured are equally in the hands of more compelling forces. Moreover, in the Temple of Venus, Scudamour's joyless words might apply as
well to any inhabitant; his is, we know, a voicing of commonplaces. And
his last word, comparing his abduction of Amoret to Orpheus rescuing
Eurydice from hell, lends unmistakable support to the idea that the
Temple of Venus is not a benign image of the realm of desire, but an
exalted and sublimated picture of the prison in which Amyas and AE-
mylia languished or the one in which Florimell lies, "In bands of love,
and in sad thraldomes chayne" (xi.1.5).

Love is hell, Scudamour says; it is his opening and closing estimation in the story he tells. And just as his initial equation of honey and
gall is immediately revised so that ambivalence gives way to obliteration, so too the Temple, in this final allusion, is a Stygian realm. We can,
as readers, attempt to maintain the ambivalence of the place, and one
way to do this is to recall that the Temple of Venus is a literary and
artistic vision, a cultural artifact in which the domination of Venus calls
forth veneration rather than the loathing or fear that a Lust or a Corflambo causes. That the two realms might be versions of each other, that
the Temple might be a transformation of the cave, is quite understand-

able. Desire is, we know, both desired and undesirable. When lovers love, they invest their love objects with power, and then these alluring objects can grow to be feared precisely because of their power. Fear is translated into awe, and love objects can become idols. We see this when the Squire of Dames kneels before (False) Florimell (ii.23) and worships her, or when the act is repeated by the knights at the tournament, who bow before her and pray to Venus (v.26). In such instances—and these moments are clearly falsifications—the object of desire is invested with all the power to make a fantasy come true, giving the lover the joy of fulfilled desire. But lovers, Scudamour and Amoret insistently remind us, have no joy. Both lover and beloved are subjected to the power of desire; the powers of the self, the powers of another, are illusions. Desire itself is the figure for power, and power is figured by Venus. In her Temple only she has power, and the only joy in the Temple is her joy. To her, lovers' sad stories might be pleasant tales.

When Venus compels desire she shows her joy and her power. As Scudamour forces Amoret to leave the lap of Womanhood, he gazes, fixated, at the goddess—in fear. And she gives him her sign, a smile: "I saw [her] . . . / . . . laugh at me, and favour my pretence" (x.56.3–4), he says. The smile shows her power and also shows that Scudamour's force is a pretense because it is really Venus who compels him to act; his way to display power, after all, is by brandishing her shield. His name is her attribute, an object she names. So much for the independence of the self. And Amoret, weeping and begging for release, carried off into that state of unending misery in which she remains throughout book IV, nonetheless stays where she was when she sat imprisoned in the lap of Womanhood inside the Temple. Either way, she is "*Venus* mayd" (54.7). What the winning of Amoret displays, in these fearful mixtures, is that in the Temple of Venus it is not only frustration that is undesirable, as one would expect, but also fulfillment. Either satisfies Venus; neither satisfies the lover.

The space of the Temple is divided to reveal these two sides of the domain of Venus. The actual space is itself a trope, a figure for the sustained oppositions that shape desire to the undoing of those who are in its power. On the one hand, we are shown an "inmost Temple" (x.37.1); its chains and sacrificial altars embody the state of "sad lovers" (37.8), frustrated because they are without their beloveds, endlessly offering gifts to the goddess in the hope that she will grant their desires. It is here that Scudamour hears "some one through loves constrayning, / Tormented sore" (x.43.7–8), who breaks forth in the monologue that voices the desire of every unfulfilled lover. He delivers a prayer to Venus, heavily overloaded with literary references, praising her vast generative powers (x.44–47). Thirty-five of its thirty-six lines praise her; the last is the request "that of my love at last I may not misse." The single voice here asks to be included in the power of Venus which manifests itself in a universe where animals and vegetables—all of lower nature, in fact—have their desires whetted and fulfilled, who "Soone as with fury thou doest them inspire, / In generation seeke to quench their inward fire" (46.8–9). The speaker simply asks for such natural fulfillment, to have his desire and not be left to languish, excluded from this generativity. Whether this voices an animalistic debasement is not asked. Is a fire quenched a fire fulfilled, we may wonder. Is this speaker requesting fulfillment or obliteration? Is there a difference? The entire speech questions the naturalness of the desire that is expressed, not only because it depends so heavily upon antecedent texts but because its image of nature itself is so fully literary. The birds, for example, are a most troubling and, perhaps expectedly (after *The Squire's Tale*), revealing instance. The birds,

> Privily pricked with thy lustfull powres,
> Chirpe loud to thee out of their leavy cages,
> And thee their mother call to coole their kindly rages.

> (x.45.7–9)

The description is a tissue of literary tropes, anticipated by Chaucer as well as by other texts. The call of kind, at the end, is the voice of genre. Venerian generation produces literary types, social modes of behavior: natural love—"kindly rages"—has all the trappings of a medieval court and *amor courtois*. The lover speaking here, asking to be inside the Venerian universe, is "inside" even when unfulfilled. Frustration is as much her doing as fulfillment; she pricks and she cools, and instead of fulfillment she gives the birds language—"thee their mother call"—and they call her their mother for doing so, not because she is.

So, when Scudamour insists that *"Cupids* man" deserves *"Venus* mayd to hold" (x.54.7), renaming himself and Amoret as generic types, he displays that loss of individuality that is the consequence of falling under the sway of Venus. This brings us back to the other locale in the Temple, to Scudamour's first view, of the Temple as a place of fulfillment. He first glimpses the Temple grounds, once he has passed across the bridge, as "a second paradise" (x.23.2) peopled with couples virtually ceaselessly treading the garden paths, merely pausing occasionally on flowerbanks to "rest the walkers wearie shankes" (25.5), and talking endlessly—eternally—of love: "Ne ever ought but of their true loves talkt" (25.8). Desire fulfilled presents this pageant of ultimate constriction in movement and speech. The garden, as a second paradise, is a construct: ". . . all that nature did omit, / Art playing second natures part, supplied it" (21.8–9). It supplies and supplements nature by going beyond nature. Strikingly, this garden goes beyond to be a garden of the dead—fulfillment touches that perfection; those named here are all dead, their names drawn from books, a litany of friends ranging from such classical exemplars as *"Hercules*, and *Hylas* deare" (27.1) to modern figures like "Myld *Titus* and *Gesippus* without pryde" (27.5), heroes of selflessness. The garden is, explicitly, a place to be compared with Elysium (23.5) and is available only to those who have been there first. "Ioyance free" (23.9) is what it offers, participation in the joy of Venus, but at a price. Nature is subverted, and the individual subsumed, to take this fatal pleasure. In the garden are those "Whose lives although decay'd, yet loves decayed never" (27.9). Upon such losses the art of the garden rests. Fulfillment supplied beyond nature makes desire yearn for an end to nature and to the self.

The Temple's garden and inner precincts, the former the place of paired lovers, the latter of despairing lovers, add up, outside and in, to a consistent picture: fulfilled or unfulfilled, all lovers are imprisoned by Venus. The center of the mystery, with its voice of despair, seems closer to the ultimate truth of the place—that the individual, subject to desire in forms that are culturally determined, is caught in prescriptions for behavior that undo the individual and dissolve the possibility of maintaining differences. The call of kind in the Temple produces obliterative coupling, marriages that lie behind the voice speaking in the text. So, not surprisingly, concomitant with this voice that is little more than a palimpsest, Scudamour sees, at this center, "the Goddesse selfe" (x.39.1). "Selfe" is used here in a way that recurs throughout book IV, not merely as the English equivalent of *ipse*, that is, not simply to emphasize, but as a genuine category.[7] Venus embodies an idea of the self, one which, in the text, selves (individuals, characters) are at a loss to embody themselves, though it is what they desire to be, and what impels them to act.

7. The *OED* lists a 1674 usage from Traherne as the earliest instance of the modern meaning of *self* as one's own intrinsic being and a 1697 usage from Dryden for the meaning of the self as what one is at a particular time or in a particular relationship. Although these usages are roughly one hundred years later than Spenser, "selfe" in *The Faerie Queene* functions more than an intensifier, and is closer to the modern definition than we might at first suppose. I am supported in this by Nohrnberg (see n.6 above) and by Michael Goldman, who arrives at similar conclusions in " 'Self' in Shakespeare and the OED," an appendix to *Shakespeare and the Energies of Drama* (Princeton: Princeton University Press, 1972), pp. 153–58; Goldman suggests at least one use of self in Shakespeare that anticipates Traherne and several that antecede Dryden. Further, Spenser's "self" needs to be read against all those tendencies in the thought of the period which make separation and differentiation—the category of the individual—problematic.

The central philosophical problem of the Renaissance, Ernst Cassirer argues in *The Individual and the Cosmos in Renaissance Philosophy*, trans. Mario Domandi (Philadelphia: University of Pennsylvania Press, 1963 [1927]) is the subject-object problem. If we take certain central epistemological notions, for instance, Campanella's idea that *cognoscere est fieri rem cognitam* (see p. 169), or Marsilio Ficino's description of the desire of the mind to merge with the universe, to enter into universal mind (see "Five Questions Concerning the

As an amalgam of opposites, Venus is represented as containing what would be in human terms the contradictions of fulfillment and dissatisfaction. Only she—unlike the lovers in the Temple—fails to experience the oppositions as divisive. Her hermaphroditism signifies a genuine power, for unlike the solitary lover or the paired lovers, she "needeth other none" (41.9). Compelling all others to the disabling desire for another, Venus is the image of a self-containment that is not so driven. The system of desire that she instigates—and "nature" is the field of operation where she works her arts—is one in which she has no part. The idol at the center of the Temple embodies a *coincidentia oppositorum* in "the Goddesse selfe" that is unavailable to humans except in the form of fantasy and desire. Venus, as the embodiment and shape of overmastering desire, puts the individual, the self, out of play at the same time as she creates the self as the instrument of desire. She generates desire, the desire that fulfills itself when a person becomes a generic type, and occupies a place in her structures, thereby being occupied by her. Hers is the genuine power that those in her power lack. "Mother of laughter, and welspring of blisse" (47.8); yet those in her power, like Amoret and Scudamour, tell the same story—they "never ioyed."

The Temple of Venus, that highly textualized place, is, as this reading suggests, a place in the text where the meeting of character and desire involves the dissolution of the self into a figure, of desire into the

---

Mind," trans. Josephine L. Burroughs in *The Renaissance Philosophy of Man*, ed. Ernst Cassirer et al. [Chicago: University of Chicago Press, 1948], esp. pp. 200–201), self-fulfillment in these terms is an obliteration of the "I" into an otherness; the object known in Campanella's terms is possessed by the knower; the knower is transformed into the object known. For Campanella, the boundary between self and other ("other" may be another person or an external object, the universe) dissolves. This principle of mental freedom (cf. Marvell's "The Garden"), in which minds ultimately meet in the One/Mind, is also, for the self, an anxiety principle, the anxiety of being overcome and of having no self. And if we recall that in Pico's "Oration on the Dignity of Man," the universe, according to God's speech to Adam, is already complete when man is created, this is, at once, the cause for celebration—man, unlike either the angels or the beasts is not fixed and limited but free to roam the universe in his mind if not in his body— and for anxiety; as a chameleon, man's protean freedom means that he is essentially alienated, split off from the universe. The self is thus established as intrinsically unstable, unlocated, and, at the same time, separated from the universe. Knowledge is the free activity of the mind in the universe from which man is essentially and existentially separated, an attempt to be at one with the world, an attempt that always fails (success would obliterate the self).

As Wind remarks in *Pagan Mysteries* (pp. 62 ff.), Pico's hardheadedness led him where Ficino dared not venture, into the realization that the desired self-fulfillment of mind-in-universe was possible only in self-destruction. The paradoxes that Wind treats are invariably versions of this central one, whether figured as the flaying of Marsyas, the dismemberment of Uranus, the rape of Chloris, the wounding of Castitas, the birth of Venus, or the chastening of Mars by Eros. These all figure the shattering relationships that obtain between the One and the Many, the Infinite and the Finite, those gaps that the human mind keeps attempting to transcend in order to establish relationships with the uni-

undesirable, of fulfillment into frustration, of nature into text, of life into death. These textual transformations, literally mapped in the geography of the Temple and the route Scudamour follows there, tell at once a story about desire, about the attempts of characters to be themselves and to have what they want. The story is paradigmatic. All of book IV seems, when we arrive at Scudamour's narration, to have been moving ahead so that it could finally arrive at this beginning story, which explains why stories never get beyond their beginnings and why selves are their own undoings. The delusion that one has one's own story to tell is matched by a delusion about the self. From the vantage point of the Temple, we can see better that the narrator's misapprehension of a pleasant tale is a delusive attempt to appropriate power for himself, and we can see why our attempts to accommodate ourselves to the story are fantasies of appropriation, too. The Temple disables discriminative powers, undoes normative distinctions. What happens to us reading it, however, has been happening in the text to those attempting to have power, to fulfill desires, to be themselves. This is most apparent at the beginning of book IV. Although it is only those overmastering figures of desire—only those, like Venus—who have joy, there is a series of characters in the text who are presented through this Venerian attribute. Like the narrator, in his attempt to control the narrative, those who display joy are caught in the illusion that they master their desires, that they can impose themselves on others.

---

verse in its otherness, in order to act freely in a universe in which such acts lead to Mind penetrating the individual. "Self" and "individual" in these circumstances are not marks of uniqueness as they will be in the nineteenth century; the terms are simply ways of demarcating boundaries in a universe in which boundaries are always dissolving. When we recall that Burckhardt virtually proclaimed the self to be a work of art in the Renaissance, we can see that this makes the "I" something manufactured; in "nature" the self would be no category at all; in Pico's terms it only exists in its doing and in activity, fulfilling itself when it is shattered into the fullness of obliterating union with God.

Many of these problems are treated by Harry Berger, Jr., in "The Ecology of the Mind," *Centennial Review* 8 (1964): 409–34, to which the reader is directed for further discussion. Equally fundamental is the discussion by Thomas Greene, "The Flexibility of the Self in Renaissance Literature," pp. 241–64 in *The Disciplines of Criticism*, ed. Peter Demetz, Thomas Greene, and Lowry Nelson, Jr. (New Haven: Yale University Press, 1968). Greene's essential argument is that Pico's optimism about self-transformation, a humanistic idea, had been undermined by the end of the sixteenth century, by such a figure as Montaigne, who saw the self as a mass of inconsistency, or by Spenser, who fashioned the self in a highly circumscribed manner. As Greene says, each book of *The Faerie Queene* fails to arrive at an ultimate metamorphosis; "within the poem itself, there is little fulfillment" (p. 262). Greene provides evidence that the humanist tradition he describes is hardly central in Renaissance thought: Pico displays an indeterminate self (p. 243); Petrarch a various self, roles that fail to coalesce in a single self (p. 248). Most tellingly, the achieved self—the integral self—is always, Greene says, an ideal, never an actuality. To have such a self would be to have no self at all; conversely, the actual self—the self to be fashioned— is itself inchoate. Mirroring oblivion defines the poles of the self.

Venus, however, is behind those who think they have this power or who entertain the delusion that they can have joy. As book IV opens, we encounter the first of these when Amoret and Britomart are challenged by a "iolly knight" (i.10.1); he is the first of several knights in book IV to be designated by this Venerian adjective. He asserts his right to Amoret, yet the "iolly" knight shows, by the virtually automatic nature of his challenge, that his assertion is not his own but rather an indication of Venus's power: a desire to have a mate—any mate—grips him. His action is limited, moreover, by precisely the same social prescriptions that underlie Scudamour's career, fundamentally, by the belief that chivalric might will necessarily reap a lady as its reward. Finally, his challenge lacks autonomous, individualized motivation because it is so clearly a response to the immediate situation. It is because the "iolly" knight has been barred entrance to a castle which admits only couples that he must have a mate if he is to have any place at all in the "goodly fellowship" (15.2). In response to his challenge, Britomart encounters the "iolly" knight, and he falls to her greater strength. But he is not ultimately denied entrance, for after Britomart has insisted that her victory means that she can enter with Amoret as her mate, to the wonder of all present she strips off her chivalric helmet and reveals that it was a mask disguising her femininity; as a woman she makes claims on the knight. He may enter as her mate. To this, the text reports the knight "doubly overcommen" (15.4) and that seems, if anything, an understatement, first because one may wonder whether the knight has achieved his desire now that he can enter the castle, and further, because it is almost impossible to say what his desire would be in this tangled situation. But equally importantly, the episode serves to undercut the assertion of power that a self might make in order to satisfy desire. When Britomart's chivalry is revealed to be a mask, the delusion in her assertion—of power, of a self—is also unveiled. And, unhelmeted, Britomart shows that the notion that power resides in another is equally false.

So the "iolly" knight is doubly overcome. He enters the castle with a mate and yet without one, and the self he asserted has been shown to be without power. This is, not surprisingly, all we see of the "iolly" knight, for he has been totally deconstructed; absorbed into the text, he soon re-emerges transformed. The text will shortly produce Blandamour, a "iollie youthful knight" (i.32.1).

We cannot proceed to him, however, without asking what we are to make of Britomart in this exchange. How, as readers, are we to evaluate her? Has she achieved her desire in this exchange? Has she displayed a self that has power? We can easily see that the "iolly" knight, "doubly overcommen," has shown up a chivalric delusion and a delusion about the self. He has been caught in that double-edged nullification that absorbs characters into the text. Is the case any different, despite all the apparent differences, for Britomart? Is this a victory? What has she achieved? Earlier, I remarked that Britomart was wearing a chivalric mask to hide a wound. The moment she defeats the knight and reveals herself, she displays that double self. This duplicity overcomes the knight. Does it sustain Britomart? At best, we can say that her actions manage to admit her to the castle of "goodly fellowship" (i.15.2), and, since the "iolly" knight disappears at this point, Britomart is able to enter coupled with Amoret. But what does such an entrance serve? Does this place satisfy their desires? Yes and no. Certainly both subscribe to the notion that they need a mate, and once inside the castle the two women can fall into each other's arms and reveal their mutual desire to each other, sharing one another's wound. But they palpably are no nearer to the objects of their desire in this exchange. Nor has Britomart's victory over the knight affirmed her self, which she stripped away in order to share Amoret's loss. Even her way into the castle, her manipulation of her hermaphroditism, was, as much as the "iolly" knight's assertion, an indication of Venus's sway; for her double-sexed form was that of the "Goddesse selfe," and hence a sign of her subjection even when she manipulated it. Her double nature, which, in book III, the reader had been encouraged to believe signified her wholeness and integrity, now reveals that she is split between her social show and the reality beneath. Unhelmeted, revealing herself, Britomart displays the fact that her *form* has power—the power of illusions, the power given to her form by others—but that *she* has not. If she wears a mask, she masquerades, and her outer self is a disguise, not her self. If she takes the mask off, then she reveals that she is still a divided self, because she is separated from her lover and incomplete without him. Either way, she is no Venus; she needs another. The assumptions of the castle, the demand to couple, go unchallenged despite Britomart's dazzling prowess and even more staggering revelation.

Amoret also needs another; her dependence, even more marked, functions as a clarifying mirror for Britomart's situation. Their embrace of friendship provides yet further illumination into the self and its lacks and its inevitable division from itself. Joining, they lose themselves in each other; they recognize their identities by identifying with each other. Both are in the same situation, overcome by desire for someone else. Having each other, they can see themselves in each other. They make a society like that in the cave of Lust:

> . . . all that night they of their loves did treat,
> And hard adventures twixt themselves alone,
> That each the other gan with passion great,
> And griefull pittie privately bemone.
>
> (i.16.1–4)

There is passion in this compassion; "twixt themselves alone" they are sharing and relating a loss. We have already seen what is at stake in an embrace of such "griefull pittie," for it is what Canacee felt for the falcon she saw lacerating herself as a token of her lost mate; and it is what the narrator felt at first about his story. Fellow feeling means sharing a loss with another, and the loss shared coincides with the desire for another. Overcome by desire and loss, where can Amoret and Britomart go? how could there be a quest for them—or, since their condition is central to book IV, for anyone in the poem? What is the motion from loss to loss? The stanza concludes with one answer to these questions by showing the path that lies before them:

> The morrow next so soone as Titan shone,
> They both uprose, and to their waies them dight:
> Long wandred they, yet never met with none,
> That to their willes could them direct aright,
> Or to them tydings tell, that mote their harts delight.

(i.16.5–9)

"Their waies" are wandering, and lead them to seek out others to give them directions, to tell them what they want to hear. Led by their desire for someone else, in need of others to direct them, moving through a landscape that does not satisfy their "willes," they lack the self-propelled impetus of the quest in this journey. "Their waies" are the structures of narration. And in answer to their motion they arrive straightway at Ate, the most menacing shape of desire in book IV.[8]

8. Lacan has spoken of a daemon that he calls the Other; and Angus Fletcher has characterized allegory by its daemonic agency. In book IV, the daemon underlying the self (Lacan's "subject") is Ate. As Werner Jaeger remarks, from her earliest appearances in Homer and Aeschylus, Ate is "a daemonic power which no man can resist" (*Paideia: The Ideals of Greek Culture*, trans. Gilbert Highet [New York: Oxford University Press, 1945], 1: 255; see pp. 27–28 for a discussion of the *Iliad*). Ate appears in the *Iliad* 9.502 ff. and 19.86 ff. Whereas in the first passage she carries her usual meaning of ruin, in the latter, when Agamemnon accounts for the theft of Briseis by blaming Ate and presents a myth about how she came to earth after Zeus exiled her for deluding him, she also represents the force of delusion. E. R. Dodds, in *The Greeks and the Irrational* (Berkeley and Los Angeles: University of California Press, 1951), emphasizes Ate's psychological meaning when he defines her as "a state of mind—a temporary clouding or bewildering of the normal consciousness. It is, in fact, a partial and temporary insanity . . . ascribed . . . to an external 'daemonic' agency" (p. 5). Significantly, Dodds shows that Ate is connected with the Fates (p. 8).

In English literature, Ate appears as the prologue in George Peele's *The Arraygnement of Paris* (ed. R. Mark Benbow [New Haven: Yale University Press, 1970]), where she is conflated with Eris (or Discordia) and arrives with the golden apple in order to start the ruin of Troy; she is aided by the Fates, "th'unpartiall daughters of Necessitie" (1.20); in act II she tosses the apple, crying (according to the stage direction) *"Fatum Troie."* The entire play concerns the judgment of Paris and its reversal when Elizabeth enters the play and receives the golden ball;

Book IV began with a grim comedy of errors, and this meeting with Ate fully reveals its implications. To Britomart and Amoret, Ate appears to be part of a little chivalric society composed of "two armed Knights," each accompanied by "a Ladie" (i.17.2, 4). Closer inspection shows that these are misreadings. One of the supposed ladies is Duessa, who "under maske of beautie and good grace" (17.7) bears the wounding power that lovers are wont to project onto their ladies. She is the embodiment of the fantasized object of desire, a fitting companion for the two knights she travels with, Blandamour and Paridell. The former, "a iollie youthfull knight," is "a man of mickle might" (i.32.1, 3); he exemplifies the chivalric self-assertion found as well in the first "iolly" knight of the poem; and in token of this, he immediately replays with Britomart the challenge she has already met and mastered. Paridell is Blandamour's double and alter ego, and for the next few cantos, these two act out a dance of exchanges, taking turns as any potentially desirable object or anyone who might limit their desire passes before them. Ate figures the power that moves these two knights in their assertive actions as well as Duessa in her masking. "Mother of debate" (i.19.1), "her monstrous shape" (26.9) amalgamates oppositions: she is double-tongued, double-eared, double in her motion, so that as one foot moves forward the other goes backward and "contrarie trode" (28.9). Like Venus, Ate embodies contradiction. Coming as the answer to Britomart's and Amoret's wandering, she seems to be nothing less than the shape of narration when the quest is no longer viable. Her enemy is, pointedly, "th'Almightie selfe"

---

she functions as an antidote to Ate and as Diana to Paris's choice of Venus. In his notes on Ate, Benbow cites Thomas Cooper, *Thesaurus linguae Romanae et Britannicae* (1578), where Ate is "the name of a hurtfull spirite, always working yll to men" (Benbow, p. 115). She also appears several times in Erasmus's *Adagia*, e.g., I.vii.13; IV.v.26. It seems more than likely that Peele's play influenced Spenser's Ate. She is first presented in the poem in book II (vii.55.5) in conjunction with the golden apples in the Garden of Proserpina, and in book IV, she is among ruins including the sign of "sad Ilion" (i.22.3); the "golden Apple" (22.5) is her emblem. Moreover, the strife she stirs centers on the possession of women; it leads in book IV to a beauty contest and the reward of the cestus, an attribute of Venus in Peele's play as well. In the *Arraygnement*, Paris confesses to an error of judgment; in book IV, it is the (False) Florimell that wins the belt. In the next chapter, I consider the possible transformation of some of these matters into Elizabethan mythology. For a discussion of Peele's play that comes to conclusions similar to mine, see Louis Adrian Montrose, "Gifts and Reasons: The Contexts of Peele's *Arraygnement of Paris*," *ELH* 47 (1980): 433–61.

It should probably be noted that Ate's name puns in the worst way; she is eaten hate, anticipating Milton's "eating Cares." In his fascinating essay, "Book VI as Conclusion to *The Faerie Queene*," *ELH* 35 (1968), reprinted in *Critical Essays on Spenser from ELH* (Baltimore: Johns Hopkins Press, 1970), pp. 222–46, Richard Neuse points to Ate as the "fullest expression" (p. 230) of the depletion of chivalry that marks the final book of *The Faerie Queene*; of chivalry in book IV, he notes that it "is reduced to empty forms" (p. 226) and that Satyrane's tournament "is the symbolic center of the courtly society presented in this book" (p. 232), an ironic center enhanced by Arthegall's savage appearance.

(i.30.2). Once again, we have one of those surprisingly modern usages of
"selfe" in the text. The "Almightie" here is God, certainly, in which case
"selfe" functions pronominally; but the "selfe" here is also a substantive, the self that fantasizes its omnipotence. It is precisely such a view of
the self that Ate promotes and then devastates by stirring figures like
Blandamour and Paridell to assert themselves and be defeated. Ate's in-
separable contradictions do not divide her any more than Venus's do her;
but they do divide those whose vast desires become their own undoing.
In the grips of Ate—virtually possessed—no man possesses himself;
what he has are illusions about himself and illusions about others, illusions that are essentially about his and others' power. Under Ate's sway,
the desire for others is the same as the desire to assert the self: selves are
possessed by the desire to possess.

Conventional readings of book IV treat the poem as the opposition
of Ate and Venus; indeed, most readings of *The Faerie Queene* fall under
similar pairs of antithetical figures. From them, it is an easy step to leave
narration behind and to homilize the text, to find it voicing the commonplaces of Renaissance culture. But this pair of figures (Ate and Venus) is like other supposed antitheses, one that is only supported by
failing to see that the text itself undermines such clear principles of ordering and discrimination. When we review the tangles that book IV
opens with—Amoret married, not single; Britomart divided by a disguise that once seemed to support her—and recognize that the first episode is bounded by the pretenses that govern behavior in the Temple of
Venus (these cover both the story of Scudamour and Amoret and its replay between Britomart and Amoret) and the nullifications that underlie
them—then Ate seems to be not the antithesis of these situations, but
their embodiment. She is where Britomart and Amoret are headed, literally; she is, misseen, precisely the principle behind misrecognition.
What the narrator misread, what Britomart misjudges, what we misap-
prehend, are all versions of the contrarieties that Ate promotes in the
name of her war against "th'Almightie selfe." Once Ate is on the scene, it
becomes clearer that the story of those moved by desire coincides with the
story of those moved by its supposed antithesis. The ambivalence of desire embraces hate. The chivalric world, motivated by Venus (for knights
act to have ladies), is reinterpreted—the story of Scudamour is reseen—
when we view the actions of Ate's knights, Blandamour and Paridell.
Again, much as any reader might want to preserve distinctions between
that pair and other pairs of knights that follow, or to discriminate behavior under the aegis of Ate from its Venerian counterpart, the terms that
the text uses fail to register these distinctions. This is not to say that the
two goddesses are one, but it is to suggest that they are versions of, figures
for, a single condition that goes under various names and devours characters in its powerful grip. Desire is the general term I have been using to

cover those antitheses. In textual terms, we can see a bit further what the desire of the text means. It functions to our undoing, for it refuses us the differentiating term that would enable us to go beyond antithesis to resolution. Desire keeps the play of signifiers going. In the text, what the desire of the text does is enacted by what desire makes the characters enact.

Blandamour and Paridell, blown by the winds of passion, challenge every knight and attempt to possess every woman who comes into their view. Why do they do this? Having no selves, they attempt to own others as a means of self assertion; yet the women they seek as prey are also objects they fear. Having no selves, they assert in order to ward off the fear that they may be possessed by others. So, Paridell and Blandamour keep egging each other on to challenge other knights; this is both self-saving and a recognition that they are alter egos sharing the same position. If they do not have, they will be had. Acting this way, human relationships are nothing but power plays; again and again, the actions of Paridell and Blandamour end in the revelation of their impotence. The first fall is typical and revealing. As soon as Blandamour is defeated by Britomart he feels "wondrous griefe of mynd, / And shame" and, as the line continues, "he shewd him selfe to be dismayd" (i.37.6–7). As the pun makes clear, his self is, quite literally, unmade. Britomart "left him now as sad, as whilome iollie" (i.36.8); his "griefe of mynd" (cf. vi.1.1), which is yet another version of *her* wounded mind (i.7.4), and his Scudamour-like joylessness, convey the recognition that the self is undone by others. A few stanzas later, Paridell challenges Scudamour; when they fall, "what of them became, themselves did scarsly weete" (41.9). The mutual lapse in consciousness, an event that recurs throughout book IV, marks an end to a conception of the self. If the only way the self has to assert its existence and autonomy is by overcoming others, either by displacing other knights or by capturing their ladies (one act leads to another in this fundamental story), then failure means that the self virtually disappears when it can no longer cling to fantasies of its omnipotence.

Oblivion and obliteration are the acts of recognition that complement the illusions about the self and its power that Ate feeds her followers. When (False) Florimell appears in the hands of Sir Ferraugh (ii.4), Paridell, trying to save himself from further defeat, refuses Blandamour's suggestion that he challenge the knight. Blandamour goes in his place and wins a preposterously easy victory, a demonstration of the unreality of the power of Ferraugh and of all aggrandizing selves, though this is, of course, not how Blandamour understands the situation, since he thinks he has asserted himself. When Paridell insists that, as his friend, he is entitled to a share of Blandamour's spoil, he is roundly refused. Stirred by Ate "twixt love and spight and ire" (ii.11.8), Paridell starts a battle that threatens to destroy both himself and Blandamour. It is stopped, we recall, only when the Squire of Dames arrives to announce that Satyrane is having a tournament to establish who properly owns Florimell's girdle; the Squire's significant entrance serves to legitimize the quarrel of Blandamour and Paridell. For three cantos, the poem will center on the attempt of knights to display the chivalric prowess requisite to win Florimell's girdle and find the lady who is beautiful enough to wear it. The conclusion to that tournament reflects back on these actions and the values underlying them: (False) Florimell, proclaimed as true, chooses Braggadocchio as her fitting mate. In response—in anger and dismay—virtually all the knights and ladies gathered at the tourney go off in pursuit of those two illusory creatures who are nonetheless, as we can now see, the definitive couple for the assumptions about the power of the self and the beloved that have been operating in the text. Although Braggadocchio, "that masked Mock-knight," has been made the "sport and play" (iv.13.4) of all those on the way to Satyrane's, of both Blandamour and his crew as well as Cambel and his, it is the mockers who are now mocked. Their jesting—and it is a recurrent feature in the text, this pleasant tale, as when Blandamour scorns Scudamour for believing that Amoret has been disloyal to him (i.51), or when Scudamour jests at Arthegall's fall to Britomart (vi.28)—is yet another sign of the lack of individual power, for it makes claims on the joy of Venus. All such moments of joy are made at the expense of others; they are meant sadistically and are ultimately self-reflexive. Only Venus can smile at pretense. Each time a character adopts her attitude, saying, in one way or another, "So you thought you had power, did you? Now you've had your comeuppance," he merely says to another what can be said to him and often is. Here, for instance, is what one of these jesters, Blandamour, receives when he has momentarily won (False) Florimell:

> Sometimes him blessing with a light eye-glance,
> And coy lookes tempring with loose dalliance;
> Sometimes estranging him in sterner wise,
> That having cast him in a foolish trance,
> He seemed brought to bed in Paradise,
> And prov'd himselfe most foole, in what he seem'd most wise.
>
> (ii.9.4–9)

He is being had and, as the final line indicates, his self is split in half— divided against it—possessed as he is by his illusions of a paradise of joy. It was for this that Paridell challenged him, and it is after these illusions that the figures swayed by Ate chase.

Ultimately, Blandamour and Paridell fully embody the contradictory nature of desire, revealing that desire is not desirable. When they appear for the last time in book IV, they and their new alter egos, Druon and Claribell, make this contradiction apparent.

> *Druons* delight was all in single life,
>> And unto Ladies love would lend no leasure:
>> The more was *Claribell* enraged rife
>> With fervent flames, and loved out of measure:
>> So eke lov'd *Blandamour*, but yet at pleasure
>> Would change his liking, and new Lemans prove:
>> But *Paridell* of love did make no threasure,
>> But lusted after all, that him did move.
> So diversly these foure disposed were to love.
>
> (ix.21)

This round robin of desire runs on the wheels of disgust. Excess meets antipathy; no other person is really desired by these four; rather it is the lost self—their own lost selves—that they seek in the whirlwind of false passion. If desire does not support the self, if, indeed, the self that asserts desire only finds itself undone by desire, caught in this destructive round, are there then no alternatives?

Here, we need to face a set of antitheses about character alluded to earlier. On the one hand, the careers of Blandamour and Paridell are an ultimate demonstration of the illusions of chivalric behavior. From the vantage point of the wounded self, the self is a wound over which the mask of chivalry functions as sheer illusion, so that, once removed, nothing remains. To have a self in this way means that there is in fact no self at all, and it also demonstrates the textual principle that creates faceless knights and interchangeable, disappearing characters. As the final tetrad of Druon, Claribell, Blandamour, and Paridell reveals, all positions taken by those dominated by desire—and by the desire to assert the self—are the same.

This sameness also raises a question: are all the positions exhausted by this tetrad? Is there no alternative, no way not to be deformed by desire and the desire to have a self? For Paridell and Blandamour, that desire is manifested in the attempt to have another; this is an answer to the call of kind, to be under the sway of Venus and Ate. What, then, would the refusal of desire be? Could a self be made not subject to desire? Could a self assert itself in the renunciation of desire? This is Druon's position, and it is at once the opposite and the same as Paridell's; to lust after all, indiscriminately, is to loathe all.

Druon's position is the other side of the misrecognition of the self. It is founded in the declaration of self-sufficiency, of not wanting another. From the beginning of book IV, once Amoret's "hole" becomes the principle of character and the integrity of the self, this position becomes insupportable. However, this position also looks like the opposite of the situation of Blandamour and Paridell, and we need to examine it more fully in order to see, once again, that we cannot tell the differences that matter. Behind the will to possess and its renunciation there still lurks the underlying figure of desire, although, obviously, this is harder to see in those who seem to oppose desire. The paradox cuts deep, however; those who renounce desire do so to preserve themselves. Amoret's story retold tells us two things. There are no single selves. And the self only exists as undone in its relation to another. What we need to understand is how this applies to those like Druon. Or, rather (for this is the telling example), we need to consider Arthegall and the *via negativa* he embraces to save himself. It is a twisted and deformed path, and through it the other side of desire and the illusion of the self manifest themselves. Moreover, through Arthegall, we trace another inevitable path, one that leads us back to a figure of overmastering desire.

Arthegall calls himself the Salvage Knight and insists that this palpable misnomer, this name for a disguise, be the name by which he is addressed. He names himself in a mask: "Call ye me the *Salvage Knight*, as others use" (vi.4.9), he tells Scudamour, who has asked him to identify himself. The statement seems to be defensive, since Arthegall is suppressing his own name, and the meaning of that seems clear. He is not owning the mask, just demanding that it be recognized. Furthermore, his name is all Britomart has of him. His name, the echo of Arthur, is the name of Britomart's lover. Denying it—denying himself (insofar as the self is designated by a proper name)—he resists desire. But, he is also holding onto his self by refusing to give it up, by refusing to give his name. That this name denotes relations to others in which the self is submerged is seen a few stanzas later when Arthegall is at Britomart's feet; Scudamour then has no trouble producing the name he has not yet been told: "Certes Sir *Artegall*," he says,

> I ioy to see you lout so low on ground,
> And now become to live a Ladies thrall,
> That whylome in your minde wont to despise them all.
>
> (vi.28.6–9)

We know what to make of Scudamour's sadistically joyful attitude, and we may well suspect its assumed superiority. But what are we to make of his reading of Arthegall's *salvagesse* as a sign of antipathy to women and, therefore, a refusal to succumb to desire?

This interpretation may be correct, since at the tournament the disguise could be said to betoken Arthegall's "sole manhood" (iv.43.2), manifested as an assertion of self-sufficiency. But at the tournament, Arthegall is defeated by another knight who is similarly disguised (Britomart, in fact); retrospectively, as we interpret the action, his mask and its meaning become lies, illusions of power. In fact, when he later explains his *salvagesse* to Scudamour, he revises its meaning so that it is no longer an emblem of his power, but a sign of his shame. It is in the context of this explanation that he tells Scudamour to call him the Salvage Knight. Now, asking Scudamour to call him what others call him, although it appears designed to safeguard his real name and, with it, his genuine "sole" self, is really an admission that Arthegall no longer calls himself what others do. Nor can he rightly name himself. Since both the disguise and the real name point to a self that lacks sufficiency, Arthegall has no way to refer to his "sole" self. Arthegall aches, he tells Scudamour, for revenge on the knight who caused his downfall. Only then will his lost self, his "sole manhood" be recovered. Yet, when revenge comes, it works against Arthegall. At the end of his battle he has his right name from Scudamour and is on his knees before Britomart, worshiping her beauty. "Sole manhood" falls, as does the disguise that at first asserted it and then became a badge and an announcement of a lost self.

When Arthegall falls to desire, he is—however lost, however far from the pretense of "sole manhood"—not very far from where he was in that initial mask. When Britomart first threw him down, he was playing a social role that belied his antisocial assertion: he was a knight at a tournament seeking a lady. More than that, however, he appeared at the tournament as "Salvage," the first character in book IV to be presented in the form that recurs throughout the second half of the book as the emblematic shape of desire—greedy Lust, Timias transformed—the desire that AEmylia finds contrary to and yet which embodies her most privy thought. The form that Arthegall wears as a costume at the tournament situates him inescapably in the power of desire. He wishes to master desire and is instead mastered by desire. Desire encloses its negation: this is what Ate's shape proclaimed. Arthegall's chosen disguise signifies at once his alienation from desire and its inevitability, the inevitability that the self constituted in desire is opposed to itself. Acting against desire and yet ultimately within its sway, Arthegall presents an even more radical version of the failure of the self than Blandamour and Paridell had done. They thought it was their desire when they desired; he thinks he does not desire when he does. These are different positions, but they do not have different effects. Either way, selfhood is subverted by the antitheses of desire, which is an otherness that overwhelms and subverts the self.

Not surprisingly, Arthegall's subsequent wooing of Britomart continues the hostility of their battle engagement; he lays "continuall siege unto her gentle hart" (vi.40.4), shooting another arrow into her already wounded breast. Having wooed her, "wrought her" (41.1), and won her, he "wonne her will to suffer him depart" (43.2). Winning her and losing her, he fulfills his mastering desire in its radical ambivalence.

And Britomart, having and losing Arthegall, is even more firmly situated where she was when the book began. Now she is revealed fully in
Amoret's position, for having removed her mask, she is entirely vulnera-
ble, totally wounded. She has had and lost. She has surrendered completely. After this, there is, as we know, only one direction for her, back
to Amoret, to share the wound and, finally, to demand that Scudamour
tell his story, for it is her story too.

Let us return now to Scudamour. To follow the presentation of his
character in book IV, to trace the career from its telling in canto i to his
telling of it in canto x, is to set before our eyes a paradigm of the process
that we have been examining thus far. His is a story that begins in a
retelling and ends in rewriting. His is a name that at once designates a
character and makes character a function of someone else—"*Cupids
man.*" As I have been insisting, to tell his story, we must not pretend that
it can stand alone; or that he can. We must move on to his marriage
partner. But that pairing does not exhaust the nature of relations. Scudamour's final position, as surrogate narrator—squire within squire—
follows a sequence, for throughout book IV he takes on various shapes
that mirror the forms of desire. When first seen (i.39), he is recognized by
Blandamour as his own alter ego—Scudamour legitimately "owns" (although he has lost) the woman whom Blandamour has just failed to
capture from Britomart. The victory that Scudamour achieves over Paridell follows upon the fall of both into an identical trance, which demonstrates the precariousness of the self. When Scudamour awakens, he
hears Ate say that Amoret and Britomart have betrayed him; their scene
of friendly commiseration becomes in her words a hallucinatory vision
of betrayal, yet another sign that the self is mastered by others.

> I saw (quoth she) a stranger knight, whose name
> I wote not well, but in his shield he beares
> (That well I wote) the heads of many broken speares.

> I saw him have your *Amoret* at will,
> I saw him kisse, I saw him her embrace,
> I saw him sleepe with her all night his fill,
> All manie nights, and manie by in place,
> That present were to testifie the case.

(i.48.7–9; 49.1–5)

Ate interprets Britomart's disguise as her self; her shield means that she
renders others impotent and that she takes what they desire. Ate sees—for
Scudamour's benefit—a vision of chivalric potency in Britomart's alliance with his lost bride.

Scudamour is first presented in the text as the legitimate "owner" of
Amoret; this is how Amoret views him in her grief and how Blandamour

and Paridell see him in their envy. When Ate puts Britomart in his place, he is undone. What Ate says she "saw" represents the very shape of Scudamour's mind, for she voices his worst fears and penetrates the frailty of his identity and his powers. Although she cannot have seen what she says she saw, nevertheless her report is true to appearances; it expresses what anyone seeing Britomart and Amoret would say of them. Scudamour is possessed by this confirmation of his inner apprehension. When the scornful sadism of Ate, the supposed objectification of his own self-wounding self-assertion echoes against Blandamour's equally malicious and joyful reproaches (i.50), Scudamour loses all self control. Overwhelming anger—the sure sign of Atean possession—leads him to strike out at his squire, Glauce. Even this act is ironically undermining, for his squire is really Britomart's squire. Having been replaced in bed by Britomart, he takes out his anger on her through her companion. He has no real object for his anger, nor is he acting for himself.

The next canto makes this transformation and loss of self clear. An elaborate simile compares Glauce's attempts to calm Scudamour to David ministering to the possessed Saul, Agrippa's soothing the maddened Roman crowd—even to Orpheus's mending strife and making friends. Yet Glauce's ministrations are rather ambiguously directed to someone simply named "that wrathfull knight":

> Such us'd wise *Glauce* to that wrathfull knight,
>   To calme the tempest of his troubled thought:
> Yet *Blandamour* with termes of foule despight,
> And *Paridell* her scornd, and set at nought,
> As old and crooked and not good for ought.
> Both they unwise, and warelesse of the evill,
>   That by themselves unto themselves is wrought,
> Through that false witch, and that foule aged drevill,
> The one a feend, the other an incarnate devill.
>
> (ii.3)

If "that wrathfull knight" is Scudamour, Glauce's words are nonetheless answered by Paridell and Blandamour, as if one of them were the knight in question. Their explicit self-destruction in these lines mirrors what has happened to Scudamour here, for he fails to appear at all, having been absorbed into his alter egos in the text, Paridell and Blandamour, those two knights stirred against him, and against themselves, by Ate. Scudamour's name appears nowhere in this or the subsequent canto, and there is no sign in the narrative that he is present. He has simply become another undifferentiated self moved to self-destruction by Ate; the silence of the text, omitting his name, eloquently enacts this loss of the self in desire. When Scudamour's name does reappear, in canto iv, it is used in place of Blandamour's (iv.2.4); his name appears only because the narrator makes a "mistake." If the naming implies that Scudamour is present at Satyrane's tournament, as described in this and the following canto, it is the only sign of it; there is no other indication that he is present. The obliteration and substitution of the name register in the text the paths of desire in generating the text in the loss of the self, to itself, and to others.

At the tournament, Amoret, although certainly there, fails to be recognized as the winner of the beauty contest; and if Scudamour is in attendance, he fails to recognize his lost wife. Scudamour reappears and is seen as himself only after the tournament; then, in the Cave of Care, he meets "the goodman selfe" (v.34.1), the inner principle of his self-alienation that has allowed him to go unrecognized and to have been absorbed in the text for so long. Care is the form of Scudamour's love, it is the word for desire that has become anxiety. The Cave of Care represents the mind of Scudamour absorbed as it is in self-wounding thoughts: it is a figure for minding. What it means to be so absorbed is displayed not only in the word "care" and in Scudamour's tormenting experience, but in the route the text takes to arrive in the cave, and to locate itself in Scudamour's minding, resituating him in the text. The narrative proceeds to him only through others and in their minds.

Here is the sequence of the transition from Satyrane's tourney ground to the Cave of Care: the tournament is over, only Britomart and Amoret do not pursue Braggadocchio and (False) Florimell. Britomart follows Arthegall, the object of her desire whom she has, unknowingly, just met and defeated—found and lost—at the tournament. Amoret, the "companion of her care" (v.30.5) likewise seeks "her lover long miswent" (30.6), that is, Scudamour, who, as the next stanza relates, is "bent to revenge on blamelesse *Britomart* / The crime, which cursed *Ate* kindled earst" (31.1–2; we might note in passing the ambiguity here; the line reports Scudamour's criminal understanding of Britomart's behavior, a reading that Ate kindled and confirmed; but it could also be affirming that reading as a valid one—then the "crime" would be what Britomart did at Ate's unrecognized prompting). "So as they travelled . . ." (32.1), the text continues, and the reader is, at least retrospectively, brought up short. Who are "they"? Britomart and Amoret, presumably; we have been following them and their thoughts as they leave the tournament. Eight stanzas later, it is clear, however, that the pronoun "they" must refer to Scudamour and Glauce; they are in the Cave of Care. They are in the place of the mutual care of Britomart and Amoret, what they mind and fail to see.

When Scudamour later tells his story, he will reveal that this is not a location that he ever leaves: "I never ioyed howre," he says, "but still with care was moved" (x.1.9). To journey to Care is to move in "sad misfare, / Through misconceipt" (vi.2.3–4), and Scudamour meets in

Care a paradigmatic embodiment of desire, his own desire as well as the absorbing thought of his fellow travelers in disquietude. Care—shaggy, ragged, and blind; busy at his forge of "unquiet thoughts, that carefull minds invade" (v.35.9)—is a composite figure, an amalgam of desire, a palimpsest; he anticipates the form of greedy Lust, but is blind as Cupid and at his forge replays Vulcan, the archetypal cuckolded husband, as well.[9] No wonder that at the end of the episode the narrator leaves the Cave of Care overcome like Scudamour with weariness; for in this location the text produces a powerful image of self-absorption and self-loss. This is a generative forge in which false visions and false selves are created. In sleepless agony and tormenting dreams Scudamour realizes that "the things that day most minds, at night doe most appeare" (v.43.9). The ambiguity of minding (it was in part the route to the cave), like the ambiguity of "care," points to the contradiction of the wounded mind that is undone by what it desires. Absorbed by Ate, vanquished by Venus, caught by Care, Scudamour registers all the positions of enslavement to desire. After the cave, Scudamour first joins with Arthegall—for they meet in mutual "sad misfare, / Through misconceipt" (vi.2.3–4)—and then sadistically exults in Arthegall's fall. The self-recovery is momentary, however, for the tables turn: Amoret, he hears, is lost again. Pursuing her in company with Britomart, he next emerges as the voice in the text telling of his own undoing, recounting the story, everybody's story, of how he became Cupid's man. Voice inside of voice, mind within mind, Scudamour, "still . . . moved" with care, figures what the self becomes when shaped by the desire of the text.

Scudamour threads his way through the text. His career traces a path through others, through obliteration, through desire, to become the voice of that destructive path. Pursuing Scudamour, we follow him into himself, into his assumption of his own voice, which is his undoing, and which is the voicing not of a character but of the end of the self

9. John Steadman provides some background for the figure of Care in two essays, "Spenser's House of Care; a Reinterpretation," *Studies in the Renaissance* 7 (1960): 207–24, and "The 'Inharmonious Blacksmith': Spenser and the Pythagoras Legend," *PMLA* 79 (1964): 664–65. His final interpretive point is apt: "The potentiality for harmony also contains the seeds of dissonance. Just as the same musical instrument can produce either concord or discord, *amicitia* can become *inimicitia*. The 'matter' of friendship and jealous hostility, like that of harmony and dissonance, is one and the same" (*PMLA* 79, p. 665). The forge of Care produces the phantasy image of (False) Florimell in v.15; as Steadman notes, "forge," like "care," is double in meaning.

One significant element in this episode is undoubtedly alchemical; Vulcan, for instance, is an alchemist in Ben Jonson's *Mercury Vindicated from the Alchemists at Court.* Alchemy has connections with psychological development according to Jung, and with poetic labor mythologically; Mircea Eliade shows the ancient connection of poet and wordsmith in *The Forge and the Crucible: The Origins and Structure of Alchemy*, trans. Stephen Corrin (New York: Harper & Row, 1962), pp. 88, 98–99.

that has been obliterated by the principle that moves him to that end. His story, woven into the context of the history of chivalric self-aggrandizement, has its complement in the history of the other to whom he is wedded when book IV begins. If he exemplifies the history of masked mock knights, Amoret's story, when it is picked up again in canto vii, summarizes the career of beauty, that dazzling mask.

When the poem returns to Amoret, it presents her story in a manner analogous to Scudamour's. Her history is woven into the various squires' tales that follow. She is briefly attached to each of the subsequent stories, first that of AEmylia and Amyas, then that of Timias and Belphoebe (her unrecognized sister); and finally, as we have seen, she ends as a figure in Scudamour's tale rather than as his regained bride. Just as Scudamour enacts his role as *"Cupids* man" Amoret plays the part of *"Venus* mayd." She is everyone's surrogate pursued by desire, misrecognized and misrecognizing, lost over and again. Saved from Lust's grips, she is abandoned by her rescuer. Saved again, she fears her savior. Finally, with her husband in sight, she disappears into his story, to be seen no more. The pattern behind this sad career is established in the cave of Lust when, as she solidifies her friendship with AEmylia, "they did discourse, / And each did other much bewaile and mone" (vii.20.1–2), and Lust appears in the mouth of the cave—and in their mouths—ready to devour them. Significantly, he is, at that moment, named in a usage we have come to expect; he is "the villaine selfe, their sorrowes sourse" (20.3). When the two women coincide in a common story, they are discovered by that overwhelming villainous force, that illusion of identity. They have been talking about how AEmylia has preserved herself, her witty trick; Lust, she says, is so indiscriminate that he will take anyone, and an old hag has satisfied him. Talking about this substitution, Lust appears to signify that he is a part of their substitution, of their compassionate identification and, most pressingly, of their illusions about how they can preserve themselves. For there is no self to save; unknowingly, but tellingly, when AEmylia identifies Amoret with herself as a "caytive" (vii.12.1) in the prison of desire, she applies a name she shares with the "villaine selfe," for Lust too is "this same cursed caytive" (24.4). Same and other, and yet the self. Lost and named in that identification, AEmylia summarizes her identity and Amoret's when she describes herself as "a wofull wretched maid, of God and man forgot" (14.9). So described, she joins all those forgotten selves that the text buries in its progress: the knights who fall into oblivion; or, to extend this to the reader, those names that the narrator tells us we "remember well" (iv.2.7) when he himself cannot and errs; or those like Florimell, whom we are told we "neede . . . to remember" (xi.2.1) just when the narrator, in producing her name, has apparently forgotten Amoret's. AEmylia's name, which means friend, and which is scarcely even a proper

name since it also alludes to a text, echoing the title of the well-known
friendship story, *Amis and Amiloun*, so little designates a self that it
refers to a relationship that idealizes not having a self, forgetting oneself.
Advising Amoret, AEmylia as the voice of friendship says in a single
ambiguous sentence a summary of all the poem has to say about the self,
its desire, and the structure of its relationship to another: she says, "Selfe
to forget to mind another, is oversight" (vii.10.9).

This illuminates the destructive ambivalences that undermine
character (and the idea of "selfe") in *The Faerie Queene*. Moreover, the
very act of reading that AEmylia's sentence entails (her sentence is a
sententia, the kind of utterance available to characters in *The Faerie
Queene*) reestablishes the position of the reader in relation to the text,
the extension of the narrative action and the thematic space of friendship
to the production of the text as a shared space of annihilation. In AEmylia's sentence, the voice of friendship—the voice of theme—speaks of
character to another and speaks of the self in relation to others. And these
relations, structured in the text, display the structure of the text. In
AEmylia's sentence we have in one line an exemplary meeting of desire
and the desire of the text.

"Selfe to forget to mind another, is oversight." A split self speaks
that sentence, for AEmylia praises and dispraises selflessness at the same
time, simultaneously taking another's place and being replaced by
another. The self is to forget itself, AEmylia says; and to achieve such
selflessness the self stands in the position of the other by having overmastering supervision, or "oversight." However, "oversight" is, at the same
time, misprision, mistaking, overlooking oneself to one's loss, an ideal
of selflessness that coincides with opacity and obtuseness. Or, the sentence can mean that to forget to mind another is to err in being wary of
another. In that construction, others present perils to the self, and AEmylia's prescription bespeaks a brand of paranoia. But although "mind"
can be construed to mean wariness, it can also, like its synonym "care,"
point to a virtue. Then the sentence advocates nothing less than the
golden rule of concern for one's fellow creatures. The syntax of this sentence is double at least, and the lexical possibilities seem, if anything,
even more extensive. The sentence is quintessentially Spenserian, and
the voice—itself diffused as a structure of relationships (as the voice of
friendship)—produces a piece of text that appears to be capable of endless reading, yet is and remains finally undecipherable. This line about
the self undoes the voice speaking—it is no self speaking—and it undoes
the reader reading—we will never come to the end of this line. Overloaded with meaning, the words hover on the margins of meaningless-
ness. Perhaps the sentence contains its contradictions: we cannot, nor
can they support a self. We are overcome, as those in the text are overcome, by a demand the text makes and we cannot meet. The text makes

its demands and presumably fulfills its own desire—Spenser's desire?—
despite us.

"Selfe to forget to mind another, is oversight." This sentence about
the self, quintessential not merely because of what it contains but also
because of how fully it disables the terms that it uses—"self," "other,"
"mind," "oversight," "forget"—the terms that establish character, interiority and exteriority, vision, self-knowledge, the knowledge of others,
and the terms that establish the possibility of interpretation, summarizes
the meeting of self, text, and the desire of another that structures the text.
It is central in its decentering, and it points to the nature of symbolic centers in Spenserian narration. They are not summary places, which contain and condense meaning. Rather, they are textual places, as unstable
as language is. The cave where we find AEmylia has its duplicates in the
poem. One, we have seen, is the Temple of Venus. But just as Venus is
complemented by Ate, so too is Ate's realm a version of the Temple. It is,
after the castle of fellowship, the first locale in book IV. Its placement is
meaningful, for the cave of Ate is a fundamental location of undoing: it
shows where fellowship leads. Not surprisingly, at least in retrospect,
its topography is reminiscent—or anticipatory—of the Temple's. It is a
place worth pausing over.

Like the Temple of Venus, Ate's realm is divided into an area within and without, here a cave and a garden. Inside, "too long a worke to
count" (i.24.2), endless destructiveness is monumentalized in broken
bands and torn garlands, the signs of friends become false, brothers
proved unnatural, lovers turned enemies, the moving contradictions of
desire. This is the inner space of nullification, the space of the wound.
Outside is a garden of weeds, the flourishing growth produced by "the
seedes of evill wordes, and factious deedes" (i.25.5). This is the space of
human action, of the masquerade.

The monuments inside the cave of Ate are nothing less than the
broken texts upon which civilizations are founded, the "ragged monuments of times forepast, / All which the sad effects of discord sung"
(21.2–3), the work of time transformed into a set of signs and names
memorializing all that has been lost, making history take the shape of a
text in which one loss replaces another; the cave takes in what grows in
the garden without.

> There was the signe of antique Babylon,
>   Of fatall Thebes, of Rome that raigned long,
>   Of sacred Salem, and sad Ilion,
>   For memorie of which on high there hong
>   The golden Apple, cause of all their wrong,
>   For which the three faire Goddesses did strive:

There also was the name of *Nimrod* strong,
    Of *Alexander*, and his Princes five,
Which shar'd to them the spoiles that he had got alive.

And there the relicks of the drunken fray,
    The which amongst the *Lapithees* befell,
    And of the bloodie feast, which sent away
    So many *Centaures* drunken soules to hell,
    That under great *Alcides* furie fell:
    And of the dreadfull discord, which did drive
    The noble *Argonauts* to outrage fell,
    That each of life sought others to deprive,
All mindlesse of the Golden fleece, which made them strive.

(i.22–23)

History traces its course from "the golden Apple, cause of all their wrong," to "the Golden fleece, which made them strive." The energy behind all the heroic names is destructive ("strive" and "strife" are one here), and finally self-destructive when the heroic drive for that object of alluring desire, the golden fleece, is forgotten, and those in pursuit of it become "mindlesse." The text in Ate's cave is a memorial erected to those who are forgotten and who forget themselves, and are only further dismissed in this reliquary of loss. The text describes itself when it arrives at the "bloodie feast," for the destructiveness that it embodies "within" it also sends "without." There the text becomes generative, planting "seedes of evill wordes." "And those same cursed seedes doe also serve / To her for bread, and yeeld her living food: / For life it is to her, when others sterve" (26.1–3).[10] The cycle represented by Ate is self-consuming. She produces generously, devours omnivorously. What she produces and devours are the words that are the life of the text, the names of these brothers, friends, and lovers, the acts of time and history that undermine the "Almightie selfe" (i.30.2).

If, as we saw earlier, the Temple of Venus brings together disabling contradictions, ambivalences that destroy the stability of selves and the possibility of meaning, Ate's dual realm reflects the meeting of the contradictions of desire and the production of texts. Garden and cave, like the garden and Temple of canto x, are places that at first seem to divide interiority and exteriority, then collapse that distinction. The words produced in the garden are reproduced broken in the cave. The breaking of relations in the cave sustains and is sustained by the seeds planted in

---

10. Perhaps Keats had this passage in mind when, in a letter of 21 September 1819, he described his relationship to Milton: "Life to him would be death to me."

the garden. Nature here—these seeds—is words, texts; natural and unnatural meet here as nature and art do in the Temple, confusing boundaries, driving distinctions toward nullifications. The circles of the cave,
like those of the Temple, are hermeneutic rounds, endlessly enclosed
upon themselves, incapable of penetration, but also words without ends.

The realm of Ate, so fully destructive, and yet so fully revelatory of
the life of the text, is productive. This cave, where the text first takes its
life, is replicated throughout book IV, so that the history of the self that
is presented is the same as the history of the broken and lost text. The
meaning for the generation of the self—and the text—of the grisly lar-
gesse that Agape learns in the cave of the Fates, when she finds that to
preserve one son she must sacrifice two, is revealed at the moment when
Diamond's spirit is received by his sole surviving brother, Triamond. He
is filled "with double life, and griefe, which . . . he felt, / As one
whose inner parts had bene ythrild / With point of steele, that close his
hartbloud spild" (iii.22.3–5). He receives life as a deadly wound. Generated from others, living on their deaths, the "double life" that distinguishes Triamond is also a terrible wound and a disabling pain. He is
born here as himself in a wound experienced as loss. Life depends upon
death, and the life received from others is experienced immediately as a
wound to the self, as self-diminishment. Triamond is twice born and
born double; "doubly overcommen" like the "iolly" knight, he is not
himself alone because he needs another to produce him and is produced
and reproduced as one of three; and because he exists desiring another,
Canacee, and opposing another, Cambel. He is nothing himself. His life
in the text figures the life of the text located in the place of loss: book IV,
after all, is born like Triamond in "infusion sweete" (ii.34.6). The spirit
of Chaucer lives in the narrator, to his pain. The life of characters—of
the self—in this text is an imitation of the narrative life of this text.

The central paradox of desire, that it brings together having and
losing, that it is generated in loss and sustained by loss (as Scudamour's
paradigmatic statement says, "I never ioyed howre, but still with care
was moved" x.1.9), is an explanation of the principle behind both the
self and the text. Selves in the text are undone by desire; undone by desire,
they become texts. This brings them no closer to their desires, but does
fulfill what the text requires, namely, that they be examples, names,
words—not selves—that can be devoured or that will devour. The characters ("selves") in the text enact verbal relationships and structures:
they show the life of words. This explains why in reading *The Faerie
Queene*, although the significance of an action often seems to depend
upon some final word—frequently the name of the character performing the action, which is withheld until the very end—when the word is
supplied, it fails to have the expected explanatory force. The explana-

tion tends to undo the action that it undertakes to define; indeed, the last word, like any word, is produced in such a way as to rob it of any definitive or representative power. An example from book III, the transformation of the jealous cuckold Malbecco into *Gealosie*, is the perfect instance of the process: he "ran away, ran with himselfe away . . . / Forgot he was a man, and *Gealosie* is hight" (III.x.54.6, 60.9). A series of negations and undoings of act and actor produce the last word. Malbecco is separated from "himselfe" before our eyes; he has suffered a "wounded mind" (55.9) and is finally reproduced in the annihilative space of that wound. Similarly, when book IV locates its first action in the mutual wound of Britomart and Amoret, it defines its sphere of operation. Generated in loss, never themselves, all the characters could name themselves as Duessa does in book I: "I that do seeme not I, *Duessa* am" (v.26.6).[11] The wounded mind, the grief of mind, the shared condition that moves selves to their undoing, generates them to be replaced by others, different characters, in different terms. Fulfilled, they are undone; undone, they fulfill the desire that moves the text and moves them in the text. The figures of desire in book IV—Ate, Venus, Lust, Corflambo—stand in the text as figures for the relation of the text to its characters. They stand for the relation of theme to character. And, as I have been arguing, what they reveal about character is not limited to book IV. Once again, the movement of desire in book IV, which is the movement of the text, reflects retrospectively on what has come before. Like the revisionary gesture that opens the poem, the marriage of Amoret and Scudamour, book IV is similarly wedded to what comes before. It continues to undo and to replace. Malbecco's wound and his transformation are echoed in Britomart's wound. They share the words and the condition. Duessa can never be finally unmasked.

Perhaps one further demonstration of these relations is needed, and it entails a return to a moment in the poem that has engaged our

11. Rosemond Tuve points in *Allegorical Imagery* (Princeton: Princeton University Press, 1968) to the withheld name as a technique of romance; as she says, by the time the name—the explanatory statement—comes it seems inadequate to the experience described, so that the last word, instead of being definitive, is simply another word; the abstract name *Gealosie* is no more authoritative than the coinage "Malbecco" (see p. 415, e.g.). In *S/Z*, trans. Richard Miller (New York: Hill & Wang, 1974) Barthes talks about the withheld name as part of the way in which narration sustains itself, luring the reader to expect that knowledge will coincide with the name; but names spawn more names (pp. 92 ff.). In *The Faerie Queene* one aim of the writerly text is achieved: there are no proper names in the text, and therefore no "persons" or selves; as Barthes says, "what is obsolescent in today's novel is not the novelistic, it is the character; what can no longer be written is the Proper Name" (p. 95). In what Barthes would call the preclassical era, the proper name does not really exist. The self is too fully embedded in structures of relationship to be individualized; a person, defined through a grid of social relationships, *is* one's family, class, occupation, etc., before being oneself.

attention before, a crucially intertextual one, when the characters from
The Squire's Tale first appear in book IV. Reviewing this moment, we
can finally see that the relationship between selves in book IV is always
intertextual and that the dominant figure for the text in the text is always
a figure of desire, the representation of an otherness that moves the self,
an otherness like the other voice that speaks through the self, an otherness that is the self in its own undoing. To pursue, once again, the first
ending of *The Squire's Tale* will lead us to see how the generation of
character in *The Faerie Queene* is accomplished.

Blandamour and his crew are presented about "to overtake"
(ii.30.2) the Chaucerian couples, Canacee and Triamond, Cambel and
Cambina. But instead of completing this action the next piece of narration, the flashback to their coupling, displaces the story of Blandamour
in order to conclude *The Squire's Tale*. When the narrative returns in
canto iv to where it broke off, Blandamour tries to assert himself, to gain
power over the Chaucerian characters by a verbal assault, "Disgracing
them, him selfe thereby to grace" (iv.4.2). He is answered, however, with
the "perswasions myld" (iv.5.1) of Cambina, and her words make for
reconciliation. What happens to Blandamour here replicates the ending
of *The Squire's Tale* in canto iii. He is caught in that textual paradigm,
for there too Cambina's persuasions brought the battle to an end. This
time, however, the battle is explicitly a war of words, and the one who
attempted "to overtake" is himself overcome (his Chaucerian name,
Pleyndamour, should of course be remembered). We can by now be sure
that Cambina's power is not attributable to some potency she possesses
as a character; nor does it figure some remarkable powers of the self.
Rather, when Cambina appears in the text, she is clearly invested with
powers that are not her own. She is dressed "after the Persian Monarks
antique guize" (iii.38.8), that is, as the prototypical tyrant. Riding in a
chariot, her theatrical entrance, "such as the troubled Theaters oftimes
annoyes," (37.9) has been costumed, staged, scripted. It is, in a word,
"such as the maker selfe could best by art devize" (38.9).

Who is Cambina then? It is clear that this question cannot be answered by saying that she is herself or that she represents some idea other
than herself. The "maker selfe" she represents is produced by the text
itself. The text has supplied her as the double of Canacee, Chaucer's lady
with magical attributes; indeed, the two names first appear linked,
paired as friends in the text, joined in an act of commiseration that Blandamour is about to interrupt:

> two Ladies of most goodly hew,
> That twixt themselves did gentle purpose make,
> Unmindfull both of that discordfull crew,
> The which with speedie pace did after them pursew.

(ii.30.6–9)

Similarly, Cambina's brother, Triamond, replicates Cambel; they are so well "lincked" in this initial appearance that they "partake" of each other (ii.30.3–4) and, like other archetypal friends in the poem, eventually prove indistinguishable. Chaucer's text generates these doubles. Or, as book IV says it, Spenser's characters are the friends of Chaucer's. They are also husbands and wives; this too satisfies a Chaucerian design. But the doubling of relationships goes even further; a deeper family resemblance is here, one promised in the conclusion of the second part of *The Squire's Tale*. The squire held out the promise of an incestuous end: "And after wol I speke of Cambalo, / That faught in lystes with the bretheren two / For Canacee er that he myghte hire wynne" (*Squire's Tale*, 667–69). The same incestuous conclusion is available to Spenser; indeed, thanks to the magic ring of Canacee, Cambel appears to enter the tournament assured of winning his sister as his bride. However, incest is avoided by producing doubles for Cambel and for Canacee. The text, doubling itself, satisfies within itself a forbidden desire, that is, a satisfaction that is forbidden *to us* (in nature? by culture?).[12]

In the text, since one name generates another in the endless chain of names, one will do for another. Cambina's name in fact appears to remind us of this, since it seems to mean "combine" and "exchange" (cf. *cambio*), and she does what she is; echoing, exchanging, and combining with her echo, she is produced by recounting, "by art," and she marries

---

12.   Nohrnberg documents the incestuous Canacee tradition, *Analogy of "The Faerie Queene,"* pp. 622–23, and connects the Spenserian marriage quaternio with Jung's discussion of the transference in *The Psychology of the Transference*, trans. R.F.C. Hull (New York: Bollingen Series, 1954), itself a reading of an alchemical text. While this quarternio has cosmological and alchemical meanings, the exchange of sisters is more fundamentally a social form, the most "elementary formula of marriage by exchange" according to Claude Lévi-Strauss in *The Elementary Structures of Kinship*, ed. J. R. von Sturmer and Rodney Needham (Boston: Beacon Press, 1969 [1949]), p. 129. As he shows clearly (e.g., pp. 14, 47–48), this form avoids incest most narrowly of all marriage exchanges; it is the least dynamic and most stable of marriage forms. Lévi-Strauss has situated the incest taboo as the "rule" by which society is formed and, as he admits, it is a rule that is outside of the system it generates, since the taboo seems to be at the same time a natural and a social prohibition. The taboo thus crosses the text/nature boundary upon which *The Faerie Queene* moves when it explores friendship. As Jacques Derrida brilliantly shows in "Structure, Sign, and Play" (in *The Structuralist Controversy*, pp. 247–65), Lévi-Strauss's discourse depends upon a central term that is a founding principle and, at the same time, a heuristic device; Lévi-Strauss practices deconstruction from within (pp. 252 ff.), preserving "as an instrument that whose truth-value he criticizes" (p. 255), founding his discourse on a difference that is also an identification. Spenser, of course, did not need anthropological discourse to arrive at this elementary form and its meanings. Besides the Canacee tradition, there are biblical references to sister-exchange; e.g., Gen. 34:16, "Then will we give our daughters unto you, and we will take your daughters to us, and we will dwell with you, and we will become one people."

Triamond, the final word generated in the cave of the Fates, that combined word/world woven in the text and figuring the life of the text.[13]

When we arrive at this marriage, we are in a familiar place. As we
work through each episode of *The Faerie Queene*, trying to understand
how things relate to one another, we pass from an initial sense of
obscurity—what, we may ask at any point in the poem, does *this* have to
do with *that*—to an overwhelming answer that blurs distinctions and
differences. Repetition and sameness absorb differences, and difference—as a textual matter and as a matter of characterization—is the most
problematic area in *The Faerie Queene*./The problem is central to the
nature of language itself, for it is composed of differences that are un-
marked and unremarkable.[14] It is this silence that somehow makes
"hole" not be "whole," or that somehow separates character from character, episode from episode. Yet,/the text never gives terms for these dif-

13. On Cambina's name, see Leo Spitzer, *Classical and Christian Ideas of
World Harmony* (Baltimore: Johns Hopkins Press, 1963), on the meanings of
cum- and *con-* as "perfective" and spatially enclosing (e.g., p. 30). These meanings sit well with the cosmological implications of book IV and its musical
language, e.g., IV.ii.1–2. See on this Spitzer's note on the cult of friendship as a
tuning of souls (pp. 15–16).

14. On this difficult point, see Derrida, *Of Grammatology*, trans. Gayatri
Spivak (Baltimore: Johns Hopkins University Press, 1974), pp. 52 ff. Saussure
proclaimed that there were only differences in language; Derrida goes on to
question the nature of these differences. The *a* in *différance* is a demonstration of
the idea that differences are absences. In "Differance," Derrida says that "the
difference between two phonemes, which enables them to exist and to operate, is
inaudible" and goes on to connect this difference to the central metaphysical
thrust of *différance*, that it violates the "founding opposition between the sensi-
ble and the intelligible" (p. 133). This is not a perception about language that
need be couched in structuralist terms, as I was reminded by an enormously
moving lecture delivered by Thomas Greene before the Tudor and Stuart Club at
The Johns Hopkins University on 24 October 1980. There, Greene suggested
that the task of historical criticism involves a battle with texts that are fundamentally irrecoverable; words in Renaissance texts, as he brilliantly suggested, did
not exist for their readers in dictionaries. We find our ambiguities in the *OED*;
for a Renaissance reader the text was probably more indecipherable because the
reader lacked those tools that delude us into thinking we can make distinctions
that were in fact not made by a Renaissance reader.

Greene dwelt on the pathos, indeed, the tragedy of our situation in relation to the text, and demanded that we recognize how much of the text we fail to
grasp, that we allow the text its otherness—its estrangement—that we not seek to
appropriate the text, but rather seek what is appropriate to it. Although he
argued against a Derridean solution to this impasse, rejecting freeplay, and
urged a historical criticism practiced with a full sense of its inevitable failures, I
believe that his position need not deny Derrida's. Indeed, the movement from
this chapter to the next is aimed at demonstrating that the two critical approaches can, in fact, meet. As Greene urged, what must be defeated is hermeneutic narcissism, and this means, essentially, to deny phenomenological approaches that make the reader's mind a place where the text can be reconstituted
whole. What I am urging is a freeplay within the text's own narcissism, which
also leaves the text playing with itself and the reader defeated; I return to these
matters in the concluding chapter.

ferences; rather, characters are absorbed into one another, while episodes fade one into another. The uniformity of the text, its structural patterns, its structures of generation, overlap with its failure to satisfy us (what is the meaning, we keep asking, how are we to arrive at a conclusive interpretation, a final reading?). But the presence of these structures is the sign in the text that it is satisfying itself, generating itself from itself. In book IV, these textual structures are the structures of relationships between selves and between incidents. The difficulty of the text is nothing other than the difficulty of sorting these structures out, establishing their differences, and, thereby, their meanings. The text proclaims, explicitly, that these differences are blurred. It demands of us what it does not do itself and what cannot be done—to move outside of the patterning of the text in its replications in order to determine the significances.

"Hard is the doubt, and difficult to deeme, / When all three kinds of love together meet" (ix.1.1–2), we are told. But rather than sort out the difficulty and assist us in making judgments, the text drives relationship into relationship, kind into kind. Kinship, marriage, friendship—the three loves here, the triple link between the two married couples in canto iii—blur and dissolve into each other. Patterns in the text, relations, relating, and its taletelling, generate this overlay. So what comes instead of difference and clarity is another story, another relation. If we look at these stories in terms of what generates them, or if we look at these selves in terms of what generates them, we find in the text that the figures of desire are figures for the text. Either way we find progenitors, what generates desire, what moves the text: Venus, "mother of laughter, and welspring of blisse" (x.47.8); Ate, "mother of debate" (i.19.1); even the narrator finds her in the text, for playing with the names of the rivers, he pays tribute to "my mother Cambridge" (xi.34.7). And surely in those central friendship stories, AEmylia's "Lord of high degree" (vii.15.2) designates both her father and Lust, a connection made more apparent when Lust's double, Corflambo, is twice called a "mightie man" (viii.47,1; 38.6), a nomination befitting AEmylia's father. In short, what constitutes the reader's frustration is precisely the principle by which the text is satisfied.

The text satisfies itself in itself. It is not an overstatement to say that the relations between characters are incestuous, or to say that incestuous desire is a root ambivalence that drives characters to their undoing. Desire generates characters to desire what undoes them; it is a figure for the profound satisfaction that the text offers and denies; offers in itself, and denies its reader. We can see the text engulfing itself; if we take pleasure in the text, it is not the pleasure of the text we take. That we have been denied, to our undoing.

When we look again at what "the maker selfe could best by art devize" (iii.38.9), we see another paradigmatic story told to our undoing, another story about selves undone. Cambina arrives on the battlefield. When Triamond and Cambel refuse to "entertaine" (47.2) her, she uses force.

> But when as all might nought with them prevaile,
>   Shee smote them lightly with her powrefull wand.
> Then suddenly as if their hearts did faile,
>   Their wrathfull blades downe fell out of their hand,
>   And they like men astonisht still did stand.
> Thus whilest their minds were doubtfully distraught,
>   And mighty spirites bound with mightier band,
>   Her golden cup to them for drinke she raught,
> Whereof full glad for thirst, ech drunk an harty draught.
>
> (iii.48)

Her wand is the caduceus, Mercury's rod of persuasion; her force is erotic, invading their hearts and minds, her "mightier band" like those "bands of love . . . sad thraldomes chayne" (xi.1.5) that imprison Florimell, or the "inviolable bands" (x.35.4) that make the universe one. Erotic, cosmic, verbal: Cambina joins Hermes and Aphrodite, the "Almightie maker" (x.35.3) and "Great God of love" (vii.1.1), compelling desire. In her cup she brings Nepenthe, the drink of the heroes "before they may to heaven flie" (iii.44.5), a drink that satisfies desire in death and exalts the self-annihilated. She brings astonishment, loss of memory, loss of mind; mindless absorption. Her drink comes from earlier texts, among them, Ariosto's:

> Much more of price and of more gratious powre
>   Is this, then that same water of Ardenne,
>   The which *Rinaldo* drunck in happie howre,
>   Described by that famous Tuscane penne.
>
> (iii.45.1–4)

Who is Cambina? To answer this finally we might take an identification that Roche has suggested; she appears, he says, in the form of Cybele, "the mother of the Gods" (xi.28.1) as described in the *Aeneid*. Textual determination may stop with that ancient progenitor, for with Cybele we arrive at a figure for the overlap of nature and text, the place where desire meets the desire of the text. Cambina, "such as the maker selfe could best by art devize," is in the text a figure produced by texts as a figure for the generative power of the text. After her work has been accomplished there are no differences; the four characters are absorbed into their paradigmatic relationships: "So all alike did love, and loved were, / That since their days such lovers were not found elswhere" (iii.52.8–9). Becoming "all alike" through their shared desire, they leave the tourney ground. But "not found elswhere," they are yet found somewhere, for in this text they are replicating an antecedent text. Where they are "not found" they are located; Chaucer's lost conclusion is also "no where to be found" (ii.32.5). This concluding and supplementary story so fulfills the condition of its antecedent that it replaces one loss with another, or, perhaps, replicates the same loss. This ending provides the model for storytelling in book IV, story inside of story, loss within loss. This is the location of the self in the text. The self is absorbed into structures of relationship, likenesses, identifications, indistinction. These are the generative models for the structures of relationship in the poem, for the relationships between stories and selves.

At the end of book IV, the text, arriving for the first time at Marinell and Florimell, finally presents an epitomized account of the self lost in the structures of desire generated by the text as an otherness that annihilates difference. By merely retelling, we can see the generation of the self under the aegis of deforming desire, the submergence of the self into the desire of the text. This ending story, which is, we know, a beginning story without an end and a story without beginning, presents two selves coming to themselves and to each other. In so doing, they come to their oblivion, fail to have a story as they stand before each other on the verge of a marriage implicit in their meeting. Before each other they echo each other, and their selves, so situated, are generated by the texts that come before them. This is a beginning of the end of the self generated by the desire of the text.

Marinell has at last felt the wound of love, that grief of mind, and compassionately, in thought, he enters the prison to share it with Florimell. Soon, however, he returns "backe to him selfe" to blame himself as "the author of her punishment" (xii.16.2,3) rather than acting as her liberator. Finding himself, he discovers his impotence; he cannot rescue her. "He had lost him selfe" (17.3) when he heard Florimell cry; he grieved, becoming, naturally, like a mother weeping for her lost child:

> Like as an Hynde whose calfe is falne unwares
> Into some pit, where she him heares complaine,
> An hundred times about the pit side fares,
> Right sorrowfully mourning her bereaved cares.
>
> (17.6–9)

Naturally transformed, he changes place and sex, entering the realm of "bereaved cares." The circles in the text are played out in what follows. Returning home, he finally agrees to impart his grief to his mother, enacting and inverting the trope that defined his relationship to Florimell, consenting to share with her his wounded mind. She, joining him "in troubled mind" (28.8), undertakes to provide him with the wife he desires, his prophesied undoing and hers too. Her appeal is to her own progenitor, Neptune, and he unravels a "double wrong" (30.2) to enable her to have her "delivered" (33.2) from "*Proteus* selfe . . . the root and worker of her woe" (29.1,2). She brings Florimell to her disabled son, "And shewed her to him, then being sore bestad" (33.9):

> Who soone as he beheld that angels face,
>   Adorn'd with all divine perfection,
>   His cheared heart eftsoones away gan chace
>   Sad death, revived with her sweet inspection,
>   And feeble spirit inly felt refection;
>   As withered weed through cruell winters tine,
>   That feeles the warmth of sunny beames reflection,
>   Liftes up his head, that did before decline
> And gins to spread his leafe before the faire sunshine.
>
> Right so himselfe did *Marinell* upreare,
>   When he in place his dearest love did spy;
>   And though his limbs could not his bodie beare,
>   Ne former strength returne so suddenly,
>   Yet chearefull signes he shewed outwardly.
>   Ne lesse was she in secret hart affected,
>   But that she masked it with modestie,
>   For feare she should of lightnesse be detected:
> Which to another place I leave to be perfected.

(xii.34–35)

Upon beholding Florimell, Marinell immediately sees her as perfect; he sees a goddess, not a woman, and sees her as an overwhelming figure of desire. Beholding Marinell, Florimell immediately puts on a mask, to protect herself from a misreading. But the misreading has already occurred; he is not seeing her, but an illusion that comes from within himself. He has not produced the (False) Florimell in the text, whom she fears he will see (has she read the poem?); he has produced a false Florimell nonetheless, not herself, but another. And so has she, by donning that mask. They are both, seeing each other, seeing each as other; instantly, they are split selves. These two figures, prisoners of desire, so weakened that they have very little that even they would call a self, so little to hold onto, even they are split by the text. They stand where others, and others' words, have been before them. Marinell, the "withered weed": is he the withered tree in the garden upon which the squire's bleeding falcon perched? Or are the revived flowers of the opening lines of *The Canterbury Tales* behind him? Or is he, identified, Florimell herself, and has she thereby become the most ordinary of tropes? Identified, have they become therefore identical in this florilegium? Marinell is "right so himselfe," looking in the mirror when Florimell looks at him in hers with "sweet inspection." Inside or outside? In the text/in nature? "in place"/replaced? Where are we? where are they? Is there "another place" than the "in place" where the text locates the self in its own desire? If they began to talk, whose story would they tell? A joyless tale of two moved still by desire? Or the story of the self structured by the Other?

THE AUTHORITY OF THE OTHER

" . . . the displeasure of the mighty" (viii.1.3)

When book IV closes, it makes a final, seemingly open-ended gesture as it points toward "another place" (xii.35.9) where a definitive ending to the story it has left incomplete might be possible. Where would such a place be? Once again, we need to consider the location of the text and to ponder its referentiality. The text situates itself in the place of a lost text, invaded by other voices, spoken in the voice of an Other, and those in the text are so constituted that there is no Other except as figured in the text. Hence, when book IV closes pointing toward "another place" it would seem to raise explicitly, but in a new form, the question that we have been considering. We know that, as narration, the "other place" toward which the last line of book IV points is always "another place" only in the sense that it is a place to be filled by another. And we know that in terms of the destiny of those in the text, the "other place" is the place of meeting others, the place of mastery by the Other: the place in the text that figures its own production.

In these ways, book IV seems to deny that there could be "another place," that is to say, a different place, a place other than the text, since it appears to affirm that all space is textual and offers repeated instances of one text replacing another. The only "places" in these formulations are *topoi*, rhetorical sites where *communes loci* are recrossed. "Another place" at the end of book IV seems, however, to glance at a world "outside" the text, someplace where endings are possible, where words finally find their referents; yet, the text has been dissolving all the world into the text, playing on the world/word *topos*. If there is "another place" at all, it could refer only to something nontextual: a gap, a failure, a break in the text, what is not in the text and not textualized. Indeed, book IV ends broken, pointing to an outside that is an absence. The story, after all, is nowhere "perfected." Yet, by naming this absence, "another place" also points to the text, that site of loss, and so even the nontextual appears to be textualized, too.

If we recall Timias, who, silent and inscrutable in his transformed and forgotten state, remains nonetheless a text caught in the need for Belphoebe's word to restore him to himself—and to her—we can find a paradigm for this situation, for the text's relationship to an "outside" of itself, its relationship to "another place." For, while the episode suggests that "another place" is always another textual situation, it nonetheless does seem to point to an "outside" in another sense, to something "outside" the text that is a nontextual sphere. Its external referent, in most readings of the episode, is the affair of Ralegh and Queen Elizabeth, his disgrace and ultimate pardon. The questions that this chapter raises are the result of the meeting of these two versions of an "outside," these other places: the text that includes the nontextual, the external as the nontextual.

What is the relationship of the nontextual and the text? How do these two "outsides" come together, as they do in the Timias episode? How are the events of the real world in *The Faerie Queene*? How does the text refer to what is "outside" itself in those terms? To anticipate what will be demonstrated: this "outside," as we might by now suppose, is taken "inside"; once again, a boundary dissolves when we locate the text. In this final location, I mean to place the text historically and socially and to suggest that what we have seen in the text, figuring its own production, extends to locate the text within the conditions of production in Elizabethan society.

The story of Timias provides the clearest paradigm in book IV for this investigation. His silence coincides with an externality that inheres in the episode. Belphoebe is Queen Elizabeth: we have, as noted earlier, Spenser's word for that in the Letter to Ralegh, wherein he admits to having found that name for her in Ralegh's verse. In Spenser's poem, those two historical figures enact a version of the creation of Ralegh's text, and Spenser's imitation seems to derive from an "outside," from both the historical events and Ralegh's poems. And in that story, history—in the queen—creates the text. Belphoebe's absence and presence, her broken sentence and her accommodating words—indeed, the very name "Belphoebe," the poet's word carved on the trees—these taken together make the absent queen the source and end and the entire substance of Timias's text. Belphoebe, whose absence creates the possibility of Timias's poetic outpouring, is, by her very absence in the text, the occupant of "another place," and "outside"; nonetheless, she *is* the text in vital ways: its producer, its substance (the word), and its reader.[1] Spenser's text has inside it this account of an outside of it, one that relocates the poem in the queen and declares hers to be the body of the text. Rather than dismiss that declaration as mere fiction, I would like to consider it as a necessary fiction, to see what it means in answer to the question of the situation of the text, its relationship to that place toward which the text points and fails to reach and which is nonetheless where it ends and finds itself "perfected." If all stories are others' stories, the text is located as the product of its own exteriority. One "outside" meets another in the absent queen who nonetheless is the text.

We can most conveniently begin our investigation into the referentiality of the text by beginning at the beginning, for it is precisely with questions about the location of the text, its place in the real "outside" world, that book IV opens. Hence, the poem not only ends by glancing at some location "outside" of itself, it begins there too, and this initial "outside" appears easily placed and quite specific. The opening lines of the proem imagine a reader who holds a position of power in the world of politics:

> The rugged forhead that with grave foresight
>   Welds kingdomes causes, and affaires of state,
>   My looser rimes (I wote) doth sharply wite,
>   For praising love, as I have done of late,
>   And magnifying lovers deare debate.
>
> (1.1–5)

1. The most explicit statement of this "fiction" about Elizabeth occurs in the proem to book VI: "Then pardon me, most dreaded Soveraine, / That from your selfe I doe this vertue bring, / And to your selfe doe it returne againe: / So from the Ocean all rivers spring, / And tribute backe repay as to their King" (7.1–5). Most of the concerns of this chapter meet in these lines: the hermaphroditic ruler, feminine, yet addressed as a king; the circle in which power is expressed and yet in which the instigator is not caught in its play; the naturalization of feudal fictions ("tribute"); and, most importantly, the location of the text in the "dearest dred," so that the circle of political power coincides with the production of the text. The ways in which this fiction was given the lie by the realities of court life have been noted by recent commentators, e.g., David L. Miller, "Abandoning the Quest," *ELH* 46 (1979): 173–92, esp. p. 182. I would not deny his point; nonetheless, the realities of court life must not be used as a way of refusing to accept the fiction as a serious one. Moreover, I cannot see that Spenser's anticourt attitudes in book VI lead him to promote himself as a teacher of manners, as Daniel Javitch argues in *Poetry and Courtliness in Renaissance England* (Princeton: Princeton University Press, 1978), pp. 141 ff. Whereas Javitch believes that a reversal of influence occurred when court morality declined (see pp. 119 ff.), I think it can be shown that influence continued to emanate from the locus of power. True, the court derived its sense of itself and a language to describe itself at least in part from the poets. But the word is overly reified, and the power of poetry is idealized if this exchange of fictions is treated as equally

Most readers' immediate response to these lines is to assign a "real," proper name to this "rugged forhead"—Burghley is usually proposed.[2] We need to pause and to examine that response. Before we leap to that identification "outside" the text, it is worth observing how completely inside the text the figure in the first line is. "The rugged forhead" is a trope, a metonymy, not a name (the reader may want to turn the trope into a proper name; the text does not perform that transformation); by the end of the first line "forhead" has triggered an alliterative counterpart in "foresight," and "rugged forhead" and "grave foresight" meet in a paradox in the play on "grave," a paradox of destructive/constructive behavior that we might recognize as a forecast of a repeated textual situation of the poem, a graveyard struggle. Here, the paradox conjures the image of a mind rushing precipitously toward an end, moving forward and backward at once, a familiar juncture, a narrative movement. The "rugged forhead" in this first line enters the poem as its antagonist—as what is outside it, refusing it—yet the terms of opposition are provided by the text's figures (he is "rugged" whereas the text is "looser," he is a welder and closer when the text is loose, dilating, and "magnifying"[3]).

---

powerful as social realities and practices. And it is in the production of these that *The Faerie Queene* must finally be located. Even Louis Montrose appears to err in Javitch's direction in his brief discussion of book VI in *ELH* 47 (1980), when he claims for Spenser a subversive power in the pastoral vision on Mount Acidale (p. 459). As Montrose knows, the terms for that subversion are part of Spenser's culture.

2. Most recently by Thomas H. Cain, *Praise in "The Faerie Queene"* (Lincoln: University of Nebraska Press, 1978), 164–65. Cain goes on to link what he regards as Spenser's Orphic assertions in the proem to the disturbing connection of Scudamour and Orpheus with—in his terms—its ironic implications (p. 166), including Busyrane's role as "a vampirelike Orpheus" (p. 167). Although I find these ideas suggestive, once again I am struck by Cain's failure to carry what he sees in the poem to the social relationship between poet and court that he believes to be central to the poem.

3. Cf. the imagery of melting and softening in the final stanza of the proem. The imagery there connects the production of the poem with the forge of Care in canto v, an apt connection, since it was there that Vulcan wrought the most valued object in the text, the belt of Venus. Moreover, canto v, with its beauty contest, enters the realm of the production of the text.

Before we arrive at the cave with its forged images in Scudamour's mind, the text offers the dazzling (False) Florimell, a "forged" thing (15.9) too, as is Duessa "with her forged beautie" (11.3). It is the aim of poetry to replicate beauty and, as the narrator says, he "needeth sure a golden pen" to portray it (12.2). The forging of beauty is the making of gold. The imagery in proem 5 initiates a pattern in which much gold is in evidence, both that of the "guilefull Goldsmith" (v.15.1) as well as "good gold" (15.4). This will, as I suggest below, intimate economic concerns. However, this imagery, in conjunction with the forge, has alchemical implications—after all, alchemists produce gold as a mystification of matter; Scudamour leaves the Cave of Care "like heavie lumpe of lead" (v.45.6), an indication in alchemical terms of failed work. In the next canto, Arthegall loses his "yron courage" (vi.17.1) to Britomart's display of "golden" hair "framed in goldsmithes forge" (20.3–4); by the end of the canto, however, he

The opposition is written into the text, and his form and location anticipate the poem's thematics and point ahead to its narrative situation.
The paradoxical meeting should be no surprise since we know the text to
thrive on antagonism. It describes "lovers deare debate." Ate, "mother of
debate," lurks in the wings, and so too does Concord, forcing Love and
Hate to join hands in friendship. In the opening lines of the proem, this
antagonistic "forhead" joins with the text in its production. "I wote"
the voice speaking says (1.3); the "forhead . . . doth sharply wite."
These opponents are also echoes, inside each other, sharing words, dif-
fering in the phonemic silence that separates "wote" and "wite." Is there
an outside to the text? Does this "forhead" refer to an outside? How does
it refer to Burghley? How does the text represent what is external to it?

To begin to answer these questions is to see that what the "forhead" represents is a *need* for an "outside" of the text, a need for the
fiction that the text has a referent there, even if by being a fiction such an
"outside" is inevitably put "inside" as a text. This need corresponds to
what we have seen before, that the text generates itself through what it
represents as Other. The poem lives on debate; and it seems necessary for
the production of this text that it be read and written as a text that neither
the writer nor the reader produces, as a text made in negation and loss,
made in undoing. Having situated the "rugged forhead," the proem
continues. "To such therefore I do not sing at all" (4.1), and the "rugged
forhead" is transformed into one of "these Stoicke censours" (3.9). The
reader (first written into the text as what is outside it and as the one who
cannot read it) is dismissed, yet, as censor, becomes the one who determines if the text will be read at all by anyone, particularly by the one
person for whom the text is explicitly intended: "To her I sing of love,
that loveth best" (4.6). In referring to this ideal reader, the line describing
her traces a familiar self-reflexive curve, for the line contains multiple
meanings: that she who loves best will say that in her judgment ("to
her"; 4.1 uses the same ambiguous grammar) the narrator sings well
about love; or that the narrator sings about love so that any expert lover
will know what he sings about; or that he sings to only one reader, the
one that loves best, and that he sings to her of his—or is it her?—love.
Through these multiple possibilities, distinctions are lost; singer, song,
and audience collapse into one. Identification is problematic. Who is

---

has "wrought" (41.1) her to his will. Alchemy, in these instances, serves as an
image of the process by which interpersonal relationships are constructed, by
which people produce images of each other or have effects on each other.

In the proem, the imagery is best glossed by a later usage, Donne's appeals
to his patrons, especially Lucy, Countess of Bedford, to perform an alchemical
miracle and turn his nothing into all. On this imagery, see John Danby, *Elizabethan and Jacobean Poets* (London: Faber & Faber, 1965 [1952 as *Poets on Fortunes Hill*]), pp. 39 ff.

this ideal reader? Elizabeth? Again, before we leap to that proper name, we should note what she is called. She is the "Queene of love, and Prince of peace from heaven blest" (4.9). These names have multiple referents, among them Venus and Mercury, Mary and Christ. Who is she? Where is she? Inside or outside the text?

She is an "outside" so deeply "inside" this text as to shape its desire, give it words. This text is inside another, located in "another place." In the fiction that moves the text, the mightiest and most authoritative Other is the figure addressed at the end of the proem.

The lines express a desire to this powerful figure, the desire to be read. And more: the desire to be rewarded. Melt, soften, give; this is what is asked: "Sprinckle her heart, and haughtie courage soften, / That she may hearke to love, and read this lesson often" (5.8–9). Stunningly, what is asked of her also transforms her. The ideal reader seems as rugged and resistant as the antagonist. Yet, inside the fiction of the production of the text, the opposition is overcome in this figure of the ideal reader, "that loveth best." The fiction that the text creates to make the request that the reader accept the text is that the one who rewards is the one who produces the text: the self-reflexive circle of the other includes the text. Yet as the Timias episode suggests, that is not necessarily a fiction. When Belphoebe asks him whether heavenly punishment, mortal anger, or his own "selfe disliked life" (viii.14.9) are responsible for his forlorn state, he can answer by naming her; it is the first he has spoken since she asked "Is this the faith" (vii.36.8): "Ne any but your selfe, O dearest dred" (viii.17.1), is his reply. That answer says it all. After that, Timias is "receiv'd againe to former favours state" (17.9), embraced by Belphoebe, and withdrawn even from his most pressing obligation inside the text; he becomes "mindlesse of his owne deare Lord" (18.4). There is no having without losing. "O dearest dred" indeed.

What the proem to book IV suggests, what its glance at "another place" reinforces, is the social situation of the text. This is where the text is produced, within certain social realities. Not the least of these was the reality of the courtly fictions that surrounded Queen Elizabeth and which had to be, and inevitably were, in the text if the poet was ever to find favor with his monarch. In such a framework she is the end of his desire, its instigator as well, and that is no fiction. Desire cannot now be viewed as a simple, straightforward romance. There is another lure; not her body, but the body of the text and its value as a "real" object in the world of the court. In short, the wise poet would not, like the Argonauts, be "all mindlesse of the Golden fleece" (i.23.9). The text has a place in society, in social production, and in the production of the fictions of society which produce it. This is a reciprocal process that must be represented as the power of an Other in the text. With this mighty figure, whose pleasure and displeasure overlap in the proem to book IV and in the episode played out between Timias and Belphoebe, we reach a final figure for the production of the text. I will return to Timias later, and will conclude this chapter by considering the proem once again, but to demonstrate what I am suggesting, let us look at more of book IV. In reviewing the actions of the poem, what I want to propose is simply this: that the social situation of the text is figured in the text. We have seen that the textual production, the situation of the poem in relation to *The Squire's Tale*, is figured inside the text. We have seen that relationships in the text, between its characters, figure a textual situation. Finally we need to see that the fiction presented in book IV also points to the situation of the text in the world in another way as well. This world/word is the reality of courtly fictions within which the poem is located. And the actions played out inside this text refer to that, not only in the episode between Timias and Belphoebe, and in the proem, but throughout. The social situation of the poet and the poem is refigured in the actions that occur within the narrative. The poet's desire—to be read and rewarded—is, we shall see, a figure for the desire in the text.

We can see this clearly by reviewing a familiar story, endlessly re-told, a squire's tale again. The lure of desire is presented as an object of inestimable value. "Beauties spoile," Scudamour calls Amoret, and their marriage is a matter of economics: "I late have wonne, / And pur-chased this peerelesse beauties spoile" (x.3.2–3). Scudamour's narrative is exemplary in this regard. Throughout the text, the lure of winning a woman is doubled with gold. Canacee, set "upon a stately stage" as "the fortune of that fray," and the "most worthie wage" of the one who can "purchase" her (iii.4.6–9), also gives double value since her magic ring insures immortality for the knight that wears it. At Satyrane's beauty contest, the knight who acquires the most beautiful woman will also win the girdle of Florimell as a token of beauty. Until then, Satyrane keeps it in a shrine—an ark—and treats it as a relic.[4] Its value is at once

---

4. Florimell's girdle is of course an attribute of Venus. Its significance in the text is manifold. At once a sign of beauty and chastity, it is, moreover, an artistic object made by Vulcan, who is thereby a surrogate artist; and, finally, since Venus is also the creator of the universe/text, the belt is inevitably connect-ed to the bands that tie the universe together, bands that also describe the rela-tionships between friends. The girdle is a version of the great chain of being, and the complexity of its cultural antecedents and their replication in *The Faerie Queene* can partly be appreciated through Ludwig Edelstein's magisterial essay "The Golden Chain of Homer," in *Studies in Intellectual History* (Baltimore: Johns Hopkins Press, 1953). Edelstein places the Homeric great chain in nu-merous contexts, and these are all suggestive for Spenser. For instance, he con-nects it to the threads woven by the Fates, but also to the binding power of Eros/Aphrodite. In book IV, the universe is held by a "lovely band" (x.33.5), which

material and symbolic; gold is a prize that confers value on those who
have it.

> That same [girdle] aloft he hong in open vew,
>> To be the prize of beautie and of might;
>> The which eftsoones discovered, to it drew
>> The eyes of all, allur'd with close delight,
>> And hearts quite robbed with so glorious sight,
>> That all men threw out vowes and wishes vaine.
>> Thrise happie Ladie, and thrise happie knight,
>> Them seemd that could so goodly riches gaine,
> So worthie of the perill, worthy of the paine.
>
> (iv.16)

The girdle is described as an object of desire ("hearts quite robbed") and
it moves "close delight," a phrase used elsewhere in the text to designate
the deepest and most private of desires, those that are found in a "privy
place" (vii.17.7). The doubling of "thrise happie," with its hermetic implications, coupled with the repetition of "worthy" in the final line,
completes the mystification of the belt, the eroticization and spirituali-
zation of "so goodly riches gaine." At Satyrane's tournament the values
of arms and beauty are tested. In the chivalric society so imagined, Florimell's girdle symbolizes the desire of society. It binds together "beautie" and "might." Satyrane's tournament, the goal toward which the
figures move in the first part of book IV, examines and tests these beliefs,
that connection:

> It hath bene through all ages ever seene,
>> That with the praise of armes and chevalrie,
>> The prize of beautie still hath ioyned beene;
>> And that for reasons speciall privitie:
> For either doth on other much relie.
>
> (v.1–5)

---

also seems to partake of adamantine necessity in the "inviolable bands" (35.4)
that keep the world "in state unmoved" (35.2). (Cf. *An Hymne In Honour of
Love*, in which Eros links the universe with "Adamantine chaines" [1.89], the
attribute of the Fates in Plato's *Republic* [616–17]). Finally, the chain also seems
to connect, as Edelstein says, with Hecate, as "sovereign over the three realms of
the cosmos" (p. 61), and with symbolism of the rope and the ring. In book IV, the
latter images may be associated with Britomart, when she loosens her golden
hair (i.13); with Canacee's ring; with Agape raped, as she combs her golden locks
(ii.45), to produce the triple world; with Cambina's "mightier band" (iii.48.7);
with the golden ribbon tied around the dove's neck (viii.6); or with the ribbon
holding the placard in the Temple of Venus (x.8). The words *band, bond, link,*
and *chain,* are threaded throughout the poem.
   On the etymology, see Onians, *The Origins of European Thought about
the Body, the Mind, the Soul, the World, Time, and Fate* (Cambridge: At the
University Press, 1951), pp. 310–51.

The prize of "goodly riches gaine" crowns the vision of chivalric society; it is the object that draws "the eyes of all," the end of a relay that begins in "privitie."

The belt is worshiped in the stanza cited above in terms that echo later in the tournament when (False) Florimell is made the object of veneration. She is placed in the middle of a circle and "all on her gazing wisht, and vowd, and prayd" (v.26.3). Still later, the trope identifying the object of desire, although somewhat transformed, is not basically altered when Amoret is finally seen traveling with Arthur "as safe as in a Sanctuary" (ix.19.6). This begins as a way of describing Amoret's familiar position in the text, under the protection of a knight; here Amoret is imagined as a fugitive who has found safety in a sacred shrine. But the sanctuary that contains this valued thing of beauty is also an ark, or reliquary, and Amoret in the metaphor now becomes the golden belt— an appropriate metamorphosis since the belt fits only her and is her attribute in the text. (Hence it is no wonder that Amoret can read Arthur's protection as menacing, for the same configuration can be found in the figure of Lust, that privy figure, who stores "the relickes of his feast, / And cruell spoyle" [vii.6.3–4] in his lower lip.) Amoret moves through book IV as a most valuable and desired object; as her story threads its way through others', she moves like a coin passing endlessly through people's hands. Having been "bought" (i.2.1), she is rightly sold; in fact, she subscribes, as we have seen, to these prescriptions of chivalric society:

> For well she wist, as true it was indeed,
>   That her lives Lord and patrone of her health
>   Right well deserved as his duefull meed,
>   Her love, her service, and her utmost wealth.
>   All is his iustly, that all freely dealth.

(i.6.1–5)

The "Lord" in these lines is Britomart, but it might as easily be Arthur or Scudamour. The lines record Amoret's recognition of the truth that she has value in the chivalric system as an object of exchange.[5] She is the beauty that chivalric enterprise regards as its reward. But the lines are

5. The economics here has been studied by Lévi-Strauss. His work depends upon Marcel Mauss, *The Gift: Forms and Functions of Exchange in Archaic Societies*, trans. Ian Cunnison (New York: W. W. Norton, 1967 [1925]), who first posited the model for society in the exchange of gifts: "Everything is tied together; things have personality, and personalities are in some manner the permanent possession of the clan. Titles, talismans, coppers and spirits of chiefs are homonyms and synonyms, having the same nature and function. The circulation of goods follows that of men, women and children, of festival ritual, ceremonies and dances, jokes and injuries. Basically they are the same. If things are given and returned it is precisely because one gives and returns 'respects' and

also about another exchange system, as "patrone" suggests, an exchange system "outside" the text and replicated in its narrative. In that case, Amoret's movement in the society depicted in book IV may be taken as an image of the place of the text in the patronage system of Elizabethan society. Amoret is like the body of the text; and the social fiction about the text is that the one who produces it is the one for whom it is produced, and who rightly owns it. To own it, the lines say, a free gift must be given: "All is his iustly, that all freely dealth."

It comes as no surprise, therefore, that when we look at Amoret's rightful, legal "Lord" and owner, we find that gifts are on Scudamour's mind, nowhere more noticeably than when he enters the narrator's place and tells his story. If we look briefly again at the story he tells, we can see that in entering the narrator's place he also describes that situation as it extends "outside" the text. He is also talking about the location of the text in society, and the story he tells—everyone's story, we know from the text—and the story told for the narrator in the text, is an essential tale about the relationship of the text to society. Its terms are economic. Not only is Amoret insistently an object of value in his account, but his own value, his chivalric adventure, is viewed in economic terms as well.

> What time the fame of this renowmed prise
>   Flew first abroad, and all mens eares possest,
>   I having armes then taken, gan avise
>   To winne me honour by some noble gest,
>   And purchase me some place amongst the best.
>   I boldly thought (so young mens thoughts are bold)
>   That this same brave emprize for me did rest,
>   And that both shield and she whom I behold,
> Might be my lucky lot; sith all by lot we hold.
>
> (x.4)

In Scudamour's lottery, everything runs by fortune. Possessed as he is by this prize, his entire language is economic. Once again, the difference between knight and lady is overcome. A possession is what is taken (prise), and the etymological circle from "prise" to "possest" in the

---

'courtesies'. But in addition, in giving them, a man gives himself, and he does so because he owes himself—himself and his possession—to others" (pp. 44–45). Pierre Bourdieu in *Outline of a Theory of Practice*, trans. Richard Nice (Cambridge: At the University Press, 1977) has used the idea of the gift as part of a study of the nature of social practices, especially the relationship between power and ideological structures. Gifts, Bourdieu argues, are demands; they present a fiction of social solidarity that in fact carries a menace. Under the guise of reciprocity is the reality of power; overt domination becomes (in an act of *méconnaissance*) socially recognized power, legitimate authority, through such fictions of exchange (see p. 192). "Giving is also a way of possessing," he concludes (p. 195).

opening lines of this stanza describes the circuit of Scudamour's desire. It encloses him. The movement out ("abroad") into society, although it widens the semantic thread (an entire language of value and valuation follows immediately: winne, noble, purchase, best), is finally clinched in emprize.[6] "This same brave emprize" is certainly the achievement of the girl; but is it not also the act of telling the tale itself, Scudamour's social obligation at the moment of utterance? The language of economics doubles back upon itself in this telling. One account answers another.

In his storytelling function, Scudamour tells a paradigmatic story, one that also carries a social meaning that extends outside the society that Scudamour himself represents. As he tells his story about that "emprize," Scudamour is also, as storyteller, engaged in a parallel social position. The story he tells repeats the sitation of telling the story. Both are social actions, and, insofar as the two are analogous, Scudamour's narration includes the expectation of a prize for telling the story, just as he literally expects one for his heroic action. Because he submits to the other—the one who commands the story and provides the text—Scudamour expects a reward. The prize, we recall, was the reading of Venus's text. What this would seem to mean is that the narrator, in the voice of another (in Scudamour's voice), is telling an additional version of the central social fiction of his text: that the text comes from another. Like his surrogate, he too expects a prize. Like Scudamour, he is inscribed in a social system, voicing others' words.

The prize is on Scudamour's mind when he starts narrating; it is his obsessive care: "she whom I behold" is the promised reward and lure. But she cannot be had—except as a thought—and so an economics of substitution and exchange is figured instead. This is another way of seeing what the text puts "in place" by replacing. We can now see that Scudamour's economic situation has implications for the production of the text, that circle of substitutions, and its social situation. When Scudamour submits to the social injunction to narrate, it seems that telling the story replaces possessing Amoret; he could have her now, she is standing before him. Perhaps there are prizes worth losing Amoret for; the prize of being rewarded for telling the story, for instance. Giving up Amoret, telling the tale, Scudamour follows social dictates, the com-

---

6. One important study that suggests the economic links between social forms and friendship and brotherhood is Benjamin N. Nelson's *The Idea of Usury: From Tribal Brotherhood to Universal Otherhood* (Princeton: Princeton University Press, 1949). Nelson is particularly insistent in tracing in modern ideas of brotherhood (from the Reformation on) the ideologizing of equality; the growth of society extends the ideology of brotherhood, but "all men have been becoming brothers by becoming equally others" (p. 136). By the seventeenth century, the medieval ideals of friendship are, as Nelson notes, fictions (see p. 155) that mask economic and social relationships between and within societies.

mands of Venus. We might think about Timias's case in these terms too, for he also was denied Amoret, and he finally got Belphoebe's favor instead. The analogy is not exact, however; greater frustration is figured in Scudamour. The leaden and wearying thoughts, rather than golden shafts, which burden him when leaving the Cave of Care, still move him in the Temple of Venus. Another way to see his greater frustration is to recall that Scudamour's history is intertwined with his mythological surrogate, Vulcan. The cave recalls the forge where Vulcan made the belt that Venus cast off when she abandoned her husband for Mars. The belt passed to Florimell (v.5) and is, at Satyrane's contest, rightly Amoret's. Like Vulcan, Scudamour is denied the wife he has lost; nor does he have the golden belt. All Scudamour can do is recite Venus's words, those golden words, and hope, like the poet, for a reward for his submission. The lost prize is translated into those words. What we might suspect from this situation of Scudamour in the place of the narrator is that his account recounts Spenser's location in society, just as the comparison with Timias might reflect on the relation of the two poets and their queen. But before we pursue these possibilities, we should stay with Scudamour's story a bit longer, for it will bring us closer to the meeting of text and society.

Money is on Scudamour's mind and is reflected in what he sees: the text of Venus hanging by "golden ribbands" and written in "golden letters" (x.8.5, 7). It is also reflected in how he sees: he passes over the bridge, hastening lest Delay "steale" his time, "the threasure of mans day" (14.8), "beholding all the way / The goodly workes, and stones of rich assay" (15.4–5), envying the lovers emparadised in each other's arms. In order "to seeke my lifes deare patronesse," he must learn that "much dearer be the things, which come through hard distresse" (28.8–9), a lesson reinforced when he arrives at the center of Venus's Temple. There her statue (or is it herself?) stands upon an "altar of some costly masse" (39.2), and she is even richer, rarer, and more valuable. Offered to her are the "thousand pretious gifts worth many a pound, / The which sad lovers for their vowes did pay" (37.7–8). And the "Goddesse selfe" (39.1) "needeth other none" (41.9) since the lover's words are hers and since the gifts presented are being returned to their source. Venus, with snakes wrapped around her feet and legs, assumes the form of the rod of Mercury; she is, then, like the patron of the text, both "Queene of love, and Prince of peace" (pro.4.9). As patron, "all is his iustly, that all freely dealth" (i.6.5). The frustrated lover is depleted, denied money and a wife; the frustrated poet would no doubt settle for cash, laying his account at her feet. When, in his story, Scudamour arrives at the altar of Venus, he names the moving principle behind his story and what lies behind the social demand to tell the story he has been recounting. As we can see by looking at the language of storytelling, and at the language in the story that Scudamour tells, it is, either way, economics that is placed before our eyes: recounting, accounting, telling, giving, and giving in place. Scudamour's paradigmatic story, told in the poet's place, tells his place indeed.

His tale of frustrated love, we know, is one side of the coin; fulfillment is its double, and it is there that book IV began, resituating itself in relation to what came before. Amoret and Scudamour married: that is how the book begins, because marriage is a form of power. This new situation—marriages do not take place before book IV—this revisionary gesture, openly carries political and social meaning. Marriages were, simply, the single most important feature in international displomacy during the Renaissance. We hardly need to be reminded that Elizabeth kept more than one prospective husband dangling in order to manage European politics. In book IV, marriages are the expression of imposing, authoritarian wills. We have already considered the power of Cambina to turn enmity into friendship and marriage—she presents another instance of Venus and Mercury combined—and late in book IV, Arthur similarly ordains a pair of marriages for the squires, Amyas and Placidas, and their ladies. But the climactic marriage, the one in which marriage is characterized most explicitly as simultaneously a poetic and a sociopolitical fact, is a marriage not between the poem's characters, but between two rivers.

This marriage is alluded to later in *The Faerie Queene*, in the proem to book VI, where the relationship of the poet to the queen is seen in this simile:

> So from the Ocean all rivers spring,
> And tribute backe repay as to their King.
> Right so from you all goodly vertues well.

(VI.pro.7.4–6)

The poet's "vertues," his subject matter and his powers of representation, are bound to the queen, and he is bound to "backe repay," to offer tribute, recounting. True as it remains that the river marriage in book IV offers an etymological fancy of the poet, an expression of his powers, his play operates within limits; it appears as the freeplay within the space granted him by Neptune. To consider those limits means to pay attention to an economics of exchange, to see that in describing the conditions of narration in canto xi of book IV, the narrator reflects the flow of tribute that opens book VI. The terms of narration are economic; to "backe repay" is to "recount" (xi.9.9), and the poet's "telling" (xi.9.6,10.6), or numbering, measures the endless fertility of the generation of Neptune. We have seen that in this situation the poet has recourse to the squire's trope; he reports his inadequacy at recounting. His retelling, which would seem to add to Neptune's generation, never approaches the fertility of the god; instead, as he affirms, less is more (xi.17). If we recast these statements about poetic production and the sphere of the poet's power and authority into sociopolitical terms, we can see that his consideration of the power of poetic representation raises basic questions about social reality and its representational forms. The very map of the rivers raises the question of whether Nature (Neptune's realm here, Elizabeth's in the opening to book VI) exists independent of the texts in which it is represented, for maps say that we can know the real world only through its representations. Reality in this formulation depends on names and locations—locutions—the "real" names of rivers, in England and in the world at large; and the poet's fancy plays with these "real" words. The structures in which the rivers are represented, and marriage is one of them, are themselves forms in which reality presents itself.

Here is one way this question is raised. Like the Temple of Venus, the river marriage presents a fantasy of power couched largely in feudal, chivalric terms, the language of tribute. These fictions provoke questions about the world "outside" the text. How did the chivalry of Elizabeth's court serve its real power in the world? How did the veneration of Elizabeth as a goddess operate practically? These are difficult issues to confront, in part because they call into question the distinction between fiction and reality. Power depends upon certain potent fictions. Conversely, the text of *The Faerie Queene* offers reciprocal versions of these social representations and expects to derive its power from them. Are we any nearer to reality when the fictions of the poem correspond to the fictions of the court? Are we any nearer to the Thames when we read its name on a map? Such representations stand on that problematic boundary where text and nature meet. The discourse that shapes the text has its place in the wider text of society: "conversation," we might recall, is sociability, living together. Language is the bond of society. No doubt this reflects back on Florimell's girdle, that valued object venerated at Satyrane's tournament. But we can best see society bound together with the text by pursuing the marriage of the rivers, the place where world and word meet.

The river procession has a marriage at its center, the union of the Thames and the Medway. Consider this union's relationship to the structures of discourse in the poem and in the world. The groom is "fresh and iolly" (xi.27.1); the latter adjective we recognize as the problematic sign in this text of the Thames's chivalric might. He is clothed in a garment that is his nature, a robe in which the threads seem to be waves, in which crystal jewels simulate, and *are*, water.

> But he their sonne full fresh and iolly was,
>   All decked in a robe of watchet hew,

On which the waves, glittering like Christall glas,
So cunningly enwoven were, that few
Could weenen, whether they were false or trew.
And on his head like to a Coronet
He wore, that seemed strange to common vew,
In which were many towres and castels set,
That it encompast round as with a golden fret.

(xi.27)

Insofar as the Thames is a representation, his clothing can only be art, cunningly woven and sequined. His costume, in fact, is likely to recall that of a figure from a courtly entertainment dressed as a river. Such figures frequently entertained Elizabeth. But insofar as he represents what he *is*—and in courtly entertainments disguises are identities, masks revelations—his clothing, which seems to be water, *is* water. In neither case is he the real river, nor could he be anything but a representation.

The Thames is the potent reality of social fiction. In token of that, he is crowned with a turban like that of Cybele (xi.28) and thus, like other figures of power in the text, he implies an hermaphroditic ideal. Spenser's "dreaded Soveraine" in the proem to book VI was a "King"; in the proem to book IV, she was both "Queene of love, and Prince of peace" (4.9). The crown the Thames wears is the city of London, here called Troynovant (xi.28.8) as a sign that, in recounting, history repeats itself. The power represented by the Thames is a summary of contained differences: at once the city and the river, land and water, civilization and nature, male and female, past and present. Text and nature coincide in this image of power and authority, drawn, as we shall see further, from the repertoire of courtly images.

Crucially, the Thames is situated in social relationships. With his neighboring rivers he offers this picture, a social landscape:

And round about him many a pretty Page
Attended duely, ready to obay;
All little Rivers, which owe vassallage
To him, as to their Lord, and tribute pay.

(xi.29.1–4)

"And tribute pay": this is a feudal vision, as the terms of vassalage make clear; it is also a pun extended into the narration. Tributary rivers pay tribute. The pun naturalizes the chivalric mode of society which the Thames embodies and supports. Naturally, the rivers repeat feudal society because of a reversal, because the rivers are images within the framework of a society that represents itself in those terms. When the rivers are so seen, paying tribute, do we have then an example of political mystification, ideological rigidity, or simply an epistemological necessity?[7] And how bound to this representational situation is the poet? Elsewhere in *The Faerie Queene*, from book IV onwards, chivalric self-promotion is problematic. Is it so here, at its source, and does the poem implicate society in its fictions? The answer to these questions seems to be that the rivers represent a "natural" beginning ineluctably intertwining nature, society, and art, a "natural" beginning in an epistemological necessity of *seeing through* (that is, both penetrating and seeing by means of) these forms. The poet is playing both with and within a fantasy, and his authority for his play lies in the way in which the "outside" of the text has become its inside.

The Thames joins the Medway, which is presented, like the belt of Venus and its seekers, in terms of economic value and transcendent valuation. In her, the waters are insistently glittering and silvery (45.5, 47.6); however, she is so artfully clothed that, like the statue of Venus, her form is "unknowen" and "uncouth" (45.2–3), a work that is yet "no mortall worke, that seem'd and yet was not" (45.9). These paradoxes echo those of the Thames. Like Venus, the Medway is veiled, more explicitly masked in token of mysteries of state that transcend nature and art. On her head she wears a crown of flowers; her morning dew makes the crown grow "as a new spring" (46.5). Is this an image of nature, or is nature here replicated in the authoritative image of social power? What

7. It is a feature of ideological mystification to act as if social forms were natural forms. Bourdieu explores such objectification in *Theory of Practice*, in which "relations of domination have the opacity and permanence of things and escape the grasp of individual consciousness and power" (p. 184). The process is studied at length by Georg Lukács in "Reification and the Consciousness of the Proletariat," in *History and Class Consciousness*, trans. Rodney Livingstone (Cambridge, Mass.: MIT Press, 1971), pp. 83–222. On the subjugation of subjects to social structures that shape their language and desires, and on the possibility of moving beyond this situation, see Rosalind Coward and John Ellis, *Language and Materialism* (London: Routledge & Kegan Paul, 1977), e.g., p. 78 on ideology as a structure, and p. 117, on the subjection of individual desire. Coward and Ellis, like Bourdieu, are intent upon arguing that the subject-in-process answers the menace of the subject subjected and that language is the key to the liberation of the subject. These thinkers are moving within poststructuralist thought, in which structuration is of crucial significance. As Terry Eagleton argues in *Marxism and Literary Criticism* (Berkeley and Los Angeles: University of California Press, 1976), texts, although limited ideologically, are not so thoroughly straightened as to be merely reflections of society; they also are part of the production of society and part of the processes of social change. *The Faerie Queene* is a revolutionary text, even if what it glimpses is an impossible revolution and the limits of possibility which force it into silence. As Harry Berger, Jr., and other critics have noted, the final books of the poem labor under the pressure of society. On the relationships between social theory, structuralism, and psychoanalysis, Fredric Jameson's essay, "Imaginary and Symbolic in Lacan: Marxism, Psychoanalytic Criticism, and the Problem of the Subject," *Yale French Studies* 55/56 (1977): 338–95, particularly the concluding section, is of fundamental importance.

crown is this? Like Venus, the Medway is a generator of the universe; like her, she is an object of desire that initiates and transcends the desire she moves. Mythologically, the bride combines Flora and Aurora; and those names cover Florimell and Amoret in the text.

In the river marriage, the fantasy that moves desire in the fictions surrounding Florimell and Amoret, the fantasy of possession and conquest, has become the center of a social situation. The marriage itself is a social event being celebrated in Proteus's hall. The procession is hierarchical, and the sea gods constitute a society. As in Elizabethan processions, the bride and groom do not come first, for the place of honor is the center of the procession.[8] Their progenitors precede them; hence the principle that gives order to the procession implies the power that will be theirs in coupling. The parade of the gods presents a *genealogia deorum*, and the marriage will insure such continuities. In political terms, this genealogical form embodies a favorite device of Renaissance monarchs to provide images of their power.[9] Renaissance princes regularly claimed to derive their authority through descent from the gods: the German, French, and Spanish royal houses, like Alexander the Great

8. On Elizabethan processions, see Roy Strong, *The Cult of Elizabeth* (London: Thames & Hudson, 1977), pp. 30–31, a book to which I am deeply indebted for my understanding of Elizabethan chivalry and what Strong calls, after Frances Yates, "an imaginative refeudalization of late Tudor society" (p. 129). Yates's studies are now brought together in *Astraea: The Imperial Theme in the Sixteenth Century* (London: Routledge & Kegan Paul, 1975).

9. It is studied authoritatively by Stephen Orgel in "The Royal Theater and the Role of King," forthcoming in Stephen Orgel and Guy Lytle, eds., *Patronage in the Renaissance* (Princeton: Princeton University Press, 1981). Bourdieu in *Theory of Practice* discusses official genealogies as a social strategy for the encrustation of power. "We cannot fail to notice that those uses of kinship which may be called genealogical are reserved for official situations in which they serve the function of ordering the social world and of legitimating that order" (p. 34). Neptune, who appears to be the most powerful god in the text, had been a symbol of political power, of *imperium*, in Virgil (see the informative study by Reuben Brower, "Visual and Verbal Translation of Myth: Neptune in Virgil, Rubens, Dryden," in Clifford Geertz, ed., *Myth, Symbol and Culture* [New York: W. W. Norton, 1971]), and he figures as an ultimate deity in Lyly's *Gallathea* (see Peter Saccio, *The Court Comedies of John Lyly* [Princeton: Princeton University Press, 1969], pp. 102–14). Especially after the defeat of the Armada, oceanic powers regaled Elizabeth at entertainments, such as those of 1591 and 1594 described in Nichols, *The Progresses and Public Processions of Queen Elizabeth* (London, 1823), 3: 110 ff., 309 ff. The seagod who presides over the river marriage is Proteus; his complex history is treated by A. Bartlett Giamatti in "Proteus Unbound: Some Versions of the Sea God in the Renaissance," in *The Disciplines of Criticism*, ed. Peter Demetz, Thomas Greene, and Lowry Nelson, Jr. (New Haven: Yale University Press, 1968), pp. 437–57. Giamatti closes his discussion, which documents the manifold transformations of Proteus from classical texts to eighteenth-century manifestations, by briefly alluding to the marriage in Proteus's house, in which "male and female, art and nature, the city and the garden" join. For Giamatti this figures the poet's powers to shape matter, a civilizing ceremony (p. 475); the dark side of Proteus, so often alluded to by Giamatti, is ignored in this reading of Spenser. Further, Proteus's absence, which I discuss below, goes unremarked, although Giamatti does note it in *Play*

before them, traced their ancestry to Hercules, and though Elizabeth's genealogists were more modest, the queen was, of course, hymned as Astraea, Diana, *Venus virgo*, and the like. Insistently, the ancestors of the rivers present in their own right images of political power. Neptune, the ruler of the sea, is crowned in his "Diademe imperiall" (11.4). His consort, Amphitrite, is a pattern for the bride:

> And by his side his Queene with coronall,
> Faire *Amphitrite*, most divinely faire,
> Whose yvorie shoulders weren covered all,
> As with a robe, with her owne silver haire,
> And deckt with pearles, which th'Indian seas for her prepaire.
>
> (11.5–9)

She is the treasure of the sea, Neptune's possession, a commercial venture that has paid off spectacularly. She embodies what drove sailors to find a route to the East: ivory, silver, pearls.

After this exemplary coupling of power and beauty, their progeny follow: first the seagods whose heroic energies give evidence of the "powre to rule" (12.9), then those seagods who overflowed the land, "famous founders . . . / Of puissant Nations, which the world possest" (15.1–2); among them is Albion making Herculean claims to the rule of France. A translation into contemporary political terms is readily apparent; the rivers present an imperialistic fantasy. In it, marriage, possession of the valued object, or the valued lands of gold, gives rise to a patriotic injunction when the narrator, arriving at the Amazon river, named after those women "which doe possesse the same" (21.9), exclaims:

> Ioy on those warlike women, which so long
>   Can from all men so rich a kingdome hold;
>   And shame on you, O men, which boast your strong
>   And valiant hearts, in thoughts lesse hard and bold,
>   Yet quaile in conquest of that land of gold.
>   But this to you, O Britons, most pertaines,
>   To whom the right hereof it selfe hath sold;
>   The which for sparing litle cost or paines,
> Loose so immortall glory, and so endlesse gaines.
>
> (xi.22)

---

of Double Senses: Spenser's "Faerie Queene" (Englewood Cliffs, N.J.: Prentice-Hall, 1975), but only in asserting that his place has been taken by the poet (pp. 132–33); as I suggest below, however, it is precisely his absence that is shared.

It is important to keep in mind a point that Giamatti begins with in his essay, that Proteus is a *deus ambiguus* (see p. 443). Like other figures of power in *The Faerie Queene*, what he reconciles in himself is not otherwise available. That Proteus is closely allied with the functions of poetry and civilization is fundamental to Giamatti's treatment, and illuminates Spenser's figure.

The voice here sounds like Ralegh's in his account of Guiana and the search for El Dorado.[10] But "inside" the text, this Brazilian fantasy refigures the river marriage: we are told that the Medway long resisted but at last relented (xi.8). The land is a woman to be purchased by spoil. The geographical fantasy is everywhere extended; chivalric power is an imperialistic venture, anti-Spanish and anti-French. And, as the final line of the stanza shows, what is at stake is money—and more; symbolic capital, what the text calls "immortall glory, . . . endlesse gaines." These are like the values conferred by Canacee's ring and Florimell's girdle.

Fittingly, the social form behind (inside/outside) the text is named at once in the meaning assigned to the action of the first figure in the marriage procession, Triton. He is said to be blowing his horn "for goodly triumph and great iollyment" (12.4). His "iollyment" we know, from the Thames and from the first jolly knight of this pleasant tale, carries a general chivalric meaning. "Triumph" designates the specific social form of this celebration of possession. The triumph celebrated conquest; Renaissance princes made their royal entrances into cities as triumphs to signify the allegiance owed to them, and not merely by conquered foreign cities. Both Elizabeth's and James's coronation processions, for instance, were cast as triumphs.[11] Elizabeth is also shown in triumph, in a late painting of a procession (the Blackfriars *Procession Picture*, c. 1600; fig. 1) that may also celebrate a marriage. The picture is too late to be a source for Spenser, but its conjunction of triumph and

10. *The discovery of Guiana*, lxv in Richard Hakluyt, *Voyages and Discoveries*, ed. Jack Beeching (Baltimore: Penguin Books, 1972), pp. 386–410. "Guiana is a country that hath yet her maidenhead" (p. 408), Ralegh writes and he urges the English to "possess" it, "for whatsoever prince shall possess it, shall be greatest" (p. 410). Feudal language also surrounds his self-presentation: "This empire is made known to Her Majesty by her own vassal" (p. 409). The connection with Ralegh is made in passing in Thomas H. Cain, *Praise in "The Faerie Queene,"* p. 168.
11. On the triumph as model for Elizabethan pageantry, see the analysis of the Blackfriars *Procession Picture* in Strong, *The Cult of Elizabeth* and Yates, *Astraea*, pp. 112 ff., on "The Triumph of Chastity." As Gordon Kipling notes in "Triumphal Drama: Form in English Civic Pageantry," *Renaissance Drama*, n.s. 8 (1977): 37–56, the term *triumph* covers a number of forms, including entries, *tableaux vivants*, Lord Mayor's shows, and weddings. One wedding that seems particularly analogous to the triumphal coupling of the Thames and Medway is that of Lucrezia Borgia. The bride wore a gown that simulated fish scales in its gold weaving (see Lauro Martines, *Power and Imagination* [New York: Alfred A. Knopf, 1979], pp. 232–33, and Joseph Chartrou, *Les Entrées Solennelles et Triumphales à la Renaissance* [Paris: Presses Universitaires de France, 1928], p. 58); Chartrou also describes a 1550 entrance of Henri II into Rouen that, with its reconstructed Brazilian forest (see p. 111), bears comparison with Spenser's triumph. The forest is illustrated on p. 63 of Hugh Honour's *The New Golden Land*. Honour also mentions and illustrates the presence of Brazilians in the Triumph of Maximilian I (see pp. 14–15), as well as actual Brazilians in the triumphal entries of Charles IX (p. 64). Full bibliography is provided by Honour on p. 275.

The Blackfriars *Procession Picture* (By courtesy of Mr. Simon Wingfield Digby, Sherborne Castle)

The *Ditchley Portrait* (National Portrait Gallery, London)

marriage is not unusual. Conquer a nation, marry a nation's princess; the ends, after all, are the same, and so is the imagery. Fortune, Machiavelli remarks, is a woman.[12]

The language of the river marriage is cast in the same language as a royal triumph, even if it nowhere explicitly replicates the royal form. Elizabeth is never mentioned in this canto, yet she is implicitly present again and again if only because the symbolic forms of the text are the forms devised for her representations. These two rivers, after all, meet in her country. The queen has two bodies and one of them, her body politic, is coextensive with the land she rules and which is mapped in the river marriage.

In the mythology of Elizabethan veneration, where the queen was so often linked to Diana, a tale implying her authority over the rivers of her land is especially appropriate; she is, as the moon, responsible for the flow of waters. So, in the famous *Ditchley Portrait* (1592; fig. 2), the queen stands on a map; the sonnet that accompanies the portrait concludes (I depend on Roy Strong's reconstruction of the text) with "Rivers of thankes" pouring into a "boundles ocean . . . / Where grace is grace above, power po[wer]." The portrait celebrates the queen, but, as we know from the position of the queen's feet, it also commemorates a visit to Sir Henry Lee, the queen's jousting champion for many years and, apparently, the inventor of the annual tournament held to commemorate her accession. Thus, the *Ditchley Portrait* visualizes the feudal conceit of the river's tribute in the context of the chivalric revival that characterized the ceremonies of Elizabeth's court. Nor is Elizabeth associated with a map only in this portrait; she is frequently depicted with a globe; and, in a 1598 Dutch engraving (fig. 3), the queen's body has become the map of Europe. So, too, in the marriage of rivers, the map coincides with the represented form of the royal power and imperial designs that move the poem.

These depictions echo the most common mode of celebrating Eli-

---

In the discussion of Elizabeth's portraits that follows, I depend upon the work of Strong and Yates cited above, and particularly on Roy Strong's *Portraits of Queen Elizabeth I* (Oxford: Clarendon Press, 1963). Also of importance is Marianna Jenkins, "The State Portrait, Its Origin and Evolution," *Monographs on Archaeology and Fine Arts* 3 (1947); pp. 23–24 deal specifically with Elizabeth's portraits, but the entire study is worth consideration for its insistence on the idealizing function of official portraits, and its ethical, political and philosophical imperatives.

12. A Shakespeare text which exemplifies many of these meanings is *Henry V*. Possession of France is embodied in the marriage with Kate which is contracted in the final scene of the play. Henry's grisly humor—that he has spared many a fair city because of this fair maid—is based on their substitutive identification, "the cities turned into a maid" (V.2.307) as the King of France says, or, as Henry says to the princess, "when France is mine and I am yours, then yours is France and you are mine" (V.2.172).

zabethan imperialism. Under Elizabeth, imperialistic ventures were always associated with sea power. The defeat of the Spanish Armada generated assertions of English power and gave these assertions the imagery and the form evident in the river marriage: after the Armada, Elizabeth entered London in triumph to commemorate that victory. Celebratory portraits of the queen depicted the Armada arriving and sinking in two windows behind her; against that background the queen presents essential forms of power, her hand rests on a globe, while her body is supported by a throne that sports a decorative sea nymph (fig. 4). Again, after 1588, the idea of empire is celebrated in engravings of *Eliza Triumphans*. In a late version of this engraving (fig. 5), Elizabeth appropriates the pillars of Hercules, which were Charles V's emblem for his imperialistic designs and his symbolic proclamation of his descent from Hercules. Although the queen's name is absent from the vast list of participants in the marriage of the rivers, she is present in all the forms that represent power: triumph, genealogy, sea dominion, and map.

We might note too that another figure, Proteus, is curiously (significantly?) absent from the list of sea gods, even though the banquet takes place in his house. Are these perhaps parallel absences, two instances that exemplify a principle of power, that what is behind the form stays hidden? If so, Elizabeth and Proteus are, in this canto, *dei absconditi*. Similarly, the narrator finds that he has power by giving less and by denying that what he gives is his own at all. He is cut after the same pattern. Hence, we could say that the names in the river marriage, like all other substitutive names generated in the text, are periphrases, supplements for a power that the text cannot name more directly, and which is yet the source of the text itself, what produces it: an absent name.

Inevitably, this text is inside yet another text, the one constituted by the fictions and representations—the "conversation" and discourse—of Elizabethan society. Such representations comprise a discourse of power, and *The Faerie Queene* is written in that language. Book IV is a most convenient guide to it because in subject and in imagery it locates itself explicitly in social forms. Although it is a commonplace of Spenser criticism to contrast the social concerns of the final books of *The Faerie Queene* with the private issues of the initial books, the revisionary gesture that opens book IV puts that commonplace in question. Book IV, we have seen, disables the notion of the self. In part, it does that because society precedes the individual and because social forms locate persons. Marriage is a basic form of social life, and, as presented at the opening of book IV, the marriage of Amoret and Scudamour reflects back on the earlier books; but it also, as we must see now, reflects accurately the practices of Elizabethan society. Moreover, the initial telling of the story places in question the relationship of social practices to the fictions they

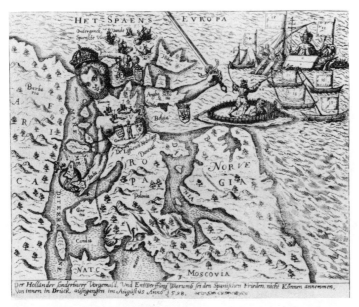

Dutch engraving of Elizabeth I as a map of Europe (Ashmolean Museum, Oxford)

The *Armada Portrait* (By kind permission of the Marquess of Tavistock, and the Trustees of the Bedford Estates),

ELIZABETA D.G.ANGLIÆ.FRANCIÆ.HIBERNIÆ.ET VERGINIÆ
REGINA CHRISTIANAE FIDEI VNICVM PROPVGNACVLVM.
Immortalis honos Regum, cui non tulit ætas   *Queis ipsa tantum superant reliqua omnia regna,*
Ulla prior, veniens nec feret ulla parem,   *Quantum tu maior Regibus es reliquis.*

Eliza Triumphans, second version (Courtesy, Trustees of the British Museum)

produce, and in which they are clothed. This story may serve again as a multiple mirror for us to regard the place of the text in social discourse. At her marriage, Amoret is carried off by Busyrane. And the crucial point is that, as the lines record the event, it is hard to judge whether this abduction constitutes a violation or a fulfillment of social practice:

> For that same vile Enchauntour *Busyran,*
>> The very selfe same day that she was wedded,
>> Amidst the bridale feast, whilest every man
>> Surcharg'd with wine, were heedlesse and ill hedded,
>> All bent to mirth before the bride was bedded,
>> Brought in that mask of love which late was showen:
>> And there the Ladie ill of friends bestedded,
>> By way of sport, as oft in maskes is knowen,
> Conveyed quite away to living wight unknowen.
>
> (i.3)

As a social form, masques are the "sport" of society; in Elizabethan society they were a form for self-representation and a means of playing at being oneself. The masque here is Cupid's, and it is therefore played under the aegis of tyrannic desire. In this light, "sport" (3.8) conveys those implications of Venus connected with joyfully sadistic imposition. In the masque, the demands of desire are reconstituted as social demands and "sport" is the form of both. Busyrane's abduction of Amoret is ambiguous because it replays Scudamour's heroic abduction of her from the Temple of Venus. The sport of the masque repeats the elaborate and ritualized society of the Temple in which the act of courting a lady is represented symbolically by Scudamour's progression through the social landscape of castle, bridge, and shrine. The architecture, in its mixture of "curious Corbes," arched porches, and Doric pillars (x.6.6–9), sounds genuinely Elizabethan. And the place, a court devoted to frustrated courting, cannot fail to recall another court and its self-sufficient queen.

If the reader's judgment is disabled by the story of Amoret's abduction, it is because the voice of society speaks through her story, and its power overwhelms the distinctions and discriminations we might wish to make. Society, the voice of authority, is heard throughout book IV; from the first, book IV is about what it means to enter society, and the terms used to understand social forms are characteristically Elizabethan. Entering society is figured in Britomart's and Amoret's reception at the first castle with its complex rules of coupling. Britomart's hermaphroditic manipulation of the situation carries weight precisely because it is socially sanctioned, a "Seneschall . . . cal'd to deeme the right" (i.12.1) accepts her mask of chivalric force as identical with her self. Throughout the book, the social world passes judgments that depend upon the ability

of others to "read" the self and place it in society. The baffling battle
between Cambel and the "-mond" brothers is adjudicated by six judges
who sit on one side of the field, while Canacee is on the other. Between
the object of desire and the voices of judgment a social space is defined in
which winning a wife is also the means of entering society. They are
"assembled . . . in field, the chalenge to define" (iii.3.9).

> The field with listes was all about enclos'd,
>   To barre the prease of people farre away;
>   And at th'one side sixes iudges were dispos'd,
>   To view and deeme the deedes of armes that day;
>   And on the other side in fresh aray,
>   Fayre *Canacee* upon a stately stage
>   Was set, to see the fortune of that fray,
>   And to be seene, as his most worthie wage,
> That could her purchase with his lives adventur'd gage.
>
> (iii.4)

This social space draws on the vocabulary of the Elizabethan tilts, those
chivalric exercises revived under Elizabeth; the allusion is most explicit
in Satyrane's tournament, in which the three-man fight for Canacee is
elaborated as a three-day battle under the supervision of the Knights of
Maidenhead. On the final day, Britomart, masked, defeats first Arthegall, disguised as the Salvage Knight; then Cambel and Triamond, the
victors in the second day's fight; and finally Blandamour, whom Britomart encounters and defeats twice more in the poem. Hers is a triumph
for the Knights of Maidenhead. The fact that Amoret can wear the girdle
of Venus demonstrates that she is Britomart's proper reward. But the
voice of society differs; the golden belt is awarded to (False) Florimell,
one forgery to another, "so forged things do fairest shew" (v.15.9)—and
(False) Florimell chooses not Britomart but the "masked Mock-knight"
(iv.13.4), Braggadocchio. That the trial of chivalry should be an endless
masquerade and a regressive battle, that it should issue in false judgments and in an unholy alliance suggests—as does the pun on "forge"—
the profound ambivalence surrounding social representation.

   Once again, we arrive at a representation of the power of the Other
shaping the text. Society here contains the oppositions that undo discrimination; society is what is "forged," constructed, made, joined together, as a set of representations that are, inevitably, misrepresentations
and misperceptions. Representing the chivalric world, the text inevitably *sees through* Elizabethan representation. Satyrane's tournament
constitutes no ironic dismissal of chivalric society, but evidence that all
power is illusion, including—perhaps, especially—the power of the text
grounded in these illusions. Since society is clothed in ritualized and

archaized forms for behavior, social judgment confronts not the difference between truth and falsity, between reality and illusion, but true and false representation, masks of various kinds, all of which are, nonetheless, masks. For those in the poem who, unlike the rivers, are presented as people—"selves"—the forms of society are baffling and defeating.

The struggle to have a self in book IV inevitably seems to dissolve the self into a text. We can now add to this the recognition that the text that stands before the self is a social one. The self is born into society and finds itself in society. Characters dissolve into endlessly substitutive language in this text. That transformation restates a social fact: that words are the way in which we enter human society. Invariably, our first words are those of another and our ability to name ourselves as ourselves depends upon another having named us. So, identification by another comes before self-identification. The "I" exists first in the eyes of another. Such social acts of identification alienate the self, make misidentification, misrecognition, and misrepresentation the norm of society. The self is lost in society under the masks that society provides, and demands, if the individual is to have a place—be "in place"—in society.[13] In the societies represented in book IV, only those who have power do not feel these social impositions as self-divisive. Those who have power are those mastering figures of desire that we have met before; now we may see them as the voice of society in the text, containing the oppositions that undo the self.

As suggested earlier, the belt of Florimell is a fitting symbol for the deeply ambivalent vision of Elizabethan culture that *The Faerie Queene* offers. Although it is the chastity belt that Venus put off when she abandoned her husband in order to commit adultery with Mars, it is meant by the Knights of Maidenhead to symbolize the union of "the praise of armes and chevalrie" with "the prize of beautie" (v.1.2–3). The tournament thus seeks, as does the proem to *The Faerie Queene*, to marry a latter-day Mars to a new Venus, not to recapitulate the marriage of Vulcan and Venus, and it intends to legitimate them with the prize. The birth of a second Harmonia, the supposed offspring of the illegitimate

13. Although my terms here are Lacanian, the argument need not be. To apply Saussurian principles to society as Lévi-Strauss does will yield similar results. See, e.g., "The Individual as a Species" in *The Savage Mind* (Chicago: University of Chicago Press, 1966), pp. 191 ff. Or, to borrow from Coward and Ellis in *Language and Materialism*, what I am describing is ideology; see, e.g., p. 76, "the function of ideology is to fix the individual in place as subject for a certain meaning." Or, to use Richard A. Lanham's terms in *The Motives of Eloquence* (New Haven: Yale University Press, 1976), what Spenser's text offers is "the rhetorical ideal of life" in which reality is always subjected to the play of texts.

coupling of Mars and Venus, is presumably sought.[14] Illegitimacy and
legitimacy keep meeting at the tournament, and the actions performed
raise insistent and troubling questions about social forms and behavior.
Is Satyrane's veneration of the belt, for example, idolatry, or the proper
worship of a symbol of chaste love? Is Britomart's victory, despite her
mask, nonetheless an avowal of chivalric society? Or is it a revelation of
male impotence, a reversal of the sexual politics in the chivalric hierar-
chies of male and female, possessor and possessed? If so, would such a
reversal be antithetical to the Elizabethan court, with a ruler who insistently called herself a prince and invoked thereby an ideal hermaphroditism? Is this beauty contest a version of the Judgment of Paris? If it is, does
it liken the breakdown of the chivalric mode to the incipient Trojan
disaster? Is it revisionary, like Peele's play, or poised like the 1569 painting of the Judgment of Paris in which Elizabeth wins the prize (fig. 6)? Is
the golden belt being compared or contrasted to Ate's golden apple? And
is the poet, when he *sees through* the fictions of his society, empowered
or rendered powerless? Is he cast, or has he cast himself, in the position
in which he depicts the prophet Nereus viewing the fall of Troy?

> Thereto he was expert in prophecies,
>   And could the ledden of the Gods unfold,
>   Through which, when *Paris* brought his famous prise
>   The faire *Tindarid* lasse, he him fortold,
>   That her all *Greece* with many a champion bold
>   Should fetch againe, and finally destroy
>   Proud *Priams* towne. So wise is *Nereus* old,
>   And so well skild; nathlesse he takes great ioy
> Oft-times amongst the wanton Nymphs to sport and toy.
>
> (xi.19)

14. On Harmonia as the child of Mars and Venus, see Wind, *Pagan Mysteries in the Renaissance* (New York: W. W. Norton, 1968), pp. 86 ff. The tradition goes back at least as far as Plutarch's *De Iside et Osiride*, a text of some
importance to Spenser; Plutarch makes the marriage of Mars and Venus congru-
ent with an Empedoclean cosmos of friendship and strife, precisely the terms
replicated in book IV of *The Faerie Queene*. It should be recalled that the fatal
house of Thebes sprang from the loins of Harmonia and Cadmus. I am grateful
to Lee Patterson for reminding me that that story was central to Chaucer; *The
Broche of Thebes*, he believes, includes "The Complaint of Mars" (spoken by a
bird) and "The Complaint of Venus"; the broach is described in "Mars," 11. 245
ff., in terms reminiscent of the description of the belt of Florimell in IV.iv.16.
Louis Montrose finds the painting alluded to below more ambivalent in its
praise than Peele's text (*ELH* 47 [1980]: 446), which, for him, affirms Elizabeth's
declarations in which "the integrity and strength of the English body politic
came to seem mystically dependent upon the integrity and strength—the
intactness—of the Queen's body natural. . . . Her control of the realm was dependent upon her physical and symbolic control of her own body" (p. 441). For
Montrose, Peele's text is an unambiguous gift, part of the system of prestation
that Montrose nicely defines, depending upon Mauss and Bourdieu, as "a tacitly
coercive and vitally interested process predicated on the fiction that it is free and
disinterested" (p. 454).

Judgment of Paris (By the gracious permission of Her Majesty Queen Elizabeth II)

Knowing that Troy will fall does not stop it. Nereus views the consequence of Paris's "prise" and then "takes" his own sexual pleasures
where he can find them. He tells what he knows, and knows what and
how he tells. "He takes great ioy / . . . to sport and toy."

When the narrator of book IV considers the court and its relationship to the lust and decadent beauty that seem to characterize the world
in its decline, he attempts to find a safe way through its ambiguities.

> And now it [beauty] is so utterly decayd,
>   That any bud thereof doth scarse remaine,
>   But if few plants preserv'd through heavenly ayd,
>   In Princes Court doe hap to sprout againe,
>   Dew'd with her drops of bountie Soveraine,
>   Which from that goodly glorious flowre proceed,
>   Sprung of the auncient stocke of Princes straine,
>   Now th'onely remnant of that royall breed,
> Whose noble kind at first was sure of heavenly seed.
>
> (viii.33)

This stanza might be a representation of Elizabeth's court, combining as it does male prince and female bountiful sovereign in one; at the very least, it depicts the symbolic form of authority which this text shares with the court. Once again, the place of power is one where social form meets nature, and the imagery here is of purely natural generation. But when "royall breed" meets "heavenly seed" nature is mystified, and the language takes on an ideological function. The production of the poem in society is perhaps figured here too. Cannot these plants be the weeds of poetry? Might not "bountie" here convey a bid for money? Those meanings and many others reside in these courtly images. Yet the stanza is finally undecipherable. Is it affirming the court or denying that any but the center of the court has the power and beauty it praises? The question cannot be answered confidently, for the syntax goes astray in a hypothetical "but if" that never resolves itself; and the vocabulary is at once open and opaque, endless in its possibilities. These lines come at the end of a place we have looked at before, the narrator's address to the reader-as-slanderer of the text. The lines are, of course, disconcerting, since one slander the text has just allowed the reader is, as we have seen, the identification of Belphoebe with Sclaunder. This final stanza seems to intend to rule out the possibility of further connections that might move the reader "outside" the text. Yet instead of stopping the chain of signifiers, the introduction of the court leaves the poet virtually tongue-tied, like Timias become dumb.

Is this what the authority behind and in social illusion demands? Is this where "the displeasure of the mighty" (viii.1.3), which is also the pleasure—and desire—of those with power, leads? Perhaps so, for Elizabeth, like Venus in the text, is a figure of desire who demands that those who desire her be unsatisfied. Nonetheless, she demands their desire. Like Venus's Temple, Elizabeth's court was a place of endless courting, where "all doe learne to play the Paramours" (x.45.5), and woe to the courtier who, like Ralegh (like Timias), sought favor elsewhere. Other marriages were betrayals in Elizabeth's eyes. Yet marriage was never a possibility that the queen really offered to her courtiers. Courting was a metaphor for the desire for power and authority, a metaphor enacted and lived. The queen granted position and power and gave gifts. These are real and symbolic acts at once. What she never gave—or said she never gave—was her body; it was mystified, too precious, virginal, untouchable. The elaborate world of the court ran on the illusion of sexual desire frustrated: "First doe the merry birds, thy prety pages / Privily pricked with thy lustfull powres, / Chirpe loud to thee out of their leavy cages" (x.45.6–8). That principle fulfilled the queen's desire and was the embodiment of the preserving fictions of her rule. The queen made herself a goddess, chivalry said she was forever young, as did her portraitists.

These are fictions to preserve the body politic. Insistently, the queen said she ruled by love.[15]

Preservation takes the form of multiple denials and undoings, reversals that signify potency although their form is that of impotence. The queen does not marry, she has no children. The desire she generates she refuses herself. Hence, the imperialistic forms of marriage and generation are manipulated as lacks. In the early part of the reign possible suitors are denied; only on her deathbed, if then, does she acknowledge James VI of Scotland as her successor. In book IV, powerful figures of desire convey these political meanings, most notably Venus who, like Elizabeth, "needeth other none" (x.41.9). A comparison to Venus is indeed a regular part of the vocabulary of Elizabeth's portraitists. For instance, in the *Raveningham Portrait* (1575; fig. 7), the queen displays a jewel in which one can make out Venus, born from the sea, standing amidst men holding fish. Similarly, in book IV, immediately after the river marriage, Venus appears as what the waters produce and what produces them:

> Therefore the antique wisards well invented,
>   That *Venus* of the fomy sea was bred;
>   For that the seas by her are most augmented.
>
> (xii.2.1–3)

Power and love are manifested here at once. Should one remember whose foam bred the goddess, or think that castration is the route to the reign of gold?

Let us look at another pictorial representation to elucidate further the complex and ambivalent power represented by the symbolism of *Venus virgo*. The queen is shown holding her favorite emblem in the Siena *Sieve Portrait* (1580; fig. 8). Roy Strong explains the iconography: "The Sieve is the symbol of the Vestal Virgin Tuccia who had carried water from the river Tiber to the Vestal Virgin Temple in a Sieve to prove her

---

15. See, for example, the most famous speech of her reign, delivered on 30 November 1601, in which Elizabeth repeatedly returns to the theme that she has "reigned with your loves" and that England has never had a sovereign "that will love you better" (cited in G. R. Elton, *England under the Tudors* [London: Methuen, 1955], p. 465); or, as Marianna Jenkins says of the *Ditchley Portrait*, "What could be more telling for the portrait of a woman who once reminded her parliament of 'the pledge of this my wedlock and marriage to my kingdom'?" (*Monographs on Archaeology and Fine Arts* 3 [1947]; 24). In a review of Strong's *The Cult of Elizabeth*, Stephen Greenblatt has written a lucid and suggestive note on Elizabeth's manipulation of love as a mode of power (*Renaissance Quarterly* 31 [1978]; 642–44), what he characterizes as her "blend of seduction and compulsion." Cf. Thomas H. Cain, *Praise in "The Faerie Queene,"* pp. 50–51.

The *Raveningham Portrait* (Elizabethan Club of Yale University)

The *Sieve Portrait* (Pinacoteca Nazionale di Siena)

chastity."[16] In the portrait, the queen is flanked by a column on the left and a colonnaded courtyard behind her on the right. One might well assume that she stands in the Temple of the Vestal Virgin, and no doubt she does. But that is not the only place she occupies: she is also situated in a marriage temple. Evidence for this can be found in the column, on which scenes from the *Aeneid* depict the story of Dido and Aeneas. These alert the viewer to the recreation of those events. A queen in a temple adorned with scenes from the past (recall Dido in the Temple of Juno) is about to be visited by a latterday Aeneas (note the chivalric retinue filling the courtyard).

These allusions and figures add a density of meaning to the portrait. The queen is situated at once in a virginal and a marriage space—a fitting space for *Venus virgo*. The *Aeneid* references explain more. No doubt, although the courtiers who are assembled in the courtyard derive from the same scene of the meeting of Dido and Aeneas in Virgil, the meaning in the Virgilian allusion has been reversed, not merely because the queen is a virgin, but because even though she is in the position of Dido in the painting, her destiny fulfills the model of Aeneas. In her, the power of chastity rewrites history to make London into Troynovant. She occupies a double space and assumes the identity of both its occupants; in herself, she legitimizes an illegitimate marriage. The picture places the queen in history, but her place rewrites the love of Dido and Aeneas; historical progress is also a reversal of history; repetition occurs, but with a difference. Rather than marry another, the queen marries herself, and marries in herself Dido and Aeneas, passion and power, just as Venus unites male and female. Her virginity is her marriage, to herself and, as she so often said, to her nation. In the picture, on the globe that stands between her and the waiting courtiers is a motto: *Tutto vede e molto mancho*, "I see everything and I lack much." The lack here joins with divine omniscience. It is her link to history; it is how she is in that text. Below the column, an inscription from Petrarch's *Trionfo d'amore*—

16. *Portraits of Queen Elizabeth I*, p. 66. In elucidating the *Venus virgo* symbolism, I am of course indebted to Edgar Wind's discussion of the trope in *Pagan Mysteries*. In Petrarch's *Triumph of Chastity*, a virtuous Dido (the "widow Dido" of *The Tempest* II.1) appears immediately after the passage in which the Roman vestal virgin proves her virtue by carrying water in a sieve (11.148–59). In an earlier appearance, Dido is presented to exemplify "amor pio" (1.11): there she has Aeneas's epithet (citations from Franceso Petrarca, *Trionfi*, ed. Carlo Calcaterra [Torino: Unione Tipografico-Editrice Torinese, 1923]).

In *Shakespeare by Hilliard* (Berkeley and Los Angeles: University of California Press, 1977), pp. 29 ff., Leslie Hotson argues against Strong's interpretation of the *Sieve Portrait*. The evidence he presents seems to me convincing, but supplementary, not contradictory. The sieve was a Sienese device, he explains (this clarifies somewhat the present location of the portrait), that implied sifting out imperfections (p. 30) and, in an account recorded in B.L. MS. Add. 116000 f. 48v, Queen Elizabeth is said to have given "for her Device a Sieve, for she had been sifted and fanned with all curious devices, but no chaff found" (p. 31).

Stancho riposo e riposato affano, "Weary I rest, and having rested, remain weary"—testifies to the queen's triumphant role in the realms of desire. Together, the complex picture proclaims Elizabeth as Tuccia, Venus, Diana, Dido, and Aeneas all at once. This replete image has its Spenserian counterparts in those mastering figures of desire who, complete in themselves, stand outside the desires they instigate and move.

So, we arrive at Belphoebe again. It is time now to review the situation of the text, to see finally how the episode with Timias presents the essential story of the relationship of the text and history and the place of the text in society. This is, we know, a paradigmatic story about the generation of the text, its most deeply embedded squire's tale. Retelling it once more, we can finally see where we are at this most metacritical moment in the poem. The text comes to Belphoebe by way of Lust; she is the final link in the story of Amyas and AEmylia, which is, as we can now see, a story as much about society as it is about desire. For AEmylia loves "a Squire of low degree" (vii.15.7) (Belphoebe, similarly, has Timias), but her father, "a Lord of high degree" (vii.15.2), will not hear of marriage. Love matches, especially when they violate the order of society, are not socially acceptable (remember Ralegh and Elizabeth Throckmorton or Donne and Ann More). The father is the great forbidder. In AEmylia's case, he wants her for his own ("My Sire . . . me too dearely well did love" 16.2), and she is an instrument of his will and his treasure as well.

Attempting to foil his will, AEmylia meets at her assignation greedy Lust, a version, we might now recognize, of Busyrane and Scudamour, those who act within her father's law of desire, who see their love objects as objects. She does not meet her desire, but the desire that overcomes her. Lust is the embodiment of the social form that coincides with her father's will. His mouth is a reliquary in which he puts ladies—his "spoyle"—not words or jewels; hence he is "greedie lust," desire that is the same as greed: "His neather lip was not like man nor beast, / But like a wide deepe poke, downe hanging low, / In which he wont the relickes of his feast, / And cruell spoyle, which he had spard, to stow" (vii.6.1–4).

As a social form, Lust figures an overpowering desire that has become undesirable by not being one's own. He figures the economics of exchange that affects women, objects, and words. He meets his end when he is slain by Belphoebe. The meaning of this is not, however, simple or straightforward, not merely a matter of Belphoebe's opposition to this embodiment of desire. For Belphoebe herself is sustained in antinomies much like those that Lust figures; and that should come as no surprise to the reader, for even more than he, she embodies the force of social authority in the shape of desire. Lust, who would take all, and who devours all who are in his grip, is overcome by the figure who already has everything and who, rather than give what she has, denies. Two versions of power and possession meet in their confrontation, one to replace the other, the lesser power to fall before the greater. When he is dead, she gazes at his body "surcharg'd with spoile and theft" (vii.32.5), spent in possession; she is fascinated: "Yet over him she there long gazing stood, / And oft admir'd his monstrous shape, and oft / His mighty limbs" (vii.32.6–8). A moment later, she sees him again when she sees—and sees through or misprises so seeing—Timias with the wounded Amoret.

The judgment she pronounces—"Is this the faith" (vii.36.8)—is made in the voice of Authority, a voice that embodies the power of society. It asserts its power as the only power, its desire as all that counts; it demands that others deny theirs. It says that those who do not have power are generated, and devoured, by those who do. Not simply sexually, however. They are produced as texts, read into the social forms that are the shape of power and desire. Timias has apparently stepped out of the frustrating script which demands that only Belphoebe be wooed, but never won. He has apparently courted another and is undone for that. His aphasia and his abandonment of Amoret signify that Belphoebe alone gives him words. Without her, silence is a suitor, "mum" (44.5) is his only word. While mumming he still wears a mask, as he does in his transformation. He is at her word. She generates him in her powerful antipathy to desire, her powerfully antipathetic desire. As much as AEmylia, Timias is overcome, found out by his disabling desire.

The complexity of these antipathies comes clear in the simile comparing Belphoebe in pursuit of Lust to Diana:

> As when *Latonaes* daughter cruell kynde,
> In vengement of her mothers great disgrace,
> With fell despight her cruell arrowes tynde
> Gainst wofull *Niobes* unhappy race,
> That all the gods did mone her miserable case.
>
> (vii.30.5–9)

Lust in this simile is identified with "*Niobes* unhappy race," mortals who dared to compare themselves to the gods. The punishment is destruction at the hands of Diana, cruelly opposed to generation ("unhappy race") in her role as goddess of chastity. But Diana plays another role; she is the goddess of the moon, and in that part she is connected to female generativity, just as, in the simile, for all her opposition to Niobe's children, she is still acting on her own mother's behalf even as she punishes another mother. The oxymoron "cruell kynde" presents this ambivalence.

Belphoebe slays Lust, male generativity; she does what Britomart's shield with its broken spears announces: her power is castrating. Yet her opposition is also a sign that she includes what she opposes, just as her fixation on Lust, that dead member, suggests her assumption of his powers; and just as the *Sieve Portrait* encompasses legitimate and illegitimate unions, bringing together desire, chastity, and virginal antipathy all at once. In this ultimately disabling moment, we can never tell whether what Belphoebe sees when she sees Timias bent over Amoret is accurate or not, recognition or misrecognition. Her seeing it makes it so, doubling representation upon itself. And what she does in the text reflects and reproduces the text's relationship to what is "outside" it.

What Belphoebe means for poetry can be seen in Timias's case. Because he is Belphoebe's lover and her poet, she is his word, all he can say, all he can write. A momentary lapse does not release him from her power but merely transforms him into another manifestation of it. Having or losing makes no difference. Abandoned, he becomes her text quite palpably, a demonstration that he has no words but hers. Restored, he remains what she makes. Her effect on him can be compared to what happens the first time Belphoebe appears in *The Faerie Queene*, that moment of conspicuous irrelevance in book II. The narrator describes her clothes. All goes well until he arrives at her gold: "golden aygulets, that glistred bright, / Like twinckling starres, and all the skirt about / Was hemd with golden fringe" (II.iii.26.7–9). Undone, he stops. A final half-line, rather than the expected alexandrine, is where the stanza concludes, broken and incomplete, "hemd with golden fringe," the limit on his power to end. Two stanzas later a rhyme is missing, and the word "play" appears when "sport" is what the rhyme calls for (28.7). Are these lapses accidental or significant? Trivial substitutions, or a reminder of who has joy and power? There are no other moments like these anywhere in the poem, and they seem to indicate a need to break the text to acknowledge the arrival of the most authoritative figure in the text. For a moment, the narrator appears to fumble, the poet is dumb. Where? When the object of desire coincides with his desire, gold, when his transformation of the *Aeneid* in book II meets the figure who gives him the pretext for such sport. "*O dea certe* . . . ." "O dearest dred."

Who produces *The Faerie Queene*? This is, of course, a complicated question, and to answer it we would need to recapitulate the course of this book, to take stock of the manifold ways in which the Authority of an Other shapes this text. To see, at least, that this is a question that the text itself engages—and that doing so it draws what we might have been tempted once to call the "outside" into the text, we can turn again to the final episode of book IV, that moment of severe reduction that nonetheless pointed us from the start to "another place" (xii.35.9) where "endlesse worke" lay "to be perfected." We recall the story: Florimell is imprisoned, and remembering her, the narrator hastens to her aid. In a parallel moment, Marinell awakens from his self-love to discover his love for Florimell; he also realizes his impotence; he can do nothing without his mother. She too discovers the limits of her power. After exhausting the knowledge of the seagods' surgeon Tryphon, after Apollo reveals—but does nothing about it—that Marinell languishes in love, Cymodoche appeals to Neptune, as the highest power, for relief. The narrator's desire to save Florimell from captivity leads through this chain of surrogates, these interconnected powers, to the ultimate power. Even Apollo, god of medicine and poetry, is surpassed by Neptune, god of the seas. "Unto great king *Neptune* selfe" (xii.29.4), Cymodoche proceeds. Arriving at this apparent end, this highest power, we must pause to consider where we are, and what power is being figured at this point. Here is Cymodoche's scene.

> And on her knee before him falling lowe,
> Made humble suit unto his Maiestie,
> To graunt to her, her sonnes life, which his foe
> A cruell Tyrant had presumpteouslie
> By wicked doome condemn'd, a wretched death to die.
>
> To whom God *Neptune* softly smyling, thus;
> Daughter me seemes of double wrong ye plaine,
> Gainst one that hath both wronged you, and us:
> For death t'adward I ween'd did appertaine
> To none, but to the seas sole Soveraine.
> Read therefore who it is, which this hath wrought,
> And for what cause; the truth discover plaine.
> For never wight so evill did or thought,
> But would some rightfull cause pretend, though rightly nought.
>
> To whom she answerd, Then it is by name
> *Proteus*, that hath ordayn'd my sonne to die;
> For that a waift, the which by fortune came
> Unto your seas, he claym'd as propertie:
> And yet nor his, nor his in equitie,
> But yours the waift by high prerogative.
> Therefore I humbly crave your Maiestie,
> It to replevie, and my sonne reprive:
> So shall you by one gift save all us three alive.

(xii.29.5–31)

The scene is courtly, the language legalistic and feudal, indications that ultimate power is being conceived in political terms, perhaps the only terms in which it can be. Neptune here is lord over life and death, the initiator and disposer of all generation, and Cymodoche is his daughter, yet also his subject. Political power receives its ultimate naturalization as the power of life. Ideology can go no further. What earlier had occurred in Agape's appeal for the life of her children in the cave of the Fates is now finally refigured and replaced as an act in a political domain. As a final location of the text, this would seem to be the ultimate place where the threads of life, and of the text, are woven. Such a conjunction had, however, been intimated before, in the Temple of Venus, in the figure of Concord keeping "all the world in state unmoved" (x.35.2); "state" carries at least two meanings here. A similar configuration informs a visual representation of Elizabeth as the *Primum Mobile*, the unmoved mover, that adorns John Case's book entitled, significantly, *Sphaera Civitatis* (1588; fig. 9). At this final moment in book IV, Neptune appears to occupy a place of ultimate power, and the narrator's desire to free Florimell would seem to have exhausted a chain of powers and to have arrived at last at the last word.[17]

In her appeal to Neptune, Cymodoche asks "his Maiestie" to give a gift, "by one gift save all us three" (31.9), and thereby to take part in the complex circulation of a most valued and desired object of possession in the text, Florimell. In order to give it, he must be allowed to have it, and thus Cymodoche invokes his "high prerogative." Since book IV began its consideration of patronage and power by saying that "all is his iustly, that all freely dealth" (i.6.5), Neptune's giving of the gift means that it is his to give. However, by giving Florimell to Cymodoche, he also "replevies" her, returns her. How are these conflicting notions to be reconciled? In what sense is this act of generosity a return? How can this be a return if Florimell is his? The answer lies in what Cymodoche has said. Neptune has Florimell on Cymodoche's word; by saying that Florimell is "yours . . . by high prerogative" (31.6), she gave Florimell to him; he, then, is returning the maid to the mother. But the return also enacts a translation and an embodiment. Cymodoche gives the word and receives flesh in return. What is this if not the poet's exchange, an enactment of his desire? Yet, can we say that Cymodoche's words are her own? When she says "prerogative," the word for Neptune's absolute power, it is royal language she uses. And the point about royal prerogative is that the king is not bound by any system. Hence, when he returns the gift—as an apparent free gift—it shows that he is not bound.

---

17. The word *friendship* is cognate with the word *free*. One of the ironies of the text is that the binding to others that occurs after liberation from prison is simply another form of the binding that took place in the prisons of desire. This too is an irony found in the word *liberi* (Lat.), the sons of the household, freemen who are free and yet bound in familial obligation. The bonds are never dissolved. Behind both *friend* and *free* there is a root that means *love*: desire is inescapable. For a fascinating discussion of the etymology, see Onians, *The Origins of European Thought*, pp. 472–80.

Frontispiece, John Case's *Sphaera Civitatis* (Bodleian Library, Oxford)

Neptune smiles as Cymodoche makes her appeal. Is this, perhaps, like the smile of Milton's God when Adam freely exercises himself in an argument that God has already given him? Or is this Venus's smile on Neptune's face, the smile that Scudamour saw favoring his pretense? Cymodoche, we know, is not inventing her own words, for she invokes all those social forms that bind individuals and come before us: the family and the state, law and love. She asks for generosity from the one who generates all, she begs a gift that will not bind the giver. He will lose nothing by giving; indeed, his power will be confirmed. She will be bound to Neptune by the gift.

Cymodoche's plea seems to mean that by giving the gift back to Cymodoche, Neptune will be giving himself a gift because all comes from Neptune. The flow of tribute, we know, empties into the ocean, the source as well. This is a pattern in nature, in society, in families, and in texts. Cymodoche is bound to Neptune in all these ways; not only is he her lord, her king, and her father; even her name, meaning a wave of the sea, is a word generated and derived from him. By giving Florimell to Cymodoche, he gives back his own to his own. They figure two forms of ownership, Florimell as a "waift," a stray good fallen by fortune into the seas, Cymodoche as what he has begotten. In giving the gift, Neptune will return what was gotten to what was begotten.

We have seen this meeting before, and will see it again, in the babe that Matilde bears. Neptune performs, giving Florimell to Cymodoche, the generative act of producing the text. He acts in that space between *"be gotten"* and *"begotten"* (VI.iv.32.7). Words and bodies are exchanged here in a circle of production. The life that Cymodoche begs figures the life of the text. Nature and text meet here in this ultimate plea, in Florimell.

Yet, we have not exhausted this argument without asking what circle of exchanges this is, and whether we have, with Neptune, come to an ultimate representation of the interpenetration of nature and text, political power and poetics. This circle is a dance of restoration, a return in at least one more way. Florimell came from Mount Acidale, the home of Venus, the place in book VI where the poet will have his broken vision. *"There Florimell* in her first ages flowre / Was fostered by those *Graces"* (IV.v.5.7–8), a fourth grace to their three. In the complex dance of exchanges and returns between Cymodoche and Neptune, the dance of Florimell's origin is retraced. Giving, receiving, returning, the essential rhythm of the dance is figured and refigured; any one of the three involved can be seen as the originator or ender of this circle: Cymodoche, Florimell, or Neptune. Cymodoche, arriving at what appeared to be the end of a chain of powers, has instead begun a circle of exchanges and replacements, the endless movement of the gift. The three function like the handmaids of an unmoved mover, a power behind them, behind even Neptune. The Graces are the handmaids of Venus, and she is the ultimate power behind their dance. These three are dancing her dance. Florimell is being returned to her source.

When Florimell left Mount Acidale she brought "that goodly belt away" (v.5.9), the belt of Venus which, we have seen, figures the bond of the universe; it ties the world, society, and the text together in an inextricable bond of production. In this last dance, Florimell functions as her attribute and as Venus's attribute; she is the binding chain of obligation and the gift that is the text and its reward. She is the prize, the word circulating; even at this moment, when she is freed, she is bound again. She remains the gift of Neptune. No longer in the prison of Proteus, she is finally, with Marinell, more than ever "in bands of love, and in sad thraldomes chayne" (xi.1.5). Her life is not her own: it is the gift of Neptune and Cymodoche and Proteus, who consent to give her up. Her desire is not her own even when she is there with Marinell, son of the sea. At the end, she is "in place" (xii.35.2), fixed by the demands of nature, society—and the text. At the end, masked and silent, she is a word to be put in someone else's mouth. In her place the voice of Authority speaks.

Here, finally, and at first, is that circle of production made explicit.

"Hearke to love, and read this lesson often" (pro.5.9), that is what the reader, "that sacred Saint my soveraigne Queene" (4.2), is asked to do. The text is a lesson, something to be read, something that has been written before. Normally, the priest reads the lesson; but this reader is a saint, what would be read *as* the lesson. A lesson instructs. It is a sermon for the queen, of the queen, to the queen. It says: the poem is yours, you are the word, return the gift. Its language is erotic. "Do thou dred infant, *Venus* dearling dove, / From her high spirit chase imperious feare, / And use of awfull Maiestie romove" (5.2–4). "*Venus* dearling dove" (5.2) is invoked, asked to come to the "Queene of love": the child, "dred infant," is asked to come and lecture the mother, "awfull Maiestie," to take her power in exchange, begotten for begetter. What exchange is figured here? Several translations are possible: read the book (submit to it, it is what you have gotten), give a gift (make the word flesh). Production and reproduction meet in this erotic scene of reading. The infant is a dove whispering in her ear, a bird telling her a story, her story, for the dove is the child of Venus too; and it is also Eros/Ascanius at Dido's ear. A bird at the ear, a bird being fed. The bird has penetrating words; it sings a siren song, saying: all is from you, of you, to you. Remove majesty, submit, nothing is lost. You remain the "Prince of peace" (4.9) and the dove is the bird of that word too, that lesson. The word is love: lip to lip. The word is "in sted"; reading replacing speaking, the text for the word:

In sted thereof with drops of melting love,
Deawd with ambrosiall kisses, by thee gotten
From thy sweete smyling mother from above,
Sprinckle her heart, and haughtie courage soften,
That she may hearke to love, and reade this lesson often.

(pro.5.5–9)

The circle of love begins and ends in Venus, "thy sweete smyling mother." This looseness, this softening, this dalliance, is Venus going to Mars, but now legitimized, made pure. It is to "reade"; then the book is "gotten" and "begotten," produced and reproduced, given and received and returned. The sexual act is reading the book, producing the book, being the book, the body of the text, exchanging body for body, value for value. The request is Timias's: to be taken into favor, to have the prize, matter spiritualized, the flesh made word. She is asked to give, for her there is no loss; the replete is never less; it can give all and never lose. And the poet? He has nothing to lose too, so complete is his loss, so full, so perfect. Were she to give all, she would still have all; he would still have nothing. In a word: "All is his iustly, that all freely dealth" (i.6.5). The poet and the queen can share that sentence. In the production of the text, those two meet.

AFTERWORDS

If the text is inevitably spoken in the voice of another's authority, and in the voice of society, what remains for the poet to do? Is what book IV represents enabling or disabling? Where does *The Faerie Queene* move from its vantage point? Where can the text go as it moves to "another place"? Book V offers one further answer.[1] The text can explicitly enter the voice of authority, giving up the fiction that the poet speaks in the text at all and that it is even his text. In book V, the voice speaking in the proem to his "Dread Soverayne Goddesse" (11.1) names himself simply as "thy basest thrall" (11.6) reciting a text that is not his own:

> Pardon the boldnesse of thy basest thrall,
> That dare discourse of so divine a read,
> As thy great justice praysed over all:
> The instrument whereof loe here thy *Artegall*.
>
> (11.6–9)

The voice, abased, tells another's story in another's text.

His "discourse" is already "read"—it is the sovereign's text, her justice, her "instrument," that is represented in his text. Here, explicitly, the power of the text lies in social authority. Book V operates entirely within Elizabethan chivalric fictions, presenting the conquest of Ireland as the last of a series of knightly rescues of maidens—Belge, Flourdelis— in distress. Elizabethan imperialism restores peace ironically; Irena is pacified, and the path to peace is the incredibly destructive one traveled

---

1. In my discussion of book V, I depend on Angus Fletcher, *The Prophetic Moment* (Chicago: University of Chicago Press, 1971). I am guided too by the dry wit of Marianna Jenkins in her comment on the appropriateness of an olive branch in the Welbeck portrait as fitting "Elizabeth's remarkable penchant for undeclared war" (*Monographs on Archaeology and Fine Arts* 3 [1947]: 24).

by Talus as he lops off heads, only to replant them after these bloody harvests. The revolutionary way to regeneration in book V is by decapitation and degeneration; this is undoing on a vast scale. Before the crown can be restored to Irena, many crowns must fall, many heads must be taxed—among them, the poet's.

> Thus there he stood, whylest high over his head,
>   There written was the purport of his sin,
>   In cyphers strange, that few could rightly read,
>   BON FONT: but *bon* that once had written bin,
>   Was raced out, and *Mal* was now put in.
> So now *Malfont* was plainely to be red.
>
> (V.ix.26.1–6)

The poet is renamed in the court of Mercilla, produced under erasure, "raced out"—erased and rooted—and thus produced in what book IV called "the displeasure of the mighty" (viii.1.3), the manifest power of the authoritative other.

In book V, language is straitened to be the text of authority; its polysemous meanings are directed to support social order. So the court becomes a law court, the quest an "inquest" (i.13.1); sentences in the text are judgments, legal sentences: "My sentence understand," Arthegall says to Amidas and Bracidas (iv.16.8) and then proceeds to pronounce sentence. And the narrator is in that voice too:

> To tell the glorie of the feast that day,
>   The goodly service, the devicefull sights,
>   The bridegromes state, the brides most rich aray,
>   The pride of Ladies, and the worth of knights,
>   The royall banquets, and the rare delights
>   Were worke fit for an Herauld, not for me:
>   But for so much as to my lot here lights,
>   That with this present treatise doth agree,
> True vertue to advance, shall here recounted bee.
>
> (iii.3)

The stanza describes the marriage of Marinell, now *Sir* Marinell, and Florimell; the deferred story from book IV is now sloughed off as a matter of indifference. The voice speaking here sounds at first like Chaucer's squire; we expect an excuse for inadequacy. But this voice has taken on authority, and paltry fictions do not concern it. After all, what is being written is not a poem but a "treatise" advancing the truth of society. At the marriage of Florimell and Marinell, poetic justice is dispensed; Guyon gets his horse back, the frauds (False) Florimell and Braggadocchio are shown up and disappear for good. By performing such justice and providing such endings, the text treats all that has come before as if it could be as easily disposed of, as if the problems of the text were all trivial matters, and as if these solutions were genuine resolutions of them.

Book V also replays the relationship between Britomart and Arthegall that occupies cantos iv–vi of book IV, and "gets it right" this time by defeating Radigund and making Britomart give up her powers to Arthegall. Britomart, in this final incarnation, becomes an instrument for the production of the text, for this text, by undoing the past; the vision in the Church of Isis reveals her "enwombed" of the "game" of a crocodile, bringing forth "a Lion of great might" (vii.16.5–6). Even as Britomart is written into history as a source of reality, she is also figuring, in this monstrous birth, the source for book I of *The Faerie Queene*, in Una's words, the story of "my Lyon, and my noble Lord" (I.iii.7.6). These acts of justice are unwritings, erasures, of the poem that comes before book V, putting it in place—the entire poem now comes after this authoritative beginning in the Church of Isis—in much the same way as Talus treats his enemies, dismembering them for the sake of peace.

The ironies of this entrance into the voice of authority are palpable. The text of book V is limited semantically, straitened so that it speaks only the language of power. The fictions of the poem are simply treated as such, and dismissed, so that Arthegall's entire career in book V is considered a digression, as he wanders from the path which he almost misses when he arrives for his last-minute rescue of Irena from Grantorto. As Angus Fletcher has suggested, book V is filled with a sense of the error of knight errancy, and the quest is a series of errors. This means, however, that the voice in the text is judging it, as if he were "outside" the text, passing doom. He takes authority for the text by dismissing it. The crushing irony is that this willed destruction of the text is a misreading of the power and the authority it assumes.

Book V speaks a doubletalk that is supposed to be the language of power. It sheds crocodile tears, saying pacification when it means destruction, regeneration when it means degeneration, mercy when it means justice. This is the language of power as Machiavelli describes it. Ironically, at the end of the book, Arthegall fails and is recalled to the court because he has been maligned, because he has been seen through. The court depends upon its fictions of justice and mercy, of pity and restraint, and it must punish those who do what it wants done. Arthegall, the instrument, is brought home for slaughter, for his just reprimand. The voice that has promoted his career is not the voice of power (power does not say it is destroying Ireland, it says it is bringing peace), but a voice continuously undone by power. At the end of book V two hags, Envie and Detraction, spew forth poisoned words. But their words are true: they say that Arthegall has been cruel, that innocents have been slaughtered. These voices beget the Blatant Beast, Arthegall's enemy;

and, in book VI, the poet's too. They are the poet's undoing. In book V, the poet, entering and failing to enter the voice of authority, is doubly undone.

In book VI, there is only one route for voice and action—withdrawal, the path marked out in book IV. The weary poet reports that his only delight lies in his text, and his "footing" (VI.pro.2.7) there describes the punning ways of the entire book. Action in book VI is verbal action and words are followed to their roots.[2] Hence, distressing events in the opening canto turn out to be just that, distressing, haircuts; bears bear babies, born from their mouths, *"gotten, not begotten"* (iv.32.7). Throughout book VI, the direction is back—back to nature, back to the past. Calidore stumbles across couples in the bushes and sends them home, back to their parents. He wanders into the green world, bearing civilization; when he leaves, there is a train of death and destruction, cannibalism and brigandage behind him. Calidore's name means good gift or good gold; he is the gift of the word and its compensation. When the word enters society, or society enters the word, the word is destroyed. Calidore, bringer of society, attempts to withdraw into a text and destroys the pastoral world; he returns children to their parents, undoing future generations. The way to save the text is to deny society. But the Blatant Beast has the last word.

"Back to nature" is itself a fiction, for it is also from nature that corruption springs. No matter how far "back" into nature the poem recedes, there is always a text, a sign of civilization, before nature, and not merely in the cannibals and brigands. Look at the regressive progression in the opening cantos, from the young adults, Priscilla and Aladine, guiltily making love, to Tristram, a boy who becomes a knight and immediately displays greed, to Matilde and the bear's baby. Not only is that infant a pun—a word going round in a circle—carried first in the mouth of the bear, delivered to Matilde as Sir Bruin's babe; so too is Aladine, the son of Aldus (the name of a leading Renaissance publisher). Words are made flesh, flesh made words. Generation is modeled on the

<hr/>

2. The textuality of book VI has been frequently remarked; I am most conscious of debts to Harry Berger, Jr., for his essay "A Secret Discipline: *The Faerie Queene*, Book VI," in *Form and Convention in the Poetry of Edmund Spenser*, ed. William Nelson (New York: Columbia University Press, 1961) and also to William Nestrick, for an illuminating essay, "The Virtuous and Gentle Discipline of Gentlemen and Poets," *ELH* 29 (1962): 357–71. What I have to say about book VI is supported by Richard Neuse's essay, "Book VI as Conclusion to *The Faerie Queene*," *ELH* 35 (1968), with its insistence that Calidore is a symptom of the ills of the time, not capable of standing for the poet's aim of fashioning a gentleman, and that the poet, too, is ultimately victimized by the society he meant to reform. The connection I offer between Ariadne's crown and Ate's house is suggested by Donald Cheney in *Spenser's Image of Nature: Wild Man and Shepherd in "The Faerie Queene"* (New Haven: Yale University Press, 1966), pp. 234–36.

production of a book. Since this is how texts are produced, Calepine, Calidore's double, is also fittingly named, for Calepinus wrote a standard dictionary. Behind nature there is always civilization and its texts: the holy hermit reveals that he was once a courtier; Meliboeus, the Virgilian and Chaucerian pastor, has the same story to tell. He is, pointedly, Pastorella's foster father, whereas her real parents are courtly. Calidore's final act of generosity is to bring her home again. These returns, not to nature but to what produces nature in texts, are at the same time attempts to avoid the production of texts.

In book VI, characters are constantly withdrawn, transformed into each other, with Calidore indifferently becoming Calepine, or one word becoming another. The epic assertions with which *The Faerie Queene* began are also withdrawn. The narrator of book VI is a pastoral poet, and his withdrawal from the court and courting returns him to Spenser's earliest persona, Colin Clout. In the scene on Mount Acidale, when Calidore stumbles across Colin and disturbs the dance of the graces—the circulation of gifts—the text discovers the poet in his essential position of loss. Who is in the center of this dance? Is it the Shepherd, piping "in the midst" (VI.x.10.9), or is it his visionary damsel "in the middest" (x.12.6)? Either way, we are in the essential position of the text, *in medias res*, or, as the Letter to Ralegh phrases it, "a Poet thrusteth into the middest" (p. 408). From one center to the other there is an echo: "she to whom that shepheard pypt alone, / That made him pipe so merrily, as never none" (15.8–9). Who is this maid in the middle? Pastorella? Elizabeth? Rosalind? Florimell? the Muse? No matter, one name will do for another; all name what is desired and never had, a dream satisfied only "deepe within the mynd" (pro.5.8), in words, "never none." Calidore stumbles into this scene of poetic reverie and loss; like any reader he demands an explication of the text, and the shepherd dilates (21.1), and supplements the text with learned baggage, dictionary knowledge— E.K.'s knowledge—about the graces and their dance of civility. This knowledge is not the center of wisdom, however. Rather, it is the poet's confession that "another Grace" (27.1) "made me . . . pipe." He apologizes to "Great *Gloriana*" (28.3) for this betrayal. Calidore, ravished by the poet's words, is now also overcome by shame: "Now sure it yrketh mee, / That to thy blisse I made this luckelesse breach, / As now the author of thy bale to be, / Thus to bereave thy loves deare sight from thee" (29.2–5). Calidore is right to lament his authorial supplementation of the poet's loss; but the dream, too, has the same shape. It was of another never had. The poet's center, where he is, is a place of loss. Having her is a fantasy which in reality is always lost bliss. When Calidore separates Colin from his vision he is doing what he did when he stumbled upon Serena and Calepine in the bushes, interrupting coitus, making bliss bale, a "luckelesse breach".

Looke how the Crowne, which *Ariadne* wore
  Upon her yvory forehead that same day,
  That *Theseus* her unto his bridale bore,
  When the bold *Centaures* made that bloudy fray,
  With the fierce *Lapithes*, which did them dismay;
  Being now placed in the firmament,
  Through the bright heaven doth her beams display,
  And is unto the starres an ornament,
Which round about her move in order excellent.

(x.13)

Ariadne: won at a bloody feast, the emblem of cannibalistic civilization in Ate's house. Ariadne: won and lost, dismade, and had again as the pattern in the heavens. Ariadne: eternally lost and eternally there, the jewel in nature, text and nature at once. Ariadne: the heavenly scales, weighing words and gifts.

The moment that Calidore disturbs and that we disturb by reading and that the poet disturbs by publishing is the moment in which the poet, united with his vision of loss, supplements it with the figures that stand in place of loss. Having that loss as his own, and words to fill it, he pleases himself if no one else. For such a poet, giving is losing. Although the plea to the queen is that she will not lose by giving, the poet knows that he will lose by giving. As long as the poem is not given, there is the illusion that it is his to give; once given it is no longer his but belongs to the reader, to the publisher; he becomes his text. As long as the poem is not given, there is the illusion that behind the poem is a reality of having; instead of the depths of loss, there is the reality of having the poem in place of loss.

Once the poem is given there is double loss. There are some palpable ironies here, not the least of which was that Spenser had more success as a professional poet than any other poet of his time.[3] No other poet was granted so large a pension—fifty pounds a year—by the queen. And that gift had been his after the publication of the first half of *The Faerie Queene*. Clearly, to Spenser the gift (a respectable yearly salary), along with his Irish positions, was not enough. He chose to view his Irish career as banishment, his pension as a paltry reward. Nothing compensates the poet for his creative expenditure.

3. A recent presentation of the career, and of the importance of Spenser's claims as poet, is Richard Helgerson's "The New Poet Presents Himself: Spenser and the Idea of a Literary Career," *PMLA* 93 (1978): 893–911. On the role of *The Shepheardes Calender* in the career, see Louis Adrian Montrose, " 'The perfect paterne of a Poete': The Poetics of Courtship in *The Shepheardes Calender*," *Texas Studies in Literature and Language* 21 (1979): 34–67, and " 'Eliza, Queen of shepheardes' and the Pastoral of Power," *English Literary Renaissance* 10 (1980): 153–82.

That had been his belief as early as *The Shepheardes Calender*, his extraordinary piece of self-promotion. Here is the first poem of "this our new Poete":

> Goe little booke: thy selfe present,
> As child whose parent is unkent:
> To him that is the president
> Of noblesse and of chevalree,
> And if that Envie barke at thee,
> As sure it will, for succoure flee
>   Under the shadow of his wing,
> And asked, who thee forth did bring,
> A shepheards swaine saye did thee sing,
> All as his straying flocke he fedde:
> And when his honor has thee redde,
> Crave pardon for my hardyhedde.
>   But if that any aske thy name,
> Say thou wert base begot with blame:
> For thy thereof thou takest shame.
> And when thou art past ieopardee,
> Come tell me, what was sayd of mee
> And I will send more after thee.
>   Immeritó.

The final myth of poetic production is here already. "Envie" barks necessarily at the text, so it flees for aid to its patron. The patron questions the text about its origins; the text is told to be evasive. The questioning patron and protector is metamorphosed into the "ieopardee" which the text must get past in order to return to the poet. The poem is given to a perilous world, and must be withdrawn. The poet keeps himself at home. There he writes, singing as he feeds his straying flock. The sheep wander astray; the poet gives words, food, and life to his words, releases them into the world. In the world, he has a false name, self-given. In public his name is Immeritó. His name is his text, begotten basely with blame. Whose blame? the poet's, the public's precedent/"president" of chivalry, jeopardizing and making possible the text's production. The circle of production, of begetting and giving, is this dance of triple loss.

In the "October" eclogue, Cuddie laments the fact that his audience "han the pleasure, I a sclender prise" (1.16), and although Piers attempts to argue that "the prayse is better, then the price" (1.19), the eclogue is surely on the side of Cuddie. For Colin is reported in that poem, as throughout the *Calender*, to be unable to write because he has failed to win the prize, his lady's love. From the broken pipes of "January" to the elegaic strains of "December," the *Calender* is a poem about the shepherd's void. As Harry Berger, Jr., has suggested, the *Calender* offers a banquet of kinds of texts; yet it is a feast in which discontinuity, not order, results. As much as *The Faerie Queene*, this first poem is one of fissures, of losses, of disconnections: a jumble of poetic kinds and attitudes, prose and verse, woodcuts and emblematics. All that unites the poet's pleasure to the demands of society is loss. What can be gotten from the poem is what the poet keeps to himself against the devastations of multiple loss: "I play to please my selfe, all be it ill" ("June," 1.72), Colin tells Hobbinoll; "One if I please, enough is me therefore" ("December," 1.120) is almost the last word. As the emblem for "September," the eclogue that provoked Johnson to comment that "surely, at the same time that a shepherd learns theology, he may gain some acquaintance with his native language," Narcissus's motto appears: *Inopem me copia fecit,*—"Plenty makes me poor"—the central line as well in the sonnet that appears twice in the *Amoretti*.[4] What Calidore disturbs is the poet's solipsism, his fantasy of having by not giving, his sense that all giving is molestation.

Throughout his career, Spenser acted as if he were a failure, as if he never got what he wanted. The world without was hostile. This poet filled a wedding song with lamentations about the lack of generosity of those in power; he wrote bitterly satiric allegories about corrupt courts; he retired to Mulla after his devastating trip across the seas. Yet, his fortunes grew; a pension was awarded; over the years there was the patronage of royal favorites, Leicester, Ralegh, Essex. The center of the need to view the life as a failure has to do with protecting the central illusion: that the words are his, not another's, that he, not another, has the text, that the value of the text is what he confers. So, he writes no language, as both Ben Jonson and Samuel Johnson say; thus the poem is kept by the poet, holding it back. Here is the characteristic gesture at first: in 1580, to Gabriel Harvey, he confesses in public (but withholds his name, he is Immeritò, the one without value because so valuable).

I minde shortely at convenient leysure, to sette forth a Booke in this kinde, whyche I entitle, *Epithalamion Thamesis,* whyche Booke I dare undertake wil be very profitable for the knowledge, and rare for the Invention, and manner of handling. For in setting forth the marriage of the Thames: I shewe his first beginning, and offspring, and all the Countrey, that he passeth thorough, and also describe

4. Johnson's remarks are found in *The Rambler,* no. 137 (24 July 1750) in *The Yale Edition of the Works of Samuel Johnson* (New Haven: Yale University Press, 1969), 3: 203. The Narcissus sonnet is 35 and 83 in *Amoretti.* In "The Narcissus Myth in Spenser's Poetry," *Studies in Philology* 74 (1977): 63–88, an essay devoted mainly to demonstrating that Spenser read the Narcissus myth in Ficinian terms (mistaking outer for inner beauty, shadow for reality), Calvin R. Edwards does note one connection significant for my discussion, that Avarice in *FQ.* I.iv.29.4 is described as one "whose plenty made him pore" (p. 76).

all the Rivers throughout Englande, whyche came to this Wedding, and their righte names, and right passage, &c. . . .

But of that more hereafter. Nowe, my *Dreames*, and *dying Pellicane*, being fully finished . . . and presentlye to bee imprinted, I wil in hande forthwith with my *Faery Queene*, whyche I praye you hartily send me with al expedition. . . . (p. 612).

From the first, this is a poet who will be the author of many lost texts. Elsewhere Harvey alludes to nine comedies; E.K. adds tragedies and a poetic treatise to thc list. But also, from the first, this is a poet who claims to have finished many texts. In 1580, the entire corpus and a good deal more is said to be done. This is the poet's fantasy; he has these lost texts to himself. Giving them will empty him into the reality of loss.

INDEX

THE JOHNS HOPKINS UNIVERSITY PRESS

This book was composed in Baskerville text and display type by the Oberlin Printing Company from a design by Alan Carter. It was printed on 50-lb. Sebago Cream Offset and bound by Universal Lithographers.